The Fatherhood Movement

The Fatherhood Movement

A Call to Action

Edited by

Wade F. Horn
David Blankenhorn
Mitchell B. Pearlstein

LEXINGTON BOOKS
Lanham • Boulder • New York • Oxford

LEXINGTON BOOKS

Published in the United States of America
by Lexington Books
4720 Boston Way, Lanham, Maryland 20706

12 Hid's Copse Road
Cumnor Hill, Oxford OX2 9JJ, England

British Library Cataloguing in Publication Information Available

Library of Congress Cataloging-in-Publication Data

The fatherhood movement : a call to action / edited by Wade F. Horn,
    David Blankenhorn, Mitchell B. Pearlstein.
        p.   cm.
    Includes bibliographical references and index.
    ISBN 0-7391-0021-1 (cloth : alk. paper). — ISBN 0-7391-0022-X
(pbk. : alk. paper)
    1. Fatherhood—United States.   2. Fatherhood—Social aspects—
United States.   3. Fathers—United States.   4. Paternal
deprivation—Social aspects—United States.   I. Horn, Wade F.
II. Blankenhorn, David.   III. Pearlstein, Mitchell B., 1948–
HQ756.F3815   1999
306.874'2—dc21   98-33382
                                                              CIP

Printed in the United States of America

⊖™ The paper used in this publication meets the minimum requirements of American
National Standard for Information Sciences—Permanence of Paper for Printed Library
Materials, ANSI Z39.48–1984.

In loving celebration of our wives and children.

WFH

DB

MBP

Contents

ACKNOWLEDGMENTS

These essays were originally written for a conference held in Minneapolis in October 1996, cosponsored by the Minnesota-based Center of the American Experiment, the New York-based Institute for American Values and the Maryland-based National Fatherhood Initiative. In addition to the approximately 30 participants who gathered in the Twin Cities, the editors wish to thank all those who made that two day meeting possible, especially its underwriters: the Achelis, Annie E. Casey, General Mills, Honeywell, JM, and McKnight Foundations.

We also very much appreciate the contributions of Susan C. Lavrakas, who served as executive director of the conference, as well as those of Brenton S. Bills, David Brenner, Matthew Buckwalter, Therese A. Faulconbridge, Virginia E. Hafner, Michael D. Moriarity, Jeffrey C. O'Brien, Malcolm Williams, and Peter J. Zeller.

For editorial assistance, we are exceptionally grateful to Deborah Strubel and Maggie Gallagher.

Introduction

Toward Fatherhood

David Blankenhorn

This book brings together many of the leading voices of the fatherhood movement.

As Wade Horn argues in the book's opening chapter, "movement" is a big word, suggesting important activity, but it has become the most appropriate word today to describe the diverse and rapidly expanding group of leaders, organizations, and grass-roots initiatives, cutting across ideological, political, and racial lines, all aimed at reconnecting men to their children. Five or six years ago, fatherlessness was still a problem with no name. Some good people were doing pioneering work, mostly at the local level—especially African-Americans such as Charles Ballard of the Institute for Responsible Fatherhood in Cleveland—but these leaders were largely isolated and unrecognized, voices in the wilderness.

The contributors to this book are among the people most responsible in the 1990s for publicly naming this problem and initiating a movement to confront it. Think of these essays, then, as working papers for the new movement, vision statements and marching orders from the conceptual frameworkers and front line leaders.

Several of these contributors are widely acknowledged as experts in their fields, but if you seek in these essays a consistently specialized or expert discourse, you should probably look elsewhere. Compared to formally academic treatments, these essays cut a wider swath and are much more intuitive and freewheeling. They also, I believe, get us closer to the heart of the matter. These authors constitute a promiscuously diverse group. Some are scholars. Some are organizers and activists. Some are clinicians and service providers. Some are think-tankers. Several are in government. Some are writers and public intellectuals. Several of them wear more than one hat. Readers will also note that these writers sometimes disagree with one another, frequently in matters of emphasis, occasionally in matters of substance.

At the same time, they are not strangers who are simply talking past one another between book covers. Most of these authors know and respect one another. Many of them actively work together and influence one another's ideas, either formally, through organizational ties, or informally, through regularly talking to one another, sharing research, or debating strategy. This broad sense of people with a common understanding of the challenge—not sameness, as in indistinct voices in a chorus, but purposeful relatedness, as in different players in an ensemble—means that these essays connect to one another, engage with one another, in ways that are often missing from multi-author volumes. This shared understanding culminates in the book's conclusion, a jointly authored "Call to Fatherhood."

Finally, most of these authors are not detached observers, dispensing allegedly values-neutral reportage from above the fray. For better or worse, these essays take the form of on-the-ground arguments, frequently marked by passion and personal commitment. The best of them—and there are a number of very good ones—combine passion and precision.

Where is the fatherhood movement going? That is the essential question. The answer is made more complicated by the fact the fatherhood movement is now much bigger than any individual or organization, or even any grouping of individuals or organizations. This fact changes the nature and possibility of leadership. Leaders in a bureaucracy typically seek to manage, decide, and claim credit. But leaders in an emerging social movement strive instead to inspire, empower, and give credit to others. Bureaucratic control is not an option. Indeed, with fatherhood now a salient national issue, and with new fatherhood projects popping up every day, it is no longer possible (if it ever was) for any one group even to monitor everything that is happening in the field.

In such an environment—which is the new and happy result, of course, of much effective work over the past few years—the main task of leadership is to develop a broadly shared vision for the movement, based on a rough consensus regarding first principles and core goals. Toward that end, informed by the insights of these authors, and also reflecting on the possibility of actually reversing the trend of fatherlessness in the years ahead, let me suggest four important challenges for the fatherhood movement in the United States as we approach the new century.

The first challenge is setting goals that are compelling and realizable. Building a movement requires winning concrete victories, beginning with small ones, but small ones that nevertheless signal progress toward an ultimate goal. But which small victories? And toward what larger goal?

Fatherlessness is a multi-faceted social problem. Moreover, the situations of

U.S. fathers today are highly diverse and increasingly problematic: many are very young, many are divorced, many are never-married, and many confront multiple problems, from racism to poor education to joblessness to drug addiction. For these reasons, the measurements of progress for a fatherhood movement must also be realistically wide-ranging and diverse, while at the same time pointing always toward a coherent vision of fatherhood.

To me, the leading indicators for evaluating progress in the fatherhood movement should include:

- The proportion of Americans who believe that all children deserve fathers and that fatherlessness poses serious risks for children and society.
- The proportion of children who have a positive, enduring relationship with at least one responsible adult male.
- The proportion of children whose fathers are legally identified.
- The proportion of children whose fathers support them financially.
- The proportion of children whose fathers regularly spend time with them.
- The proportion of children whose fathers live with them.
- The proportion of children who spend their childhood living with their two, married parents.
- The proportion of children whose fathers responsibly love and nurture them to adulthood.

Of these eight indicators, the last is the most important—the ultimate vision of the fatherhood movement—as well as the only one that is almost impossible to measure empirically. In one sense, then, perhaps all the other indicators can be viewed as proxies, indirect but hopeful pointers toward this final objective. In all likelihood, the proportion of children who grow up with their two married parents will prove to be the single most reliable indicator of how many children have responsible fathers who help to love and nurture them to adulthood.

The second challenge for the fatherhood movement is racial reconciliation. Twenty or even ten years ago, fatherlessness was largely seen as a black problem, with specific causes and dimensions that were distinct from trends affecting the larger society. Moreover, from the mid-1960s until quite recently, many opinion leaders, both white and black, have insisted—a few still insist today—that calling attention to father-absence amounts to little more than racism, an attempt to blame the victim. In short, fatherlessness in recent decades has been a racially charged and racially divisive issue.

No longer. The extent of fatherlessness among whites today matches almost exactly the extent of fatherlessness among blacks in 1965—the year that President Lyndon Johnson declared a War on Poverty aimed largely, he said in his famous Howard University speech of that year, at redressing "the breakdown of the Negro family structure."[1] Fatherlessness is currently increasing faster among whites than among blacks. No longer, then, according to any reasonable measurement, can fatherlessness be viewed as a black problem, a poverty problem, a "them" problem. It's an "us" problem.

For this reason, more than almost any other issue, fatherlessness can be an issue that bridges the racial divide, a crisis that brings us together for a common purpose. Our guiding premise should be: one challenge, one movement.

The third challenge for the fatherhood movement is supporting marriage. As several of these essays suggest—and as the diverse views expressed in this volume clearly demonstrate—the "m" word is often controversial in discussions and programs regarding fatherhood. Some people feel that marriage itself is a problematic institution. Others worry about "imposing values" or sounding too preachy.

Others worry about being unrealistic. In this view, marriage may be a fine thing, but like it or not, many fathers today are divorced or never-married. Is the fatherhood movement ignoring them or writing them off? Besides, why single out marriage as a necessary support system for fatherhood? Aren't there other viable ways for men to care for their children?

Well, at least in my view, not really. Across history and cultures, nurturant fatherhood has rested securely on two foundations: co-residency with children and a parental alliance with the mother. All human societies have recognized these living arrangements as structural pre-conditions for effective fatherhood. All have created public ceremonies to legalize and sacralize them. Everywhere, the name given to this pro-child way of living is "marriage."

Certainly, there are exceptions. Some never-married fathers, against all the odds, stick around and make it work. Some divorced fathers, at great personal cost, continue to be good fathers to their children. It is also true that something —a name on a birth certificate, a child support check in the mail, a weekend visit—is better than nothing. But let us be honest. There are not many exceptions. And these small things, these faint reminders of fatherhood, are only a little better than nothing. For the child, what really makes the difference is an in-the-home, love-the-mother father.

For this reason, the fatherhood movement ought to aim high. Sometimes, of course, our reach will exceed our grasp. Sometimes the best is not possible. But surely this movement ought to know, and be unafraid to say, what the best is.

To me, a marriage strategy is also the most realistic strategy. For there is little reason to believe—there is almost no empirical evidence to suggest—that we as a society can ignore or dispense with marriage while simultaneously renewing fatherhood. Everywhere, the two rise or fall together. That's one reason why marriage is often called a "natural" institution. It fits us as fathers. It best suits what our children need. That's also why Charles Ballard is not merely moralizing or engaging in sentimentality when he says that the most important job of a father is to "love the mother of his child" and the most important job of employees of his Institute for Responsible Fatherhood is to "model excellence in marriage."

The fourth challenge for the fatherhood movement is recognizing the moral and religious dimensions of fatherhood. Several years ago, I wrote a book about fatherlessness. I tried to use social science research and cultural analysis to show that fatherlessness is the most harmful social trend of our generation. In that book, partly due to ignorance and partly because I wanted to make my argument in conventional terms, I said almost nothing about the relationship between human fatherhood and the fatherhood of God. I only asked: Do children need fathers? But what if the deeper question is: Do fathers need God? More precisely, does knowledge and love of God help a man to be a good father and a good husband? If so, why and how? The more I learn about contemporary fatherlessness in modern societies, the more I am persuaded that these are not only the hardest questions, they may also be the most important.

In this book, several authors approach this subject. Glenn Stanton and David Gutmann, from quite different but fascinatingly congruent perspectives, confront the issue directly. In the larger fatherhood movement, many (though certainly not all) of the current leaders are people of faith, and much of the movement's energy and most effective grass-roots activity is based in churches, synagogues, and other faith-based organizations. This is more, I would suggest, than a coincidence.

But if the faith dimension of fatherhood renewal is not a coincidence, what is it? Read Gutmann and Stanton for the good stuff, but here is a starting point. Fatherhood calls men to purposes larger than themselves. In this sense, the essence of fatherhood is the giving of oneself, connecting to others, and recognizing truths that are bigger than any one man. Having and loving a child thus becomes for the male a flesh-and-blood signal of the possibility of transcendence—perhaps his best chance to glimpse, even in his weakness and shortsightedness, that spark of the divine that is in every human person. For being a good father is as close as men can come to participating with God in creation.

Notes

1. "To Fulfill These Rights," Remarks of President Lyndon B. Johnson at Howard University, Washington, D.C., June 4, 1965.

Chapter One

Did You Say "Movement"?

Wade F. Horn

> *The single biggest social problem in our society may be the growing absence of fathers from their children's homes because it contributes to so many other social problems.*
> —Bill Clinton, President of the
> United States, 1995

> *We have arrived at a consensus that fathers have been lost and must be found.*
> —Ellen Goodman, syndicated columnist, 1996

> *Dan Quayle was right.*
> —Barbara Dafoe Whitehead, *Atlantic Monthly*,
> 1993

Fatherlessness in America today is an unprecedented reality with profound consequences for children and civil society. In 1960, the total number of children in the United States living in father-absent families was less than 10 million. Today, that number stands at *24 million.*[1] Nearly four out of ten children in America do not live in the same home as their father. By some estimates, this figure is likely to rise to 60 percent of children born in the 1990s.[2] For the first time in our history, the average expectable experience of childhood now includes a significant amount of time living absent one's own father.

For one million children each year, the pathway to a fatherless family is divorce.[3] The divorce rate nearly tripled from 1960 to 1980, before leveling off and declining slightly in the 1980s.[4] Today, 40 out of every 100 first marriages end in divorce, compared to 16 out of every 100 first marriages in 1960. No other industrialized nation has a higher divorce rate.[5]

The second pathway to a fatherless home is out-of-wedlock fathering. In 1960, about 5 percent of all births were out of wedlock. That number increased to 10.7 percent in 1970, 18.4 percent in 1980, 28 percent in 1990, and nearly 33 percent today.[6] In the United States, the number of children fathered out of wedlock each year (approximately 1.3 million annually) now surpasses the number of children whose parents divorce (approximately 1 million annually).

No region of the country has been immune to the growing problem of fatherlessness. Between 1980 and 1990, nonmarital birth rates increased in every state of the Union.[7] During this time period, ten states saw the rate of nonmarital births increase by over 60 percent. Furthermore, births to unmarried teenagers increased by 44 percent between 1985 and 1992.[8] In fact, 76 percent of all births to teenagers nationwide are now out of wedlock. In 15 of our nation's largest cities, the teenage out-of-wedlock birth rate exceeds 90 percent. Overall, the percent of families with children headed by a single parent currently stands at 29 percent, the vast majority of which are father-absent households.[9]

African Americans are disproportionately affected by the problem of father absence. Sixty-three percent of African American children live in father-absent homes. But fatherlessness is by no means a problem affecting minorities only. The absolute number of father-absent families is larger—and the rate of father absence is growing the fastest—in the white community. Currently, nearly 13 million white children reside in father-absent homes, compared to 6.5 million African American children.[10]

Research consistently documents that unmarried fathers, whether through divorce or out-of-wedlock fathering, tend over time to become disconnected, both financially and psychologically, from their children. Forty percent of children in father-absent homes have not seen their father in at least a year. Of the remaining 60 percent, only one in five sleeps even one night per month in the father's home. Overall, only one in six sees their father an average of once or more per week.[11] More than half of all children who don't live with their fathers have never even been in their father's home.[12]

Unwed fathers are particularly unlikely to stay connected to their children over time. Whereas 57 percent of unwed fathers are visiting their child at least once per week during the first two years of their child's life, by the time their child reaches seven-and-one-half years of age, that percentage drops to less than 25 percent.[13] Indeed, approximately 75 percent of men who are not living with their children at the time of their birth never subsequently live with them.[14]

Even when unwed fathers are cohabitating with the mother at the time of their child's birth, they are very unlikely to stay involved in their children's lives over the long term. Although a quarter of nonmarital births occur to cohabiting couples, only four out of ten cohabiting, unwed fathers ever go on to marry the mother of their children, and those that do are more likely to eventually divorce than men who father children within marriage.[15] Remarriage, or, in cases of an unwed father, marriage to someone other than the child's mother, makes it especially unlikely that a noncustodial father will remain in contact with his children.[16]

The absence of fathers in the home has profound consequences for children. Almost 75 percent of American children living in single-parent families will experience poverty before they turn 11 years old, compared to only 20 percent of children in two-parent families.[17] Children who grow up absent their fathers are also more likely to fail at school or to drop out,[18] experience behavioral or emotional problems requiring psychiatric treatment,[19] engage in early sexual activity,[20] and develop drug and alcohol problems.[21]

Children growing up with absent fathers are especially likely to experience violence. Violent criminals are overwhelmingly males who grew up without fathers, including up to 60 percent of rapists,[22] 75 percent of adolescents charged with murder,[23] and 70 percent of juveniles in state reform institutions.[24] Children who grow up without fathers are also three times more likely to commit suicide as adolescents[25] and to be victims of child abuse or neglect.[26]

In light of these data, Urie Bronfenbrenner, noted developmental psychologist, has concluded:

> Controlling for factors such as low income, children growing up in [father-absent] households are at a greater risk for experiencing a variety of behavioral and educational problems, including extremes of hyperactivity and withdrawal; lack of attentiveness in the classroom; difficulty in deferring gratification; impaired academic achievement; school misbehavior; absenteeism; dropping out; involvement in socially alienated peer groups, and the so-called 'teenage syndrome' of behaviors that tend to hang together—smoking, drinking, early and frequent sexual experience, and in the more extreme cases, drugs, suicide, vandalism, violence, and criminal acts.[27]

If ever there was a problem in need of a broad-based social movement, it is fatherhood. For the evidence suggests that we can expect little improvement in the well-being of either our children or our communities without a restoration of responsible and committed fatherhood as a valued, respected, and widely practiced institution. In short, if a fatherhood movement does not yet exist, someone better start one.

Characteristics of a Social Movement

A social movement has been defined by sociologist John Wilson as a "conscious, collective, organized attempt to bring about or resist large-scale change in the social order by noninstitutionalized means."[28] Social movements are important because they frequently are the means through which new ideas and practices enter the social fabric. Indeed, the very appearance of a social movement is a sign that the old social order is being challenged.

Social movements typically view existing institutional structures as part of the problem, and hence unlikely avenues for achieving social change. Social movements have broad goals and incorporate diverse groups of people as they seek to affect not just their own constituency, but society as a whole.

Social movements do not emerge or succeed by accident. Although they may capitalize on fortuitous events to further their goals, their founding is purposive and their activities transcend the vagaries of day-to-day events. In this way, they are different from temporary coalitions or mere aggregate action.

Successful social movements frequently go through a three-stage developmental process. The first stage is the setting of an agenda, during which the problem is defined and given urgency. Sometimes, this occurs through the appearance of an influential book. The modern environmental movement was, for example, largely triggered by the publication in 1962 of Rachel Carson's book *Silent Spring*. Alternatively, a social movement may have its agenda set by a major speech, a focusing conference, or even a television program. Some, for example, credit the airing of a 1990 Bill Moyers television special "A Gathering of Men" for kick-starting a modern men's movement.

This does not mean, of course, that there were no organizations or individuals working on behalf of the issue prior to the birth of a social movement. All social movements have roots that predate themselves. For example, as pointed out by noted columnist William Raspberry,

> [e]very single element of what was to become the Civil Rights Movement was already being carried out by someone, somewhere. Before there was a movement there were voter registration drives, demonstrations against segregated parks and swimming pools, attempts to desegregate residential areas, restaurants and other places of public accommodation.[29]

What defines the birth of a social movement, therefore, is that the disparate activities of various organizations and individuals are, for the first time, brought together under one overarching philosophical or organizational umbrella. In doing so, the movement is able to heighten the public's awareness of the issue in ways that no single group or individual would have been able to achieve, while at the same time giving new significance and power to the various organizations and individuals comprising the movement. In other words, with the birth of a movement, the total becomes greater than the sum of the parts.

The second stage is recruitment of members from outside the initial group of originators. These members are recruited by various groups, whether formally or informally. Most successful movements do not draw their members using one charismatic leader, for when membership recruitment is too reliant on the activities of an individual, gathering converts is likely to be slow or highly episodic. Instead, the most successful social movements are those that develop more generalized strategies for membership recruitment, thereby enhancing their reach. The 19th-century temperance movement, for example, developed the strategy of convening revival-style gatherings to encourage individuals to take a pledge of abstinence as a signal of their allegiance to the temperance movement. In fact, over-identification of a single leader with a cause can be one distinguishing feature between a social movement and a cult or fad.

The third stage is the development of organizational structures capable of sustaining the movement. In some cases, one preeminent organization emerges, serving as the main vehicle for coordinating the movement and communicating its message. In other cases, several relatively autonomous organizations emerge, but with each dedicated to an overarching goal. As the movement progresses, the development of local chapters can help sustain it and nurture new leaders.

Given this understanding of social movements, is there a fatherhood movement?

The Birth of a Movement

If there is a fatherhood movement, one of its early stirrings revolves around 39 words delivered by a public figure widely perceived at the time as an intellectual lightweight—Vice President Dan Quayle. While campaigning for re-election, Dan Quayle made a speech on May 19, 1992, at the Commonwealth Club of California in San Francisco, during which he asserted: "It doesn't help matters, when prime time TV has Murphy Brown—a character who supposedly epitomizes today's intelligent, highly paid, professional woman—mocking the importance of fathers, by bearing a child alone, and calling it just another 'lifestyle choice.'"

The importance of this event was not that Dan Quayle himself went on to lead, or even propose the formation of, a fatherhood movement. In fact, prior to Quayle's speech, several national commissions, including the National Commission on Children and the National Commission on Urban Families, had already concluded that father absence was one of the most significant problems facing America. Rather, the importance of the Quayle speech was that it galvanized others to come to the defense, if not of him, at least of the larger point he was trying to make—that fathers matter to the well-being of children and that society experiments with father absence at its peril. His speech was not the creative moment, but rather the defining moment.

One of the first spirited defenses of Quayle's point was the appearance in the *Atlantic Monthly* magazine of an influential article by Barbara Dafoe Whitehead entitled "Dan Quayle Was Right." In this article, Whitehead laments that "every time the issue of family structure has been raised, the response has been first controversy, then retreat, and finally silence." Undaunted, she continues:

> The debate . . . is not simply about the social-scientific evidence, although that is surely an important part of the discussion. It is also a debate over deeply held and often conflicting values. How do we begin to reconcile our long-standing belief in equality and diversity with an impressive body of evidence that suggests that not all family structures produce equal outcomes for children? . . . How do we uphold the freedom of adults to pursue individual happiness in their private relationships and at the same time respond to the needs of children for stability, security, and permanence in their family lives?[30]

The themes laid out in Whitehead's article were further refined and expanded in a series of compelling articles and books, including *Life Without Father* (1996) by David Popenoe; *New Expectations: Community Strategies for Responsible Fatherhood* (1995) by James Levine and Edward Pitt; *FatherLove* (1993) by Richard Louv; "Marriage in America: A Report to the Nation" (1996) by the Council on Families; and, most especially, *Fatherless America: Confronting Our Most Urgent Social Problem* (1995) by David Blankenhorn. These writings, in turn, spawned a renewed interest in programmatic activity on the fatherhood issue, including skill-building programs, outreach programs for unwed fathers, the development of public service announcements, and legislative advocacy. In fact, the most compelling evidence for an emerging fatherhood movement is the dramatic increase in the number of books and programs, both secular and sectarian, addressing fatherhood that have appeared over the past several years. In just a few short years, fatherhood has grown from a topic worthy of derision to an important and legitimate subject for serious journalists, social commentators, philanthropists, and social programmers.

But to be considered a social movement, the fatherhood issue must be more than a collection of disparate activities—more than a search for new knowledge about the institution of fatherhood, seminars to increase the skills of fathers, or the pursuit of legislative victories for divorced and unwed fathers. To be considered a social movement, there must, at a minimum, be evidence of a purposive, collective effort to organize under a single theme, and, in doing so, to seek broad social change.

On this score, there is evidence that we are witnessing, if not the actual birth, then at least the labor pains, of a fatherhood movement. Increasingly, fatherhood advocates, researchers, analysts, and programmers are coming together to seek common cause. Although these leaders and organizations certainly maintain a primary interest in their own activities and agenda, increasingly there is a sense that each is a part of a larger whole—that the work of each is contributing to a greater social good. Despite widely divergent perspectives on the causes of and strategies for overcoming fatherlessness, leaders in the fatherhood arena are demonstrating an increasing willingness to put aside their differences in the pursuit of a common goal—ensuring that an increasing proportion of children grow up with an involved, committed, and responsible father.

Probably the earliest manifestation of this desire to seek common cause under the fatherhood banner was the convening of the first-ever National Summit on Fatherhood in Dallas, Texas, in October of 1994.[31] Hosted by the newly formed National Fatherhood Initiative, an organization of which I am president, this gathering attracted over 200 fatherhood advocates, researchers, and public policy analysts, along with fathers' rights advocates, fathering education and skill building experts, advocates for low-income fathers, and religious leaders involved in fatherhood promotion. Other gatherings followed, including the formation in 1995 by the philanthropic community of the Funders Collaborative on Fathers and Families; a 1995 Father's Day gathering in the District of Columbia of major fatherhood activists; an Interfaith Summit on Fatherhood in June of 1996; state-wide, governor-sponsored fatherhood conferences in California (1995), Massachusetts (1996), Indiana (1996 and 1997), and South Carolina (1997); and a conference on the fatherhood movement in 1996 in Minneapolis, Minnesota, that resulted in this book.

The Elements Needed

A bona fide movement requires more than simply a series of meetings and conferences. It also requires sufficient ideas, numbers, distinctiveness, and organization. The answer to the question of whether or not the fatherhood movement has these qualities is, at best, maybe.

The fatherhood movement certainly has no paucity of ideas. Everyone involved in the fatherhood issue believes passionately in their own perspective and idiosyncratic agenda. Religiously oriented advocates believe fatherhood is part of God's plan, without recognition of which the institution of fatherhood will not be recovered. Fathers' rights advocates consider the current focus on deadbeat dads inaccurate and counterproductive and lobby for divorce and child custody reforms. Advocates for low-income men believe poor economic circumstances are a primary cause of fatherlessness and see the solution in job training and education programs for disadvantaged and minority men. Culturalists believe fatherlessness is a failure of our culture to reinforce a compelling fatherhood script and seek the definition of one. Marriage advocates believe only a restoration of the institution of marriage will lead to a renewal of

fatherhood. The list of ideas concerning the nature of fatherhood and the cure
for father absence goes on and on.

Is There a Core Idea?

But for a social movement to survive, it must eventually coalesce around a
single core idea, while at the same time respecting diversity of opinion. This is,
perhaps, the most immediate challenge facing the nascent fatherhood
movement. It will require achieving a delicate balance between having a set of
firmly-held beliefs and accommodating a diversity of viewpoints. If, on the one
hand, the movement is too rigid and uncompromising, it will have difficulty
attracting followers and building momentum. If, on the other, the movement is
overly accommodating to differing opinions, it will have difficulty sustaining an
energized, passionate, and committed leadership and communicating a clear and
unambiguous message to the public at large.

So, if there is a fatherhood movement, what is its core idea around which its
member organizations can coalesce? Although there is certainly room for
legitimate debate on what the core idea ought to be, here is my candidate:
Every child deserves the love, support, and nurturance of a legally and morally
responsible father. This core idea is based on three assumptions: (1) responsible
and committed fatherhood ought to be a norm of masculinity; (2) fathers are
different from mothers in important ways; and (3) the father-child bond is
important to the healthy development of children. It is also the core idea
expressed in the "Call To Fatherhood" at the end of this book.

But social movements are not just about establishing a core idea or mere
consciousness raising. They are about changing behavior. Abolitionists in the
19th century were not content with having the public agree with them that
slavery was wrong; they wanted it abolished. The temperance movement was
not content with the public agreeing that alcoholic beverages, and especially
"hard" liquor, were bad for one's moral and physical health; it wanted alcohol
consumption dramatically reduced, if not stopped. So too, the fatherhood
movement cannot be about getting the public to agree that fathers are "good"; it
must be about changing the behavior of men and women to ensure that a greater
proportion of children grow up with involved fathers. This goal requires that the
movement settle on at least the broad outlines of an agenda for social change.

But if achieving agreement on a core message is difficult, attaining a
consensus on an overarching agenda for achieving broad social change will be
even more difficult. Will, for example, the divorced men's groups be able to
reconcile their agenda to improve access of divorced and noncustodial fathers to
their children with the agenda of those who seek greater accountability from
noncustodial fathers through stronger child support enforcement? Will
organizations dedicated to advancing the interests of noncustodial, unwed
fathers be able to coalesce with a movement that also includes advocates for

stronger statutory rape laws? And will those organizations that advocate marriage as the institution most likely to deliver fathers to children be able to coalesce with those that seek greater involvement of noncustodial fathers in the lives of children?

The answers to these questions are by no means clear. But social movements succeed only when their member groups, while still pursuing their own individual agenda, see themselves within a larger context. The alternative is a return to focusing on the parts, at the expense of the whole. If this happens, the nascent movement will surely be stillborn.

Is There Broad Appeal?

There do seem to be signs of a developing grassroots dimension to the fatherhood issue. Most notably, Promise Keepers, an evangelical Christian enterprise seeking, in part, to inspire men to be better husbands and fathers, routinely draws tens of thousands of devotees to football stadiums across the nation. Similarly, the Million Man March in the summer of 1995 drew over a half million African American men and their sons to the nation's capital. The message from these gatherings that fathers matter certainly does seem to have some resonance with the general public. What is still needed is a means for converting grassroots participation in these special events into mass identification with the core message and agenda of a fatherhood movement.

Thus far, this goal is unmet, primarily because the sponsoring organizations of these special events emphasize other issues in addition to fatherhood. Promise Keepers encourages not only responsible fatherhood, but also, and more centrally, reconciliation with God and the acceptance of Jesus Christ as one's personal savior. Speakers at the Million Man March organized by Louis Farrakhan preached not only the importance of responsible fatherhood, but also the need to organize politically to thwart the plans of a Republican-led Congress to downsize the federal government. Certainly it is legitimate for these organizations to have a broader agenda than fatherhood. But doing so dilutes the fatherhood message at these gatherings and makes it harder to develop a grassroots membership specific to and identified with a fatherhood movement.

In addition to developing a strategy for greater identification of the grass roots with the core message and agenda of the movement, the fatherhood movement must also find ways to broaden its appeal beyond its natural constituency of men. Historically, many successful social movements found creative ways of forging coalitions with other organizations and constituencies. The abolition movement was able to forge an alliance with pro-union sentiments in its battle against slavery. Similarly, the women's movement creatively found connections with fathers of daughters in its pursuit of equal rights for women. So too, the fatherhood movement will need to garner the active support of women and women's organizations if it is to be successful.

Is It Distinctive?

While the fatherhood issue has a number of historical roots, including the men's, fathers' rights, civil rights, and mythopoetic movements, it is distinct from these movements in a number of critical ways. First, the men's, fathers' rights, and mythopoetic movements tend to be inner-directed (toward the feelings, needs, and well-being of men and fathers), whereas the fatherhood movement is largely other-directed (toward the feelings, needs, and well-being of children). These former movements also tend to be focused on the "rights" of men and fathers, whereas the fatherhood movement is largely focused on the "responsibilities" of fathers. Thus, the fatherhood movement does not appear to be merely a branch of some other men's movement.[32]

A more critical issue is whether or not the fatherhood movement is distinct from a marriage movement. Many people, including several contributors to this book, argue fatherhood and marriage go hand in hand. One can not have the former, they argue, without first having the latter. Indeed, some even argue that ultimately the fatherhood movement's importance lies in its being a "stalking horse" for a marriage movement. If these critics are correct, there is no fatherhood movement; only the stirrings of a marriage movement. If so, some groups and leaders currently seeking to help establish a fatherhood movement will surely splinter away. In fact, we are already seeing the marriage issue develop into a dividing line within the fatherhood movement. Resolution of this issue is, therefore, one of the most critical challenges facing the fatherhood movement.

Is There Organizational Structure?

The establishment of a number of national fatherhood groups over the past several years, including the National Fatherhood Initiative, the National Center for Fathers and Families, the National Institute for Responsible Fatherhood and Family Revitalization, and the National Center for Fathering, suggests that the rough outlines of a movement "infrastructure" are starting to emerge. Although there is an attempt by a group of private philanthropic foundations to nurture and organize the fatherhood "field," thus far the chief organizational features of the emerging fatherhood movement are decentralization and specialization, not centralization and hierarchical command-and-control. Some fatherhood groups specialize in increasing public awareness, others in teaching fathering skills, others in stimulating research, and still others in public advocacy. No one national fatherhood group commands the allegiance or deference of any other.

Given this penchant toward specialized and decentralized organizational structures, it seems unlikely that the fatherhood movement will galvanize around a single organization, akin to the way the women's movement coalesced around the National Organization for Women. Instead, it appears likely that the fatherhood movement will function through a broad array of like-minded, and often specialized, organizations, similar to what has developed within the environmental movement.

The lack of a centralized organizational structure creates certain advantages for movement making, including a more flexible, diverse, and pluralistic movement; less reliance on any one leader or small group of leaders; and the ability to try different approaches and solutions. But a decentralized organizational structure also creates certain disadvantages. First, it makes the clarification of a core message all the more critical, without which the movement may simply become an ever-shifting series of temporary alliances among the various member organizations. Second, it makes it harder for member organizations to move beyond their idiosyncratic agendas and embrace a common overarching agenda for achieving social change. Third, it makes it more difficult for the grass roots to identify primarily with the broader fatherhood movement, as opposed to the parochial interests of a single organization. Still, as evidenced by the success of the environmental movement, it is an organizational structure that can work. But it does make movement building more difficult.

The Measurement for Success

One critical issue for all social movements is how to measure success. One possible measure is the degree to which the movement is able to increase public awareness of the importance of fathers to the well-being of children. Progress toward this goal could easily be measured through public opinion surveys. There are, in fact, already indications that an increasing majority of Americans view father absence as the most significant social problem of our time. But while attitudinal change is helpful, it is not sufficient. Enhancing public awareness of the fatherhood problem does not guarantee that an increasing proportion of children will grow up with an involved, committed, and responsible father. In fact, numerous psychological and sociological studies indicate that while attitudinal change is frequently a precursor of behavior change, it is neither necessary nor sufficient.

Another possible measure is whether or not the number of children living with their biological fathers has increased. On the surface, this goal seems self-evident. If the problem is father absence, the solution must be father presence. As such, one would assess the success of the fatherhood movement by declining divorce and out-of-wedlock birth rates. But while reversing the historically high divorce and out-of-wedlock birth rates would logically reduce fatherlessness, father presence alone is not sufficient as the goal of the fatherhood movement. For a father to have a positive impact on the development of his children, he must not only be present, he must be involved. It is only when fathers are engaged in the lives of their children, not just as co-residents, but as nurturers, disciplinarians, teachers, coaches, and moral instructors, that their children evidence greater self-esteem, higher educational achievement, a more secure gender identity, and greater success in life. If the present father is, in actuality, psychologically and morally absent, or worse still, abusive, his presence may well make things worse, not better, for children.

Ultimately, I believe the most important outcome measure for a fatherhood movement is improvement in the well-being of children. As such, increasing father presence is really an intervening or process variable, one that may or may not improve the true outcome measure of interest: the well-being of children. Focusing on improving the status of children as the goal for the fatherhood movement holds the best promise for achieving a broad-based coalition of both men and women dedicated to revitalizing responsible and committed fatherhood as a respected and valued social institution.

Promoting fatherhood, then, is really a strategy for improving the well-being of children, just as promoting abstinence from alcohol was really a strategy for promoting civic virtue through moderation. In fact, an interest in improving the well-being of children is the entire rationale for the fatherhood movement, for if father absence did not increase the risk of poor outcomes for children, there would be no need for a fatherhood movement. If, in the end, increasing the proportion of children growing up with fathers does not enhance child well-being, the fatherhood movement ought to be judged a failure, and we all ought to move on to something else.

A Movement Enemy

A final issue is whether or not the fatherhood movement needs an enemy—an opposition against which the troops can be energized. Abolitionists railed against the evils of slavery; the temperance movement against demon alcohol. What should fatherhood advocates rail against?

Some are tempted to designate absent fathers as the "enemy." Certainly there are too many men who desert and abandon their families, and such men ought to be ostracized. But designating absent fathers as the bogeyman will undoubtedly alienate one potentially important constituency of the fatherhood movement: divorced fathers. Indeed, with a good measure of truth, divorced fathers frequently contend that they very much want to remain actively involved in the lives of their children, but are prevented from doing so by a court system that treats them like "cash machines" and by ex-wives who deny them access to their children. Unless the fatherhood movement is ready to write off this constituency—and some appear willing to do so—it designates absent fathers as the "enemy" at its peril.

Others assert that the enemy is feminism. But a fatherhood movement which seeks simply to turn back the hands of time to an earlier period when men were patriarchs and feminists were rare will surely fail. It is only by forging a movement that seeks a revitalization of fatherhood within a modern understanding of the enhanced choices, rights, and prerogatives of women that the fatherhood movement has a chance to succeed.

If an enemy there need be, here is my candidate: family relativism—the notion that all family structures are morally and socially equivalent, all equally deserving of support, and all equally good for children. Elevating family relativism to "bogeyman" status does not mean that one has to demean other family structures. One can assert that children do best when they are reared with the love and commitment of a mother and a father, bound in marriage and dedicated to each other, and still demonstrate compassion for the fatherless and provide support for widowed and abandoned mothers. But the argument must be made—frequently and with great passion—that society needs a critical mass of married two-parent families, both to raise their own children well and to serve as models for children growing up in alternative family structures. Tragically, we are in great danger today of losing that critical mass; in some communities it has already been lost. Whatever else it does, the fatherhood movement must be, in large measure, about reclaiming that critical mass.

A Work in Progress

For those who seek a fatherhood movement, there is evidence of one in the making. Delicate, certainly. Ill-formed, of course. In need of definition, yes. But a movement nonetheless. Its leadership is clearly committed to effecting broad-based social change, and it does seem to have sufficient ideas and a growing grassroots presence. Furthermore, the rough outlines of an organizational structure are appearing—although no one organization appears likely to emerge to lead it.

But critical issues remain. Can the movement achieve consensus on a common core message and, even more importantly, on a core agenda for achieving social change, without undue fragmentation and splintering of its member organizations? Can an effective grassroots membership be cultivated that will identify with the core message and agenda of the movement? Will the highly decentralized organizational structure that seems to be emerging serve the fatherhood movement well, or will it increase the pressure toward fragmentation? Is the fatherhood movement really only a stalking horse for a marriage movement?

Given the uncertain resolution of these questions, perhaps it is best to consider the fatherhood movement a work-in-progress. But important work it surely is. Let us get on with that work.

Notes

1. Wade F. Horn, *Father Facts, 3rd ed.* (Gaithersburg, Md.: National Fatherhood Initiative, 1998).

2. Frank F. Furstenberg Jr. and Andrew J. Cherlin, *Divided Families: What Happens to Children When Parents Part* (Cambridge, Mass.: Harvard University Press, 1991).

3. U.S. Bureau of the Census, *Statistical Abstracts of the United States 1997* (Washington, D.C.: U.S. Government Printing Office, 1997).

4. U.S. Department of Commerce, Bureau of the Census, "Statistical Abstract of the United States, 1993" (Washington, D.C.: U.S. Government Printing Office, 1993).

5. National Commission on Children, "Just the Facts: A Summary of Recent Information on America's Children and Their Families" (Washington, D.C.: U.S. Government Printing Office, 1993).

6. Harry M. Rosenberg, Stephanie J. Ventura, Jeffrey D. Maurer, Robert L. Heuser and Mary Freedman, *Births and Deaths in the United States, 1995*, Monthly Vital Statistics Report 45 (1996).

7. Stephanie J. Ventura et al., "The Demography of Out-of-Wedlock Childbearing," in U.S. Department of Health and Human Services, National Center for Health Statistics, "Report to Congress on Out-of-Wedlock Childbearing," DHHS Pub. no. (PHS) 95-1257, (Washington, D.C.: U.S. Government Printing Office, 1995): 105.

8. *Kids Count Data Book: State Profiles of Child Well-Being* (Baltimore: Annie E. Casey Foundation, 1995): 125.

9. Ibid.

10. U.S. House of Representatives, Committee on Ways and Means, "1993 Green Book" (Washington, D.C.: U.S. Government Printing Office, 1993); Arlene Saluter, U.S. Department of Commerce, Bureau of the Census, "Marital Status and Living Arrangements: March 1993," Current Population Reports: Population Characteristics P20-478 (Washington, D.C.: U.S. Government Printing Office, 1994); Stacy Furudawa, U.S. Department of Commerce, Bureau of the Census, "Diverse Living Arrangements of Children: Summer 1991," Current Population Reports: Household Economic Studies (Washington, D.C.: U.S. Government Printing Office, 1994).

11. Frank F. Furstenberg Jr., and Christine Winquist Nord, "Parenting Apart: Patterns of Child Rearing After Marital Disruption," *Journal of Marriage and the Family* (November 1985): 896.

12. Furstenberg and Cherlin, *Divided Families: What Happens to Children When Parents Part.*

13. Robert Lerman and Theodora Ooms, *Young Unwed Fathers: Changing Roles and Emerging Policies* (Philadelphia: Temple, 1993): 45.

14. Ibid.

15. Kristin A. Moore, "Nonmarital Childbearing in the United States" in U.S. Department of Health and Human Services, "Report to Congress on Out-of-Wedlock Childbearing," DHHS Pub. no. (PHS) 95-1257 (Washington, D.C.: U.S. Government Printing Office, 1995): vii.

16. Linda S. Stephens, "Will Johnny See Daddy This Week?" *Journal of Family Issues* 17 (1996): 466-94.

17. National Commission on Children, "Just the Facts: A Summary of Recent

Information on America's Children and Their Families" (Washington, D.C.: U.S. Government Printing Office, 1993).

18. Debra Dawson, "Family Structure and Children's Well-Being: Data from the 1988 National Health Survey," *Journal of Marriage and Family* 53 (1991); U.S. Department of Health and Human Services, National Center for Health Statistics, "Survey of Child Health" (Washington, D.C.: U.S. Government Printing Office, 1993).

19. U.S. Department of Health and Human Services, National Center for Health Statistics, "National Health Interview Survey" (Hyattsville, Md.: U.S. Government Printing Office, 1988).

20. Irwin Garfinkel and Sara McLanahan, *Single Mothers and Their Children* (Washington, D.C.: Urban Institute Press, 1986); Susan Newcomer and J. Richard Udry, "Parental Marital Status Effects on Adolescent Sexual Behavior," *Journal of Marriage and the Family* (May 1987): 235-40.

21. U.S. Department of Health and Human Services, National Center for Health Statistics, "Survey on Child Health" (Washington, D.C.: U.S. Government Printing Office, 1993).

22. Nicholas Davidson, "Life Without Father," *Policy Review* (1990).

23. Dewey Cornell et al., "Characteristics of Adolescents Charged with Homicide," *Behavioral Sciences and the Law* 5 (1987): 11-23.

24. M. Eileen Matlock et al., "Family Correlates of Social Skills Deficits in Incarcerated and Nonincarcerated Adolescents," *Adolescence* 29 (1994): 119-30.

25. Patricia L. McCall and Kenneth C. Land, "Trends in White Male Adolescent Young-Adults and Elderly Suicide: Are There Common Underlying Structural Factors?" *Social Science Research* 23 (1994): 57-81; U.S. Department of Health and Human Services, National Center for Health Statistics, "Survey on Child Health" (Washington, D.C.: U.S. Government Printing Office, 1993).

26. Catherine M. Malkin and Michael E. Lamb, "Child Maltreatment: A Test of Sociobiological Theory," *Journal of Comparative Family Studies* 25 (1994): 121-30.

27. Urie Bronfenbrenner, "What do Families do?" *Family Affairs* (winter/spring 1991): 1-6.

28. John Wilson, *Introduction to Social Movements* (New York: Basic Books, 1973).

29. William Raspberry, "Start With The Boys," *Washington Post,* April 19, 1996.

30. Barbara Dafoe Whitehead, "Dan Quayle Was Right," *Atlantic Monthly* (April 1993): 47-48.

31. One might argue that Vice President Al Gore's meeting in Nashville, Tennessee, in July of 1994, was the first fatherhood gathering. Initially, that conference was to focus on fatherhood. As planning progressed, however, the focus changed from "fatherhood" to "male involvement," reflecting just how politically sensitive the topic of fatherhood was at the time. But encouraging *male* involvement in the lives of children is quite different from encouraging *father* involvement. Hence, Vice President Al Gore's meeting may have been an important precursor to the fatherhood movement, but its broader focus argues against portraying it as the initiating event of a fatherhood movement.

32. In its emphasis on responsibilities over rights, the fatherhood movement appears to be distinct not only from the men's and fathers' rights movements, but many modern social movements as well. In fact, most large-scale social movements in the 20th century have mostly to do with expanding the rights of a designated group, whether that group be minorities, women, or homosexuals. It remains to be seen whether or not the fatherhood

movement's emphasis on personal responsibility and obligation to others will resonate with a culture more accustomed to calls for expanded rights.

Chapter Two

Challenging the Culture of Fatherlessness

David Popenoe

To understand how to renew fatherhood, we must turn to marriage. Marriage is the institution that holds men to their children. Both the economy and the government have no doubt played some part in the marriage decline of the past three decades. But by far the most important factor is the culture, changes in the realm of values, attitudes, and beliefs. "At no time in history, with the possible exception of Imperial Rome," Kingsley Davis, the eminent demographer, says, "has the institution of marriage been more problematic than it is today."[1] As we know, Imperial Rome collapsed, and family difficulties are typically invoked by scholars to help account for its demise.

The Culture of Modernity

The importance of cultural change for marriage decline and fatherlessness, in contrast to effects of the economy and public policy, can clearly be seen through a comparison of modern nations. The modern nation that today leads the pack in fatherlessness and marriage instability, including having the highest divorce rate, is the United States. If family problems are mainly the result of economic deprivation, as is often asserted, it is difficult to reconcile that idea with this nation's status as the world's wealthiest in terms of consumer purchasing power. To be sure, poverty is no friend of marriage. But neither is affluence. In general, affluence breeds personal freedom and opportunity that is corrosive of traditional institutions and social obligations.

Perhaps the American problem, then, rests in the arena of public policy. Government intervention into the economy and the culture is considerably less in the United States than in any other Western nation, and many consider this to be a fundamental cause of our family decline. But consider Sweden, which is widely recognized to have the world's most comprehensive welfare state. Sweden has today what is probably the world's lowest marriage rate, and it also has one of Europe's highest levels of fatherlessness. One reason is the negative effect of welfare provisions on marriage formation, an effect which we have seen clearly in America's "welfare population."[2] The lack of welfare programs should not be considered a contributor to stable family life. But just as important are the unintended consequences of government welfare programs and the welfare culture that grows up around them in discouraging marriages and making them easier to dissolve.

So what can we conclude from the Western world's most laissez-faire nation and its most government-interventionist nation both having serious problems of marital instability and fatherlessness? Let us add one more fact: As the other nations of the West grow wealthier—more modern—their family structures weaken. The common denominator in all of these situations is the ever-expanding culture of modernity, which exists at a mature stage in the United States and Sweden and is rapidly advancing in the other Western nations.

The culture of modernity emphasizes personal freedom and opportunity apart from traditional values and social structures. The reason it is advancing so rapidly is that almost everyone desires it. Who doesn't wish for more freedom and opportunity to do what they want to do, when they want to do it? The problem is that when people's individualistic drives proceed so far that their social responsibilities and obligations are neglected, the social order weakens. And a stable and secure social order is necessary if freedom and opportunity are to be both pervasive and enduring.

The culture of modernity has been gaining momentum in the West for several hundred years. Yet only in the past few decades have we seen signs of an imbalance, in which the individualistic impulses have begun seriously to impinge upon the necessary components of community and order. This recent period, indeed, has been witness to an abrupt and extraordinary transformation of people's values, world view, and even self-definition, the ground rules by which we live. Large segments of the population have come to regard pure "self-fulfillment" as their dominant life goal, pushing aside such traditional "Victorian" values as self-sacrifice, commitment to others, and institutional obligation. This cultural shift has been widely documented by public opinion surveys. Daniel Yankelovich found, for example, that people today place a much lower value on what they owe others as a matter of moral obligation, and a much higher value on self-realization and personal choice.[3]

One of the most important repercussions of advanced modernity, with its radical individualism, is that the traditional moral legitimacy and authority of almost all social institutions, such as education, religion, and the professions, erode. People lose trust and faith and confidence in them. In this respect, no institution in the past few decades has been harder hit than marriage. Trust and confidence in marriage as a stable, lifelong social endeavor have plummeted.

Marriage is the historical basis of family life; as marriage goes, so goes the family. The authors of a recent history of the American family opined: "What Americans have witnessed since 1960 are fundamental challenges to the forms, ideals, and role-expectations that have defined the family for the last century and a half."[4]

Americans still believe in the importance of finding a lifetime mate and in "getting married someday." But marriage has become less a social institution that expresses society's goals and much more a personal, voluntary relationship which individuals can make or break at will in their search for self-fulfillment. "Till death do us part" has been replaced by "so long as I am happy" or "until I change my mind."

The Path to Fatherlessness

Let us briefly review the history of fatherhood in America.[5] In the colonial period, families tended to be heavily fathered. The father was the acknowledged family leader, and he was primarily responsible for his children's education and moral development (which was primarily religious in nature). Both fathers and mothers were in the labor force as farmers or small shopkeepers in or near their own homes, with their children working alongside them.

Then, associated with the rise of industry and towns in the early 1800s, what historians call the "modern nuclear family" arose. The new wage labor in factories and offices required the man to be away from home during the work day, and his income enabled him and his family to leave the farm and live in a town. It also enabled his wife to become a full-time housewife and childrearer. Fathers began to take a backseat in childrearing, leaving the task mainly up to women. But the town-living mothers typically were surrounded by caring relatives and neighbors to help them. Starting in the higher classes and gradually filtering down to the lower classes, this is the family form that predominated in the United States in various guises until the 1960s.

In the 20th century, however, and especially after 1960, more and more mothers entered the labor force and, like the fathers before them, left the home during the day. Moreover, they now lived not in towns but in suburbs or cities where the supportive "village" was largely absent. Fathers moved in two directions. Some, the so-called "good dads," helped to fill the vacuum left by the working mothers by becoming more involved in day-to-day child care than their own fathers ever had been.[6] But they were outnumbered by others, the "bad dads," who found great difficulty coming back into domestic life after more than a century of fathers having moved in the opposite direction. Many essentially abandoned their children via divorce and out-of-wedlock births, leaving the care of children solely up to women in single-parent families, which dramatically increased from 9 percent in 1960 to today's 27 percent.

The net effects of these shifts were not only a rapid increase in the number

of fatherless children, but a general decline in the amount of time that both
parents spend with their children in active childrearing. Children now spend less
time than ever before in family interactions, and more time with peers,
watching TV, and in school.

Two other cultural shifts in the late 19th and 20th centuries, both
fundamental components of the culture of modernity, had a great effect on
fathers and fathering. The first was a change in the nature of marriage.
Marriage was once a mostly economic and partly arranged relationship. Many
husbands and wives undoubtedly loved one another, but love was not the main
basis for the marriage, nor was the loss of love a reason to break up. Divorce
was mostly out of the question, and out-of-wedlock births were strongly
stigmatized. Beginning in the last century, however, romance became the main
reason for marriage, and divorce became a possibility. The result is that most
marriages today are based entirely on love, and marital partners are expected to
be intimate best friends. While this probably has generated many marriages
which are more satisfying than those of the past, especially for women,
affection alone has proved to be a weak link on which to hang such an important
social institution. Should affection in a marital relationship wane, which it does
in almost every marriage at least for short periods of time, divorce is now not
only a legal possibility in all cases but it is culturally approved as well.

The second recent cultural shift of great consequence is the sexual
revolution, in which sexual norms have moved from restrictive to permissive. A
central theme of the sexual revolution was to give women many of the same
sexual freedoms long granted to men. The rapidly accelerated version of this
revolution, beginning in the 1960s, was made possible by the widespread
availability for the first time of relatively cheap and reliable contraceptives, plus
abortion. The revolution was extended through widespread acceptance of the
idea (heavily promulgated by the therapeutic community) that good sex lies at
the root of self-fulfillment, through the commercialization of sex, and through
the extreme sexualization of popular culture by the media.

Cultural Conditions of Fatherlessness Today

The end result of the various trends just discussed is a society that is
surprisingly unsupportive of fatherhood. Indeed, if one were specifically to
design a culture and a social system for the express purpose of undercutting
fatherhood and men's contribution to family life, the resulting society would be
a close approximation of our own. Consider the following five dimensions of
contemporary society.

Marriage

The principal function of marriage is to hold men to the (inherently stronger) mother-child bond. For men everywhere, marriage and parenthood tend to be a package deal. When marriage weakens, as it has today in modern societies, men will inevitably get the message that they no longer are needed or even wanted in family life, and they will remain detached from their children.

The high divorce rate is a major and woefully underdiscussed problem. Because of it, both men and women are increasingly reluctant to enter into marriage, even when children are involved, helping to account for today's extraordinarily high rate of out-of-wedlock births.

But there is an even more potent reason for the dramatic rise of nonmarital births—the decline of "shotgun weddings." Not so long ago it was culturally expected that men would marry the women they impregnated; now it is not. New evidence suggests that the decline of this norm was strongly associated with the introduction of birth regulation technologies, including abortion, in the 1960s. This made the birth or nonbirth of a child a choice for the mother alone, and therefore marriage or nonmarriage a choice for the father alone.[7] At the same time, of course, the stigma against illegitimacy markedly decreased.

Sex

The effect of the sexual revolution on fatherhood has been devastating. Men marry partly, if not mainly, to have a stable sexual life. If men can get as much sex as they like outside of the marital relationship, they will be much less inclined to marry. In addition, the glamorization of nonmarital sex by the mass media has inevitably weakened the marital bond through making such sex seem more appealing. A less widely discussed, but no less important, problem is this: Men are less likely to marry the mothers of their children if they do not have confidence that the children are really theirs. There can be no doubt that the sexual revolution has generated a decline in "paternity confidence," a concept now widely invoked by the new field of evolutionary psychology.[8]

Education

Educational trends have had a serious impact on the preparation of young people for fatherhood and family life. At one time in American history, education was mostly a family affair, and parents were the main teachers. Families were large, and the great majority of households included children. With a strong parental interest at stake, children—both boys and girls—were taught about family life and parenting on a regular basis. Today, much of education has been formalized, taken over by schools, and is mainly concerned with preparing the young for jobs that require a high level of skill and knowledge. In general, our educational system, including higher education, disregards childrearing as a major adult responsibility and marriage as important to childrearing. Men, especially, are growing up with little preparation for adult family life, and little realization that their family life will be as important to them—if not more so—as their work life.

The Economy

The market economy, for all its virtues, has never been a great friend of fatherhood or the nuclear family. The rampant material consumerism that is engendered, especially through advertising, overshadows other important dimensions of people's lives. And the single-minded pursuit of profits is often conducted with little thought for its effect on family life.

The mature market economy in modern societies is encumbered with a formidable contradiction.[9] Bombarded by incessant urging to spend money, have a good time, travel, drink beer, and continuously enjoy life, workers find these messages to be in conflict with the older virtues of hard work, frugality, personal responsibility, and moderation. The manipulated desire for instant gratification is a constant threat to the workers' predisposition for social obligation, including obligation to family members and, indeed, to work itself. With the withering away of civil society, which has always served to insulate people from the market, the culture of materialism and instant gratification is making stronger incursions into people's daily lives. Because they are more individualistic to begin with, and also typically more involved in market activities, men are more affected by this than women.

Government

Although a major purpose of government in modern times has been to offset the dysfunctional impacts of the market, in many ways government has also helped to undermine fatherhood and the nuclear family. We can see this in no-fault divorce laws, in the marriage penalty tax codes, and in welfare policies that discriminate against two-parent families.

Cultural Changes Needed

With a modern culture so strongly stacked against it, what are the best levers of social change to renew fatherhood? Let us be clear that the culture can be changed. Just as the Progressives had a major societal impact early in this century, and the race and gender liberationists had a major impact in the second half of the century, so is it possible that pro-nuclear family forces can have a major impact in the early part of the 21st century.

The renewal of fatherhood, marriage and the family, and civil society is a tall order. It directly contradicts the dominant cultural ethos of our time: radical individualism that places at center stage the untrammeled self, loaded with a vision of individual rights and in full pursuit of self-development at all costs.

What is needed is a new balance of forces which can maintain the best of the individualistic spirit while reinvigorating those social and cultural structures able to provide the kind of social order without which civilization, including personal freedom and opportunity, cannot survive. Here are three key areas on which to focus change efforts.

First, dampen the sexual revolution. Schools, churches, and parents should urge young people to postpone sexual intercourse through the high school years. Men and women should be encouraged to restrict their sexual activity to marriage, or to relationships that may lead to marriage. Enormous pressure should be placed on the media and the entertainment industry to decrease the sexual content of their products.

Second, teach in every school in the land information about marriage and parenting. This should include the understanding that fathering is as important as mothering and that fathers are expected to play a major role in their children's upbringing. For young adults, educational programs should stress the negative effects of divorce on children and show the value of premarital counseling and marital enrichment programs.

Third, government policies should privilege marriage and the two-parent family. We can no longer afford to be neutral toward all alternative lifestyles.

Renewing Fatherhood

Rethinking and revising the institution of marriage, and especially marital gender roles, in a way that better combines the three essential traits of friendship, passion, and justice, is central to any renewal of fatherhood. Most women, and many if not most men, do not want to return to the male-dominated marriages of the past. Only when marriage is revitalized—when men and women want to marry again and stay married—will fathers in large numbers stay involved with their children.

Renewing fatherhood is ultimately about infusing into our culture a stronger sense of moral obligation for the well-being of others, especially children, and thus counterbalancing the radical strains of individualism. It may be that a fully restored sense of moral obligation can be accomplished entirely through secular means, but I doubt it. Religion has always been the main cultural repository of morality, and it is not likely that we can have permanent moral renewal without a society-wide religious reawakening. What form that reawakening might take, and should take, is an open question.

Notes

1. Kingsley Davis, "The Meaning and Significance of Marriage," in *Contemporary Marriage,* ed. Kingsley Davis (New York: Russell Sage Foundation, 1985), 21.
2. See David Popenoe, *Disturbing the Nest: Family Change and Decline in Modern*

Societies (New York: Aldine de Gruyter, 1988).

3. Daniel Yankelovich, "How Changes in the Economy are Reshaping American Values," in *Values and Public Policy,* ed. Henry J. Aaron, Thomas E. Mann, and Timothy Taylor (Washington, D.C.: Brookings Institution, 1994), 16-53.

4. Steven Mintz and Susan Kellogg, *Domestic Revolutions: A Social History of American Family Life* (New York: Free Press, 1988), 204.

5. For more on this topic, see David Popenoe, *Life Without Father* (New York: Free Press, 1996), Part Two.

6. Frank Furstenberg Jr., "Good Dads—Bad Dads: Two Faces of Fatherhood," in *The Changing American Family and Public Policy,* ed. Andrew Cherlin (Washington, D.C.: Urban Institute, 1988), 193-218.

7. George A. Akerlof, Janet L. Yellen, and Michael L. Katz, "An Analysis of Out-of-Wedlock Childbearing in the United States," *Quarterly Journal of Economics* 111, no. 2 (May 1996): 277-317.

8. For an overview of evolutionary psychology, see Robert Wright, *The Moral Animal* (New York: Pantheon, 1994).

9. Daniel Bell, *The Cultural Contradictions of Capitalism,* 20th anniversary ed. (New York: Basic Books, 1996).

Chapter Three

No Democracy without Dads

Don Eberly

American citizens and their leaders across the political spectrum have arrived at an astonishing degree of consensus: American society is undergoing a potentially devastating erosion of social cohesion and democratic health. In a few short years, public attention has shifted markedly from economic recession to social regression, a real decline in the health of our social institutions, especially the family, and an erosion of the psychological and spiritual strengths required to sustain a free society.

The decline of fatherhood is not the only reason, of course, for the fraying of our social fabric, but I believe it is a central one. Thanks to the diligence of social scientists, we are now able to pinpoint and to acknowledge the relationship of father absence to specific pathologies in society, such as crime, drugs, and teen pregnancy. Boys without fathers disproportionately grow up to become young men who threaten themselves and the social order.

What we have not yet fully captured, however, is the positive everyday contribution fathers make in nurturing boys and girls. Such things as trust, cooperation, and social generosity among citizens are preconditions of a vigorous civil society. A democracy requires of its citizens not only that they refrain from committing crimes but that they possess enough faith, energy, imagination, and self-control to work actively together to solve common problems, to help one another, and, if necessary, to sacrifice for their own future well-being and the nation's. Fathers play a key role in developing and sustaining the kind of personal character on which democracy depends.

The Democratic Character

Democracy, we are frequently reminded, is an "experiment." The continued use of the term experiment after over two centuries of practical success implies persistent doubts over democracy's basic durability. From the beginning, the founding fathers of American democracy assumed that it was, as Madison put it, "chimerical" to assume a republic could endure without a rich supply of virtue. The American democratic experiment presupposes the existence of individuals possessing democratic habits and dispositions.

"Civil Society" is the term coined to describe the seedbeds of democratic virtues, the voluntary, private character-building associations upon which democracy ultimately depends. "[F]eelings and opinions are recruited, the heart is enlarged, and the human mind is developed only by the reciprocal influence of men upon one another" noted Alexis de Tocqueville on the importance of voluntary associations.[1]

As Mary Ann Glendon, a professor at Harvard Law School, put the same truth more recently, "Governments must have an adequate supply of citizens who are skilled in the arts of self-government." According to Glendon, these arts consist of "deliberation, compromise, consensus-building, civility, [and] reason- giving."[2]

There is such a thing as democratic character, and it flows not from formal constitutions and Congressional acts, but from vital, character-shaping institutions in society. Free people need written constitutions and representative institutions, of course, but they also need unwritten social bonds that make the work of deliberation and compromise in democracy possible. Countries that are moving successfully toward democracy, such as the recently liberated nations of Eastern Europe, are also recognizing the need to rebuild the social institutions that supply democratic habits and skills. Because many of these fledgling democracies have badly weakened institutions of civil society, they are being crippled by a range of social diseases, from pervasive public corruption and crime to private greed and distrust among citizens.

Recent research by Robert Putnam of Harvard University and Francis Fukuyama of the Rand Corporation points to the unbreakable link that exists between strong social institutions and the healthy functioning of both democratic government and the market economy. Putnam, whose research focused on the relationship of regional governments in Italy to robust civic life, found that democratic government was far more effective when surrounded by strong civic communities.

Citizens in civic community, Putnam said, "are helpful, respectful and trustful toward one another." In effect, they take upon themselves much of the work of democratic deliberation and consensus-building. Individuals in civic community are bound together, not by rigidly enforced rules or "vertical relations of authority and dependency," says Putnam, but by "horizontal relations of reciprocity and cooperation."[3]

Francis Fukuyama has looked at the role that trust and collaboration now play in empowering individuals to compete in a rapidly changing, interconnected global marketplace. Economic life, he says, is maintained on "moral bonds of social trust," which he describes as an "unspoken, unwritten bond between fellow citizens that facilitates transactions, empowers individual creativity, and justifies collective action."[4] Fukuyama concludes that societies with strong bonds of social trust and collaboration will increasingly gain important advantages over those characterized by individual isolation and social fragmentation.

The success of capitalism, as we are beginning to discover, depends on a rich supply of social capital, consisting of knowledge, aptitude, skills, and positive habits. A nation's reserves of social capital, like its stock of more tangible and measurable economic capital, can be drawn down. The common phrase "living on borrowed capital" speaks to the failure of one generation to renew and pass on the social endowments it inherited. The result is a decline in what Fukuyama calls "spontaneous sociability," rooted in the loss of social trust, all of which portends worrisome consequences for a democratic society.

In Dad We Trust?

The seedbed of social trust is the family. James Coleman, who popularized the term "social capital," used the term to describe a range of personal strengths that are cultivated in the family, especially the ability to form ties of cooperation and to work toward common purposes.[5]

The decline in fathering, whether through the growing prevalence of physical absence or merely emotional disengagement by fathers, contributes to socially underdeveloped citizens who often lack the necessary disposition for healthy participation in society. Fathers can be a powerful influence in making better citizens.

Fathers in particular view their role as representing the family to the world, and fostering their children's successful relationships within it. Concerned fathers strive to cultivate in their children a spirit of reasonableness and compromise, a capacity to trust and be trustworthy, a willingness to be helpful and empathetic, and a capacity to act with self-restraint and respect toward others. When children grow up without an involved father, as is frequently the case when parents divorce, they often have a hard time establishing and maintaining relationships later in life, due in large part to a lowered capacity to trust others.[6]

Finally democracies require citizens with a sense of public virtue—with a commitment to the needs and interests of others rather than their own. Functioning families and communities are able to subordinate individual interests to the concerns and needs of the larger group.

The good society requires good institutions, starting with good fathers, pursuing good ends. For years we have seen that large majorities of Americans are distrustful of their public institutions. Less than one out of five Americans say they trust the government in Washington to do what is right at least most of the time.

Now we have discovered the unsurprising fact that American citizens are more and more distrustful and suspicious of each other. For example, a 1995 survey by the Kaiser Foundation found that only 35 percent of respondents thought that "most people can be trusted most of the time.[7] Our discontents are not confined to governmental malfeasance and feckless politicians. While public discourse focuses on procedural political reforms, the primal source of our cynicism is likely the rupture of our primary relationships within the family, of our marriages and our fellowship with our fathers. When sad experience has taught you that you can't trust your own father, who are you likely to trust?

The capacity to collaborate in trustful and helpful ways with one's associates is clearly affected by patterns of trust and interdependency learned in families. When parents are trustworthy, children are more likely to feel the world is a trustworthy place. Conversely, when a parent abandons a child, physically or psychologically—or when parents visibly dislike or mistrust one another, as often happen when marriages collapse—children learn anxiety and suspicion, a sense that the world itself is a dangerous and unpredictable place. In this way, disillusionment with our primary relationships leads to distrust of kin and community.

As inherently social and meaning-seeking creatures, human beings possess a need for membership in human community, for connection, and for coherence. Tocqueville captured this when he said: "Without ideas in common, there is no common action. There may still exist human beings, but not a social entity. In order for society to exist and, even more, to prosper, it is necessary that the spirits of all citizens be assembled and held together by certain leading ideas."[8]

When the social norms that bind people together weaken, people feel an acute sense of unease—what Emile Durkheim called "anomie." While there are other causes of America's anomie, namely, the fast pace of life and the danger of being assaulted in public places, the principal culprit is the erosion of trust produced by a growing number of parents who fail to preserve the bonds of trust with their own children. Since most absent parents are men, we are referring primarily to fathers.

Trust is nurtured in the family. In bonding to the child, the parent puts in place the rudiments of trust: a process which, according to Urie Bronfenbrenner, conveys "a strong, mutual, irrational, emotional attachment" offered through a person who is "committed to the child's well-being and development, preferable for life."[9] Who can doubt that a child will be less trusting and cooperative as an adult if he has experienced a painful loss of trust in the person in whom he thought he could surely place his trust, his own father. Sadly, for many children this betrayal occurs not once, but several times during childhood: a father drifts in and out of their life, bringing new hopes and fresh disappointment. A stepfather or boyfriend makes friends, but disappears when his relationship with the mother ends.

By the time an adolescent develops impressions of the institutions beyond the home, he or she has already developed attitudes based upon relationships that exist in the home. If the child's experience of adults and the exercise of authority in the home was positive, attitudes about authority in the broader society are likely to be positive. If adults in the home were generally caring, fair, and reliable, then that is what the child will usually expect of others (including authorities) beyond the home.

Conversely, if the experience the child had of home was one of abuse, neglect, or betrayal, the projection of attitudes of cynicism and distrust toward the broader society is not surprising. It is hard to imagine attitudes of general trust taking shape toward more remote political and social institutions when a child is abandoned or betrayed by a mother or father.

Fathers Are the Bearers of Outside Norms

Fathers are also the first encounter kids have with male authority, and perhaps authority generally. How interaction with that intimate form of authority takes shape will likely determine the child's success at navigating his or her way through the more challenging territory of authority and conflict in the school, on the playground, or at the mall. In many ways, healthy fathers serve as a bridge between the more protected life of the home and the more demanding environment of the world beyond. Fathers raise their children mostly with an eye toward their inevitable encounter with the rules and norms of the world beyond the nest. Good fathers tutor their children toward developing positive habits of self-control and respect toward others.

Committed fathers perform other important functions in the socialization of children. Wade Horn, president of the National Fatherhood Initiative and child psychologist, points out that proper socialization requires the development of the ability to delay or inhibit impulse gratification. According to Horn, "well-socialized children have learned not to strike out at others to get what they want; undersocialized children have not. Well socialized children have learned to listen to and obey the directions of legitimate authority figures, such as parents and teachers; undersocialized children have not."[10] He notes that studies, which demonstrate the differences between the way fathers and mothers parent, indicate that fathers are essential in helping the young develop impulse control.

Fathers give to society children who are capable of self-restraint and cooperation with others, precisely the personal qualities that polls indicate people feel are on the decrease in contemporary America. Calls for a more civil society reflect the desire for a more humane and socially cooperative culture.

Meeting these expectations will require a deep new respect on the part of men, women, and society for the work of fathering. A renewed commitment to the common good over private self-interest and wider civic participation are both laudable goals, pathways to rebuilding civil society. But they will not be approached, much less achieved, without a renewed commitment on the part of society to fatherhood, and on the part of fathers to their children.

Fathers Model Involved Citizenship

Fathers make an important contribution to creating citizens and community members, but it also works the other way: These community-based institutions create important roles for the father, and recognize and reward his work.

Attitudes about the importance of fathers are imbedded in communities: in a community's civic associations and social give and take. These attitudes quickly surface in local schools when a school board is asked to decide whether it should advocate childbearing exclusively among married fathers and mothers or whether it is acceptable to offer programming to teen mothers while completely withholding judgment on father absent households. Attitudes about the importance of men as fathers quickly surface when the Boy Scouts and Boy's and Girl's Clubs are asked to address young people as generic future parents, not as future fathers and mothers bearing unique responsibilities.

Until recently in the vast majority of communities few, if any, major civic, educational, philanthropic, or religious bodies tried to explicitly reach out to fathers, to send a strong signal that fathers matter. Fortunately, that is changing somewhat, although most communities have a long way to go.

The National Fatherhood Initiative recommends 10 steps to make a community father-friendly. These 10 steps include: organizing fatherhood forums, distributing information to civic and media outlets on the importance of fathers, encouraging employment practices that are supportive of fathers, developing special community events for Father's Day, and putting fathering as a topic on the local civic and service club agenda.

Renewing Fatherhood As a Social Norm

If the renewal of fatherhood is central to the restoration of civil society, we cannot afford to be ignorant or agnostic about the conditions under which strong, committed fathers are most likely to occur: when they are married to and living with their children's mother. Of course any call to fatherhood must address all fathers, even those divorced and unwed fathers not currently living with their kids.

But the danger is that de-emphasizing marriage out of a legitimate desire to improve today's fathering may have the unintended consequence of making the job harder to accomplish in the future, raising the likelihood that more children will be raised without fathers. To put the problem plainly, the immediate consequence of "expanding" the definition of family is that fathers are the first to be written out of the family script. When the cutting and pasting begins on the ever-changing family portrait, it is the father who is typically thrown away. In the vast majority of cases, children from fragmented families live apart from their biological father and, in many cases, see him infrequently.

Fathers are viewed as dispensable because they are assumed to play no unique, gender-specific role in raising children. Little in the modern cultural script favors the father, and thus, not surprisingly, little in the law favors the father either. Frequently, dad is presented in popular culture as an extra set of hands, a deputy mom, a provider of child support payments, possibly "the nearby guy,"[11] more akin to a relative than a devoted, nurturing father.

Not infrequently, popular entertainment portrays the father as a dunce. Still worse, literature from the women's movement often raises the ugliest specter of all: Dad is a danger. Domestic abuse is nothing to be trifled with, it is a criminal offense and should be treated as such. But factual distortions should not be permitted to become yet another wedge between fathers, mothers, and children.

The weakening of the ideal of fatherhood in culture and the disappearance of fathers from the home are not unrelated phenomena. One of the many differences between mothers and fathers is this: Fatherhood depends more on social and cultural components. Motherhood is the far more durable institution. Voluntary-mother absence on a large scale has never been a problem in our society or any other that we know of. Fatherhood must be understood, in part at least, as a cultural institution. Fathering, says John Miller, family sociologist, is "a cultural acquisition to an extent that mothering is not." Since there are few biologically compelling reasons for the male to care for his offspring, "a set of overlapping largely cultural developments" are required. When a culture "ceases to support a father's involvement with his own children (through its laws, mores, symbols, models, rituals) powerful natural forces take over in favor of the mother only family."[12]

Of course, increased economic opportunity is important, and policy reforms recognizing fathers and supporting marriage will help. But the restoration of fathers to their children will happen primarily as the result of a profound cultural, moral, and spiritual shift: when an all-fronts mobilization takes place within society to reinforce adult male responsibility for children. Durable social structures, including stable families, cannot be legislated into existence. They derive their strength from a people's habits, customs, and social ethics, which are drawn partly from social norms, partly from religious and moral beliefs.

Is such a powerful countercultural revival likely? Periodically in American history, strong social reform movements have moved individuals toward restraint and social obligation. In the 19th century, for example, society witnessed an explosion of voluntary associations and organizations aimed at social reform and moral uplift. Spiritual awakenings, temperance movements, and many private and public efforts were made to strengthen character and responsibility. These were dynamic movements that transcended politics and partisanship.

James Q. Wilson, who has tracked social reforms, says that "throughout history, the institutions that have produced effective male socialization have been private, not public." If this is true, he adds,

> then our policy ought to identify, evaluate and encourage those local, private efforts that seem to do the best job at reducing drug abuse, inducing people to marry, persuading parents, especially fathers, to take responsibility for their children, and exercising informal social controls over neighborhood streets.[13]

There is evidence that the moment for such a social renewal may have arrived. "Today's culture is evolving a different notion of the self," points out Daniel Yankelovich, one of the nation's leading analysts of public opinion,

> . . . A shift is now occurring toward a perception of the self as a moral actor with obligations and concerns as well as rights. . . .In our tracking studies we are beginning to measure a shift back toward absolute as distinct from relative values. . . .The focus is less on rights and more on community and society. There is less preoccupation with "me" and more concern for children, civil society, quality of life, and the spiritual dimension.[14]

The renewal of fatherhood and the renewal of civil society go hand in hand. Fathers have much to offer in strengthening communities, and community-based institutions can be mobilized to strengthen fathers—to reinforce their importance, to offer training and assistance, and to help them pass on to their own children a strong fathering heritage.

Notes

1. Alexis de Tocqueville, *Democracy in America,* vol. 2, ed. and trans. Henry Reeve (New York: n.p., 1954), 114.

2. Mary Ann Glendon, "Forgotten Questions," introduction to *Seedbeds of Virtue,* ed. Mary Ann Glendon and David Blankenhorn (Lanham, Md.: Madison Books, 1995), 4.

3. Robert B. Putnam, *Making Democracy Work: Civic Traditions in Modern Italy* (Princeton: Princeton University Press, 1993), 88.

4. Francis Fukuyama, *Trust* (New York: Free Press, 1995), dust jacket, see also p. 10.

5. James S. Coleman, "Social Capital in the Creation of Human Capital," *American Journal of Sociology* 94 (1988): 95-120.

6. See, for example, Paul R. Amato, Laura S. Loomis, and Alan Booth, "Parental Divorce, Marital Conflict, and Offspring Well-Being During Early Adulthood," *Social Forces* 73 (1995): 895-915.

7. *Trust in Government Survey.* Princeton: Princeton Survey Research Associates,

1996.

8. Alexis de Tocqueville, *Democracy in America*, vol. 2 (New York: Vintage Books, 1945), 1-2.

9. Urie Bronfenbrenner, "Discovering What Families Do," in *Rebuilding the Nest: A New Commitment to the American Family,* ed. David Blankenhorn, Steven Bayme, and Jean Bethke Elshtain (Milwaukee: Family Service America, 1990), 29-32.

10. Wade Horn, "Character and Family," in *The Content of America's Character: Restoring Civic Virtue,* ed. Don Eberly (Lanham, Md.: Madison Books, 1995), 80.

11. For further analysis of the cultural scripting of fatherhood, see David Blankenhorn, *Fatherless America: Confronting Our Most Urgent Social Problem* (New York: Basic Books, 1995), 65-185.

12. John Miller, *Biblical Faith and Fathering: Why We Call God Father* (New York: Paulist Press, 1989), 2.

13. James Q. Wilson, "Culture, Incentives, and the Underclass," in *Values and Public Policy,* ed. Henry J. Aaron, Thomas E. Mann, and Timothy Taylor (Washington, D.C.: Brookings Institution, 1994), 74.

14. Daniel Yankelovich, "How American Individualism is Evolving," *Public Perspective* Feb/March (1998): 3-6.

Chapter Four

Not Just Another Pair of Hands

Armin Brott

Almost from the moment his son, Teddy, was born, my friend Mark has held him facing out. "It's easier for him to see the world that way," he says. Mark's wife, Jennifer, on the other hand, always holds Teddy with his chest against hers. When Teddy started walking, Mark would let him stagger a few paces ahead on their strolls in the park. But whenever Jennifer takes Teddy out, "I always hold his hand," she says. And on those cold, rainy weekends at home, Mark spends a lot of time wrestling with his son and throwing him into a pile of pillows on the bed. When they're done, Teddy and Jennifer smell spices together in the kitchen.

That Mark and Jennifer interact with their son in different ways probably won't shock anyone. After all, they have different backgrounds and life experiences. What's interesting, though, is that many of their parenting differences (as well as the ones you've probably already encountered in your own home) have more to do with the gender of the parent than anything else. Mark, it seems, handles his baby in the way that men everywhere do, while Jennifer behaves like a fairly typical mother.

Babies are better off when they have two parents to love them, cuddle them, and contribute to their college fund. And even though moms are the ones who breast-feed, get up in the middle of the night, and undoubtedly change more than their fair share of newborn diapers, dads play a unique—and very important—role from the start. Babies benefit developmentally in all kinds of ways from having dads do dad-type things and from the oh-so-different-from-mom ways of being that dads have.

How Fathers Are Different

So what, exactly, do dads do differently? A comparison in parenting styles reveals at least three differences. Like my friend Mark, "fathers tend to allow their infants more freedom to explore, while mothers are usually more cautious," says Ross Parke, a pioneering researcher on fatherhood and the director of the Center for Family Studies at the University of California, Riverside. By encouraging exploration, says Parke, fathers are also encouraging their children's independence. For many men, the general philosophy of childrearing is "I let him do pretty much anything he wants as long as he isn't posing any danger to himself or to me or to anyone else."

Second, fathers speak to their children differently than mothers. Mothers tend to chat with their babies about what's going on, where they're going, what they're doing. Fathers, on the other hand, usually speak less, listen more, mimic their children, and respond to their attempts at speech. Overall, fathers seem more interested in *doing* practical, educational things rather than *talking* about doing things.

But the area in which fathers' special parenting style is most obvious—and most important—is play. Women tend to play more visual games with their babies and are, often, more verbal with them. Men, on the other hand, are far more physical, even from the time their kids are infants. Both my daughters, for example, spent most of their first year on an extended piggy-back ride, and could stand up on my shoulders—without using their hands—before they were 18 months old.

Not surprisingly, babies are among the first to notice that their parents have very different styles; and they react accordingly. "Babies know that men and women behave differently and they seek out their mothers and fathers for different reasons," says Gary Levy, director of the Infant Development Center at the University of Wyoming. "Even as young as seven months old, when babies want to be comforted, they look for their mothers. But when they want to play, they look for dad."

Infants aren't the only ones who prefer dad's more physical play style. Alison Clarke-Stewart, a researcher at the University of California, Irvine, offered two and a half year olds the choice of playing with their fathers or their mothers; more than two-thirds picked dad.

The differences between fathers' and mothers' parenting styles certainly make for fascinating conversation, but the big questions still remain: Who really benefits from these differences and how? The answers are simple: Just about everyone benefits and in a wonderful variety of ways.

Overall, children who live with involved, sensitive, and responsible fathers are better off than kids whose fathers are uninvolved or insensitive. They get along better with their peers, stay in school longer and do better while they're there, are less likely to abuse drugs or alcohol or to get pregnant (or get someone else pregnant) while in their teens, and they grow up to be more caring and sensitive adults.

Women, too, benefit from father involvement. Division of labor issues are the number one marital stressor, and the more support mothers get from their husbands, the less depressed they are, the happier they are in their marriages, and the better they perform their parenting duties.

Finally, men themselves benefit from their own increased involvement with their families and children. Involved fathers tend to be more "generative" (giving, nurturant, and helpful), more occupationally mobile, more successful in their careers, and more likely to choose jobs that are people-oriented. In addition, men whose wives are happy in their marriages tend to be happier themselves. And men who are happy in their marriages are generally more involved in their fathering role. Overall, fathering may be as good for men as it is for their wives and children.

Sadly, far too little attention (even within the academic community) has been devoted to the profound difference that fathers make in the lives of everyone around them. So let's take a thorough look at the various ways fathers matter— to children, to mothers, to men themselves, and to all of us.

Kids, Fathers, and Cognitive Development

"The evidence is quite robust that kids who have contact with a father have an advantage over kids without that kind of contact," says Norma Radin, a professor emeritus at the University of Michigan who has conducted research on fathers for over 20 years. And these benefits are evident very early in life. In one study, Radin found that children who were raised by actively involved fathers scored higher on verbal ability than children raised in families with less involved fathers. In another study, toddlers whose fathers took a special interest in child care were consistently rated two to six months ahead of schedule on tests of development, problem-solving skills, and even social skills. In addition, Radin believes that "there's a strong connection between kids' math skills and the amount of contact they have with their fathers."

And remember fathers' general tendency to encourage their children's independence and exploration? That is significant as well. In several studies, Ross Parke found that how early the father expected his child to be able to handle a pair of scissors or take a bath alone was positively related to the child's cognitive development.

Then there's the importance of play. According to Clarke-Stewart, fathers' skill as a playmate is one of the primary predictors of children's cognitive development. Fathers who were good at peek-a-boo, ball toss, and bouncing bouts had more cognitively advanced children than those who couldn't keep their children interested in their games.

Several researchers have looked at fathers' impact on their children's cognitive skills by comparing kids who don't live with their fathers to those who do. Frank Pedersen, another major figure in fatherhood research, found that baby boys from father-absent homes reached for, grasped at, and followed objects less. They also spent a lot less time playing with new toys and objects in their environment than boys from father-intact homes. All these sensory-motor behaviors are generally accepted as indicators of future intellectual development. Although girls are less often included in such studies, when they are examined, their cognitive development seems to be detrimentally affected by the father's absence as well.

A reasonable person might well ask whether the negative way fathers impact their children when they're absent might be mitigated by introducing another adult into the home. After all, there's no way that a single parent can possibly provide as much intellectual stimulation to (let alone spend as much time with) kids who live with two parents. But according to Pedersen, this isn't the case. Fathers, he says, are not just another adult; they have "an impact that is qualitatively different from other adults."[1]

How long does the father's impact on his children last? A long time. More than 40 years ago, three psychologists, Robert Sears, Eleanor Maccoby, and Harry Levin, studied over 300 mothers and their five-year-old children. A quarter of a century later, a new set of researchers studying empathy contacted some of the children from the original study. They found that high levels of empathy were associated with higher levels of paternal involvement in childrearing when the kids were five. In fact, paternal involvement turned out to have been a far more important predictor of empathy than any maternal factor.

Ten years later (when the original children were 41 years old), "those who had better social relationships in mid-life (for example, having a long, happy marriage; having children; engaging in recreational activities with nonfamily members) had experienced more paternal warmth as children," writes Ross Parke, in his critique of this research.[2]

Kids, Fathers, and Social Development

A father's influence on his children's future development extends far beyond the cognitive. A variety of studies have shown that boys whose fathers are absent (for a variety of reasons, including prolonged periods of business travel) make fewer friends and generally have poorer relationships with their peers. Why? It's possible, suggests Ross Parke, that boys who grow up without fathers have less chance to learn the behavior that other boys in their culture value. "They tend, for example, to be shy, timid, and reluctant to play rough games—traits that may make a boy a less-desirable playmate to his peers."

As in so many other areas, one of the primary ways fathers influence their children's social skills is by playing with them. In one groundbreaking study, Kevin MacDonald and his associates studied a large number of three- and four-year-old boys and girls at play. The children's teachers were asked to rank the children in terms of their popularity among their preschool classmates. For both boys and girls, the children of fathers who played with their kids a lot were consistently rated as being popular with their peers.

Playing Nerf basketball in the living room or doing somersaults on the bed is always good for a laugh, but fathers' active, rough-and-tumble play style is a lot more than a good time. On the most basic level, by wrestling and rolling around on the floor, fathers give their children some valuable lessons in self-control. They're also learning how to express and appropriately manage their emotions and to recognize others' emotional clues, and that biting, kicking, and other forms of physical violence are simply not acceptable.

Other studies show that children who play a lot with their fathers make a more successful transition from preschool to elementary school. Lisa Youngblade and Jay Belsky have found that the better the father-child relationship is when a child is three, the longer-lasting relationships the child will have with friends when he's five. And the worse the relationship, the worse the quality of future friendships.

Fathers' influence on children's social skills is evident even with infants. Pedersen measured the reactions of five-month-old boys to a strange but friendly adult. Babies who had experienced more contact with their fathers were friendlier to the strange adult. They cooed and vocalized more, expressed more interest in getting picked up, and enjoyed physical play more than boys whose fathers weren't as involved. Interestingly, the effect wasn't nearly as strong for girls. This doesn't mean that fathers ignore their daughters or that fathers aren't as important to girls as they are to boys. Fathers do have plenty of influence on their girls, but the impact tends to be seen somewhat later. Other studies confirm that kids whose fathers are actively involved in caretaking and childrearing are more secure when left alone with a friendly stranger.

Another researcher, John Gottman, who has spent several decades studying families, found something even more interesting: "While the quality of mother-child interactions were also important, we found that, compared to the fathers' responses, the quality of contact with the mother was not as strong a predictor of the child's later success or failure with school and friends." Given that mothers spend more time on child care and child-related activities than men do, Gottman's statements are surprising. But he stands by them. "We believe the reason fathers have this extreme influence on their children is because the father-child relationship evokes such powerful emotions in kids."[3]

Gender Differences

Although there's plenty of overlap, fathers impact their sons and daughters in very different ways. The more socially and emotionally nurturing a father is to his young son, for example, says John Snarey, who followed fathers and their children for nearly 40 years, the better the boy's academic skills, success in school (and, later, in college), and scores on IQ and other standardized tests. Generally speaking, adds Radin, the more involved a boy's father, the more empathetic the boy will be—and the better behaved.

Part of the reason these differences exist is that fathers (somewhat more than mothers) treat—and thus impact—their boys and girls differently. To start with, fathers tend to play and interact more physically with their boy infants than with their girls. And later on, they give their boys more encouragement to be independent and to explore. Boys are allowed to cross the street alone earlier, to stay away from home more, and to explore a wider area of their neighborhood than are girls. And these opportunities may make a difference.

While it seems somehow intuitive that dads would have an influence on their sons' development (after all, they both share that pesky Y chromosome) girls, too, have a great deal to gain from high levels of contact with their fathers. Girls especially seem to benefit from play. Girls who experience high levels of physical play with their fathers tend to be more popular with their peers, more assertive with their peers (making it less likely that they will passively accept their environment later in life), more interested in higher levels of education, and more active in sports.[4] And girls who stay active in sports are much less likely to get pregnant as teens. Other research has found that extremely competent and successful women frequently recall their fathers as active and encouraging, playful and exciting.

How Involved Fatherhood Impacts Men

Fatherhood also has a dramatic impact on men themselves. "One of the first things a father learns from his children is that his needs can match theirs," observed Maureen Green over 20 years ago in her book, *Fathering.* "They look to him for instruction; he can enjoy giving instruction. The children look to him as a model and being a model adds an extra dimension to his decisions. His ambitions and achievements look different to him if he can learn to look at them through their eyes as well as his own."[5]

John Snarey, professor of human development at Emory University, has spent his career studying fathers and their impact on those around them. "Fathers who provided high levels of social-emotional support for their offspring during the childhood decade (0-10 years) and high levels of intellectual, academic, social, and emotional support during the adolescent decade (11-21 years) were themselves as men at mid-life, more likely to be happily married," says Snarey. Snarey also found that, contrary to men's fears that putting their families first will harm their careers, "fathers who cared for their children's intellectual development and their adolescent's social development were more likely to advance in their occupations."[6] Fatherhood also seems to promote men's abilities to understand themselves as adults and to sympathetically care for other adults. According to Snarey, men who take an active role at home are—by the time their children are grown—better managers, community leaders, and mentors. Overall, they're more concerned with the generation coming up than with themselves. The bottom line? Men who are involved fathers tend to have happier marriages and more successful careers.

Daddy's Hands

As discussed elsewhere in this book, many of the problems affecting our children and our society seem in some way correlated with the absence of a father. Oddly, though, the experts haven't yet figured out exactly why fathers have such a major impact on their children's development. Many speculate that when it comes to play, fathers' more stimulating approach makes children more interested in and receptive to new information and experiences and that being more physically confident increases psychological confidence as well. And when it comes to cognitive and math skills, researchers are not studying the connection anymore. "It's pretty much a given," says Norma Radin.

Magically dropping an involved father into every household won't cure all society's problems, but neither will dropping a wad of cash into every home. The real truth about how to help our nation's fatherless children lies between the extreme views of some in the political and academic communities.

Despite what some politically-motivated social critics would have us believe, children being raised without fathers are *not* fine. On the other hand, for a father to simply be there is not enough. The quality of his relationships with his children is far more important. Incompetent fathering—just as incompetent mothering—can have a variety of negative effects. Children whose fathers were cold and authoritarian, derogatory, and intrusive often have the hardest time with grades and social relationships. They are, says John Gottman, even worse off than kids who live in homes with no father at all. "Kids with humiliating, nonsupportive dads were the ones most likely to be headed for trouble," he says. "They were the ones displaying aggressive behavior toward their friends, they were the ones who were having the most trouble in school, they were the ones with problems often linked to delinquency and youth violence."[7]

The evidence is overwhelming that fathers can and do play an enormous and valuable role in every aspect of their children's lives. Fathers aren't just another pair of hands; they play a critical role and are a source of strength from which children can learn and draw love.

Notes

1. Frank Pedersen et al., "Infant Development in Father-Absent Families," *Journal of Genetic Psychology* 135 (1979): 51-61.

2. Ross Parke, *Fatherhood* (Cambridge, Mass.: Harvard University Press, 1996),

citing C. E. Franz et al., "The Family Origins of Empathic Concern: A 26-Year Longitudinal Study," *Journal of Personality and Social Psychology* 58 (1990): 709-17.

3. John Gottman, *The Heart of Parenting: Raising an Emotionally Intelligent Child* (New York: Simon and Schuster, 1997), 172.

4. Kevin MacDonald and Ross D. Parke, "Parent-Child Physical Play: The Effects of Sex and Age of Children and Parents," *Sex Roles* 15, no. 7-8 (1986); see also John Snarey, *How Fathers Care for the Next Generation: A Four-Decade Study* (Cambridge, Mass.: Harvard University Press, 1993).

5. Maureen Green, *Fathering* (New York: McGraw Hill, 1976), cited in Parke, *Fatherhood*.

6. For more on this, see Snarey, *How Fathers Care*.

7. Gottman, *The Heart of Parenting,* 172.

Chapter Five

Promises Worth Keeping

Ken R. Canfield

In my office, I have a print of a Victorian painting entitled "Worn Out," which portrays an earlier period when plagues swept through Great Britain and families clung to each other for strength. In this painting, a sick curly-haired boy is asleep in the room's only bed. In the chair next to the bed, the boy's father is leaning back with his eyes closed. His legs are thrust out and crossed at the ankles, revealing his heavy boots. I imagine the father has been there all night. There is a small bowl below his chair. Perhaps he used it to feed broth to the boy or had water in it to dampen his son's forehead. There is an open book at his feet—maybe he read to his child.

The most poignant detail of the painting, however, is the boy's tiny hand—it is grasping tightly to his father's shirtsleeve just above the elbow. The child, drawing strength from his father, has survived another night.

It is a moving portrait that speaks volumes about what is missing in contemporary America, a void which fathers must fill. If fathers are to fill that void, it is incumbent that an updated, enriched, and practical framework for fathers be fleshed out to encourage dads to be more actively and responsibly involved in the lives of their children.

The key is to remind us that *father* is a verb, as well as a noun. Fathers who father are essential for the dreams of children to be realized. Indeed, fathers, by their deeds and actions, are the only evidence that a fathering movement has, or has not, materialized.

Many social commentators have concluded that the most prudent way to promote responsible fatherhood is to promote and restore marriage. This is wise, and it would be naive to fail to consider new strategies which seek to reverse the tide of divorce and strengthen the marriage bond. But a fathering movement must also offer a broad and redemptive view of fatherhood which can help all men, married, divorced, and single, to make the best out of their individual situations. The view of fathering must be broad enough to encourage all men to be responsible father figures and redemptive enough to admit there are no perfect fathers.

When Harvard psychologist Samuel Osherson described father absence as "one of the great underestimated tragedies of our times," he was not just talking about the physical absence of those fathers, but also the "psychological" absence.[1] The effects of psychological absence are harder to quantify, but no less real, as shown by the emergence of "Adult Children of . . ." recovery groups and by the psychological damage Osherson found in his examinations of supposedly successful Ivy Leaguers. The answer to that tragedy lies in defining what fathers must do, and then enabling them to just do it!

The 1994 blue-ribbon National Research Council's "America's Fathers and Public Policy" workshop report begins, "So diverse are America's fathers that participants in the workshop agreed there is no consensus on what constitutes the proper role for fathers today."[2] These experts may be correct that there is no such consensus, but it is vital that we forge one. If we cannot offer imperfect men a rich vision of what fathers do, then much of the recent energy and attention we've given to fatherhood—and the publicity we've garnered on its behalf—will be largely ineffective.

Commitment to Fathering

The desire to commit one's heart to fathering must come either from within or from beyond; dads must sense a higher purpose—what some would term a transcendent calling—which serves as powerful motivation. Changes in government policies, business practices, economic conditions, or media portrayals could all assist in encouraging motivation. But our research has shown that the most salient factor in a father's fathering rests in his commitment.[3] Even deficits resulting from his family of origin or current family situation can be overcome when a dad has a high level of commitment.

There are many useful frameworks for describing a father's role. If we are to encourage and aid dads, we need to offer one which is an easily transferable description of the activities of a father—the practices that give a man confidence and joy in his role. The background of the framework being offered includes a search of social science, biological, historical, and theological indexes, as well as reviews of thousands of fathers' experiences through detailed survey instruments and further thousands of children's essays about their fathers.

Before summarizing those practices which emerged, let us first acknowledge that the precursor to fathering—and for that matter, mothering—is a relationship with the opposite sex.[4]

Historically, fatherhood and motherhood have been rooted in a marital covenant, so that, in an ideal situation, marriage and parenting are inextricably interwoven. Strengthening marriages will strengthen fathering, but not all fathers—or responsible fathers—are currently married.

Second, we must resist the notion of describing a father's duty in terms of "breadwinning" or "providing" alone.[5] There is an ongoing social dynamic of couples working through the proportion of contribution that mom and dad each make, whether it be through household tasks or through a paycheck. There are wide variations, from the voluntary at-home dad, to the unemployed dad, to dual-earner couples working different hours, to two parents working full-time outside the home, to stay-at-home moms. We must think more broadly about this dimension, given Robert Griswold's conclusions from history: When fatherhood is described in breadwinning terms, fathering becomes too easily reduced to a one-dimensional role, with the result often being a father's psychological absence from his family in pursuit of a career.[6]

Four Dimensions of Fathering

After reviewing the literature, synthesizing the data, and interacting with thousands of fathers, we can summarize what fathers must do in four dimensions: involvement, consistency, awareness, and nurturance—the I-CANs of fathering.

These dimensions are not peculiar to fathering. They could be applied to mothering as well. But they would be applied differently—and should be. The evidence is increasing that it is misguided to think of "parenting" in a generic sense. Yet the key is in not focusing on the differences in approach (between a mother and father), but rather in focusing on the differences in outcomes for a child who has an involved, responsible father. A father's actions play a unique role in shaping a child. For instance, a recent study suggested that the greatest predictor of whether a child would grow into an adult demonstrating "empathetic concern" (love) as a 31-year-old adult was whether the father was involved in active care of the child as a preschooler.[7] Other research shows that while a father's aims or goals are similar to a mother's, his approach and focus will be substantially different from a mother's. For instance, a mom may talk to an upset child, soothing his or her feelings, while a dad takes steps to fix the situation which caused the upset.[8] Most importantly, in men's minds, "parenting" oftentimes is synonymous with mothering. Therefore, it is critical that we promote "fathering" and not only "parenting" if men are to be recruited for skill-building programs.

Involvement

"T-I-M-E spells love." Again and again, we see this truth fleshed out, for good or bad, in the lives of children: The strength of children's relationships with their father is often proportional to the amount of time he spends with them, time which may be precarious for a noncustodial father, yet is essential. In essays we have collected by children about their dads, children tend to remember the mundane, day-to-day activities they do with dad.

- Timmy: "My daddy loves me. He plays with me. He takes me to the park. He takes me for ice cream. He takes me swimming. Daddy helps me with my homework. He likes to listen to me read my reading books. He plays baseball with me. He takes me on walks with my dog. He tickles me a lot."
- Bethany: "He chases me. He tucks me in bed at night and prays with me. When we go to the beach I get on his back and he swims."
- Robby: "At his job he always hurries home just to see us. He tries to coach every sport that he can. Last year people asked him to be mayor and he said, 'No, I'm going to spend more time with my kids.' That's why he is the best dad."

The debate between quality versus quantity time is unfortunate. This often leads to the assumption that intense, quality time is a cure-all for lack of quantity time. The problem with this perspective becomes clear if phrased as a matter of conscious choice: "Going to Disney World every other year is better than shooting hoops several times a week." While some misguided parents may believe Disney World is better, children do not reason that way. They take joy in the small details, for it is in their involvement in the common everyday activities that children know their fathers love them.

Michael Lamb, a long-time fathering researcher, gives three facets of fathering involvement: engagement, accessibility, and responsibility.[9] During engagement a father and his child are doing something together, where the purpose of the activity (on the father's part, at least) is to be with his child. Dad enlists his teenage son to help change a tire; he suggests a walk down the street for ice cream to his daughter; he attends his children's choir performances and basketball games.

In contrast, accessibility is unstructured time—being in the vicinity of the child without necessarily doing an activity together. One can enjoy presence even while being focused on something else. Accessibility refers to the child's sense that dad is reachable. A dad could, for example, give his child his work phone number and say, "Feel free to call any time you need me," in a way that the child knows he means it.

Responsibility covers the daily routines of fathers caring for their children—wiping noses, giving allowances, driving them to lessons and games, and insuring they get a physical examination. Dads are there to meet their children's needs, whether those needs are basic or life-threatening.

The fathering movement can tell men who feel inadequate for fathering that they can be equipped with these skills. Consider sons who grew up with emotionally distant or addictive fathers. They will, in all likelihood, feel emotionally distanced from their own children or be at risk of other addictive behaviors unless there has been some intervention or change in their lives. As a result, their confidence is often lacking and their fathering is deferred to a mother, teacher, coach, or pastor.

These fathers can be taught to examine how their fathers or father figures were lacking in involvement, consistency, awareness, and nurturance. By learning new skills, such hesitant fathers can overcome their past and become better fathers than their own father was to them. Such fathers can pursue fathering resources—books, seminars, or other proactive instruction.

Another key ingredient in involvement is the influence of others. We have surveyed thousands of fathers across the country and asked the question, "Who has most influenced you in your fathering?" The most frequent answer by far has been, "My wife."[10] A wife's encouragement gives a dad strength to persevere when he's made a mistake, or when he struggles to overcome his own past or when the rewards of fathering seem faint.

Wives can also inhibit fathers by placing their parenting standards and approaches on their husbands. If a wife wants little Timmy dressed "just so," then her husband will only fail once or twice before giving up altogether. She has unknowingly discouraged him from being involved in that part of his fathering role.

Dads also receive a mixed bag of support and discouragement from other sources. When a father wants to go home to his family instead of elsewhere, he may be teased: "Going home to change the diapers?" Many parenting events, such as PTA meetings, doctor's appointments, or childbirth classes, may make fathers feel out-of-place.[11] The airlines' normal practice of reducing fares for longer stays forces dads who travel for a living to make a cruel choice.

The workplace, however, is often where a father meets the most resistance to his fathering commitment.[12] Men are encouraged to seek their identity in their work, rather than the home. The workplace, even though it can demand a great deal of a person, also offers reasonably quick rewards, such as bonuses, raises, and new titles. In addition to the extra money, these rewards also fulfill deeper needs for power, recognition, achievement, and identity.

In short, the work world can offer fast food for a starving ego. In comparison, fathering is much less immediate in terms of rewards. How many times, for example, have children told their dad thank you in the last year? When did an important member of society tell a dad what a good person he was for driving his child to soccer practice? This area of external support for fathering rapidly blends into the area of motivation—as the motivation of those around a dad will affect how they encourage him.

Consistency

Children depend on their fathers to be predictable and reliable so they can grow up with confidence and security. Children are natural explorers; they need to discover. Toddlers explore objects by putting them in their mouth. In grade school, children discover how to behave in class and what's allowed at recess. Teenagers explore the bigger issues of self-identity, faith, and the opposite sex. On their never-ending journeys of discovery, children need reference points. They need parents who are consistent in their attitudes, beliefs, and actions.

How do dads see their own role? Five of the top twelve areas identified by dads as being important to their fathering in our 1990 national research study focused on consistency: Fathers felt they played a vital role in modeling good behavior, promoting moral and spiritual development (of children), dealing with family crisis, developing parental confidence, and fostering male identity.[13] Research surrounding adolescent behavior reveals that teens who have consistent parents are more secure—boys are usually more well-adjusted, intellectually oriented, and have stable relationships with others; girls show more self-assurance and vitality, less anxiety, and conform less to rigid gender-based stereotypes.[14]

Self-discipline is required for dads to be consistent in both external and internal realms. External realms are those connected with what children see fathers doing. Dads need to be consistent in their presence, schedule (including "free" time), and responses.

Children also look for consistency in dad's internal realms. Is he consistently self-controlled, emotionally stable, and able to keep a promise? Calmness has been identified as a key factor distinguishing effective fathers.[15] Emotional stability emerged again in a longitudinal study spanning 11 years which concluded: "Fathers who maintain a close and stable emotional bond with adolescents over time protect adolescents from engaging in delinquent behavior."[16]

Awareness

Awareness is an obvious need. For fathers to father they must know who their children are. They must recognize them by their appearance, their interests, and their abilities—both those unique to the individual and common for the child's developmental level.

High-schooler Nikki Anderson longed to be known by her father. In an essay about her father, she wrote:

> If he would just try to get to know me, my father would like me because I'm not a bad person, but he won't even try. So, I get tired of being good because nobody cares anyway and then I get in trouble in school. Last time I got in trouble they couldn't reach my mom so they called my father. He drove 70

miles, and when he got here, I was standing outside with a bunch of kids, and I was so proud because my daddy was coming to see me. Then he went up to some other girl and hugged her. He didn't even know who I was.[17]

"He didn't even know who I was." These are words that should strike fear into the heart of every father. Indeed, in a 1996 National Center for Fathering/Gallup Poll, fathers were least likely to rate themselves highly in the area of awareness. Mothers also rated dads lower in this area.[18] Here, perhaps more than any other of the three dimensions of fathering, the fathering movement can raise a standard calling for better performance by our society's fathers.

An awareness of children tempers and molds our expectations. Dads have been termed the challenger—the parent who calls a child to reach beyond his or her current abilities and performance.[19] With awareness, dads are less likely to push too hard or try to mold children into someone else's image. Both are dangers which can be avoided by knowing one's children and their dreams.

Nurturance

Nurturance means to form intimate bonds with our children, responding to their emotional and social needs. Nurturance is both an action and the primary motive. It is expressed through a father's actions of touching, comforting, encouraging, affirming, and listening to his children.

Several factors influence a dad's ability to nurture his children. First, a father's ability to nurture his children depends a good deal upon how he was nurtured by his own father.

Second, the area of physical touch is a key part of nurturance. For a father, touch is often easier once children become capable of play. Daddy will pull the kids off the couch and shout, "It's time for a . . . dog pile!" and wrestle around on the floor with them. Not only is such roughhousing a peculiarly fatherly activity, but it also provides a critical form of nurturance. Through this rough-and-tumble play, our children learn about risk-taking and problem solving. Kevin MacDonald, associate professor of psychology at California State University at Long Beach, found that children who are rejected by their classmates tend to come from homes where father's roughhousing is too insensitive and aggressive. Shy and introverted children, on the other hand, tend to come from homes in which there is little or no healthy roughhousing.[20]

The fathering movement needs to paint pictures for men like this real-life example: Gary was in his military uniform, ready to board a plane. He was leaving home. While Gary's mother and sisters took turns hugging him, his father stood by watching. Finally, the father approached his son. Placing his hands firmly on the boy's shoulders, he gave him a couple of squeezes before standing back. Beaming, he stared at his son for several seconds. Then he reached up and took his son's hat off, leaned close, kissed him on the forehead, and then replaced the hat. Such purposeful and loving touch creates bonds and connections between father and son in ways that nothing else can.

Discipline is another critical ingredient of childrearing; some consider it primarily a fatherly role. For instance, David Popenoe suggests this framework for looking at the unique aspects of the fathering role: "[F]athers are irreplaceable as protectors, challengers, disciplinarians and guides."[21] Others may be surprised at classifying discipline as part of nurturance.[22] Discipline does involve elements of all four dimensions: A dad has to be involved to want to discipline; he has to be consistent in the standards he sets and enforces; he has to be aware of attitudes and what's reasonable for the child's level of development.

Yet, clearly it is nurturing to give children defined guidelines to follow, and to establish consequences when they step out of those guidelines. The purpose should be to help children become confident and well-adjusted. Healthy discipline presupposes a good relationship with one's children and is based upon one's care for them. And having a good relationship requires the sharing of emotions, other than displeasure. Our research reveals that 51 percent of men are hesitant to share their emotions, with the exception of anger.[23] It would be helpful for these men to meet with and observe other men who model healthy emotional expression.

Sources of Motivation

To have a good relationship with his children, a man must be motivated to do so. He must be interested in someone other than himself. What causes a father to choose to become other-centered? How do we raise boys to be motivated fathers?

One answer to these questions was summed up this way by a report in the *Portland Oregonian:* "A shadow has fallen over the secular men's movement, and it looks a lot like a cross." The article went on to detail the dramatic numbers of men impacted by the Promise Keepers movement.[24] In October 1997, Promise Keepers held without a doubt the largest gathering of men in a single location, as well as locations across the United States. They stress with integrity the importance of personal responsibility with respect to a man's fathering.

I vividly remember standing on the Mall that day, observing hundreds of thousands of men being challenged to be responsible father figures. At one point, a speaker said, "Take out a picture of your family!" One man in particular, in his mid-thirties, took out a picture of his wife and two children. When the speaker reminded him to pray for the welfare of his wife and children, he burst into tears. He squeezed his eyes tightly, praying with all his heart, as if he were alone on the Washington Mall. That is the kind of commitment, personally expressed, an effective fathering movement needs to elicit and to direct.

Promise Keepers is more representative of American men than one may think. The men who thronged to the event were not just the righteous but the broken, in many cases seeking healing for themselves, their fathering, and their families. According to ongoing samples of promise-keeper participants the National Center for Fathering has conducted from 1995 through 1998, about half of promise keepers have college degrees. The median age is 37. Almost 76 percent are currently married, although about a quarter have been divorced at some time. The median length of current marriage is 11 years. Sixty percent of promise keepers have working wives, about 43 percent of whom work part-time. Thirty percent of those attending reported they were converted after age 25, evidence of a new relationship between fathering and spiritual awakening. Almost 27 percent of the men consider themselves a workaholic. A majority say it is mostly or somewhat true that "I feel like my job consumes me."

A majority of Promise Keepers say they had a good relationship with their own father. Almost 60 percent agreed with the statement "I want to be like my dad." But even among these, considerable ambivalence and a longing for a more emotionally warm model of fathering was evident. Less than a third, for example, agreed that the following statement was mostly or somewhat true: "It was easy to get close to my father." And faced with the statement, "My father regularly shared his affection with me," about 57 percent disagreed.

Asked, "Did you feel that your father was largely absent when you were growing up?" almost 53 percent of men said, "yes." Almost 28 percent of promise keepers are products of broken homes, experiencing parental divorce at an average of about 11 years of age. About a third of all promise keepers reported drug or alcohol abuse in their family of origin and about the same proportion say they experienced emotional abuse. Eleven percent reported being physically abused, and six percent say they were sexually molested.

The Promise Keepers movement flourishes because it recognizes a basic truth: Despite these devastating personal experiences, many, if not most, fathers are searching for ways to strengthen the moral and spiritual underpinnings of their fathering and their families. This is not a movement of the righteous seeking perfection, but of broken men looking for healing for themselves and their children.[25] We must recognize the need to discuss the spiritual dimension of fathering. Ralph Smith puts it this way in discussing fathering: "A long-term strategy must require attention to the role of community-based organizations and churches in rebuilding the social infrastructure and natural networks within neighborhoods with the resources upon which families can depend and to which they can turn."[26]

Like many modern American cultural movements, there is a rallying phrase which provides a clear directive to the historic faith community. This one is found in prophetic Hebrew literature: "See, I will send you the prophet Elijah before that great and dreadful day of the Lord comes. He will turn the hearts of the fathers to their children, and the hearts of the children to their fathers; or else I will come and strike the land with a curse" (Malachi 4:5-6, NIV).

Ideas for Change

To encourage that faith which leads to action, here are several civil "projects" which could contribute to focusing attention on fathering. These efforts can flow alongside that river which is already emerging from the faith community and can contribute to what is the only fathering movement worthy of mention: individual dads focusing new attention on their children. Here are several ideas:

• Establish a practical, life-course curriculum for fathers called Father's University which can be accessed through the Internet, correspondence, and day-long seminars.
• Promote community-wide "Father of the Year" essay contests involving institutions like media, school systems, and professional sports teams.[27]
• Establish a "Fathering Hall of Fame" to systematically honor America's"everyday" heros.
• Offer vouchers for all children, particularly young males in middle and high school, to receive fathering awareness and skills building education. Different groups (YMCAs, counselors, colleges, faith communities) could offer the instruction, and parents could choose which group they would like their children to learn from about this crucial topic.[28]
• Establish fathering training programs with an I-CAN curriculum for those public school systems and community colleges with parenting education already in place.
• Designate a "Year of the Father."
• Conduct a broadly-coordinated "Take Your Daughter to Work Day" followed by a "Take Your Son to Work Day," both during summer vacation.[29]
• Begin "Fathering Awareness Training" for leaders and for children in such community organizations as Boys and Girls Clubs and Boy Scouts.
• Develop a program targeted toward high school boys which prepares them for the responsibility of being a father.
• Conduct "The Essence of Fathering" training for coaches, policemen, and other officials who are key surrogate fathers.

David Popenoe and others have detailed the reasons for hope that change in fathering is possible. He points to evidence that baby boomers are becoming more family-oriented, the cultural pendulum is bound to shift from focusing on individuals back to families, and economic changes like downsizing are forcing more reliance on family networks.[30] Additionally, there is evidence that the coming generation of men will be more committed to their children's welfare because they have experienced the results of paternal neglect in their own lives or the lives of those around them.[31] The success of the fathering movement can contribute to this ground swell of change by giving men specific encouragement and direction. Our success depends ultimately on our ability to help men grasp the power inherent in their role, their potential to influence the next generation, and the overwhelming fulfillment that is found in ongoing sacrifice for the benefit of children. In so doing, those who have drunk at empty wells can be offered hope of lasting satisfaction.

Notes

1. Samuel Osherson, *Finding Our Fathers* (New York: Fawcett Columbine, 1987), 6.

2. Institute of Medicine, National Research Council, Commission on Behavioral and Social Sciences and Education, Board on Children and Families, *America's Fathers and Public Policy: Report of a Workshop* (Washington, D.C.: National Academy Press, 1994), 4.

3. Gale Roid and Ken Canfield, "Measuring the Dimensions of Effective Fathering," *Educational and Psychological Measurement* (spring 1994): 216.

4. Rape, incest, and artificial insemination may all result in pregnancy, but do not represent the male relationship implicit in the meaning of the words *father* or *fathering*.

5. Effective fathers are distinguished from national norms by a slight margin on the dimension of "protecting and providing." See Roid and Canfield, "Measuring the Dimensions," 217.

6. Robert Griswold, *Fatherhood in America* (New York: Basic Books, 1993), 134-42, 185-210.

7. E. M. Koestner and P. D. Fairweather, "The Family of Origin of Empathetic Concern: A 26-Year Longitudinal Study," *Journal of Personality and Social Psychology* 58, no. 4 (1991): 709-17.

8. Tori DeAngellis, "Fathers Strongly Influenced by Culture," *American Psychological Association Monitor* (April 1996): 1, 39.

9. Michael Lamb, ed., *The Father's Role: Applied Perspectives* (New York: Wiley and Sons, 1986), 8.

10. Ken Canfield, *The Seven Secrets of Effective Fathers* (Wheaton, Ill.: Tyndale, 1992), 129-30.

11. For further development of this theme and corrective steps, see James A. Levine et al., *Getting Men Involved: Strategies for Early Childhood Programs* (New York: Scholastic, 1993).

12. The lack of work can be an even greater challenge. In a brochure titled "Core Learnings," Vivian Galsden states, "When normal venues to obtain work are unavailable or inaccessible, many fathers—particularly young fathers with few skills and few years of schooling—either avoid the responsibility of supporting their children or often turn to informal economies" (Philadelphia: National Center on Fathers and Families, 1996), 2.

13. The top 12 (out of 27) are (1) showing affection/affirmation; (2) parental discussion; (3) role modeling; (4) dealing with a family crisis; (5) involvement in discipline; (6) moral and spiritual development; (7) knowing the child; (8) involvement in education; (9) wife's role; (10) parental confidence; (11) male identity; (12) marital interaction. See Ken Canfield, *The Heart of a Father* (Chicago: Northfield, 1996), 233-35.

14. Jeanne Block, "Parental Consistency in Child-Rearing Orientation and Personality Development" (paper presented at the Annual Convention of the American Psychological

Association, Anaheim, California, August 26-30, 1983).

15. Bart Fowler, "The Relationship Between Communication Practices and Marital Quality Among Religious Fathers in the U.S.A." (paper presented at the Moscow Center of Psychology and Psychotherapy International Conference, "Psychology and Christianity: A Way of Integration," Moscow, Russia, September 7-9, 1995).

16. Kathleen M. Harris, Frank Furstenberg Jr., and Jeremy Marmer, "Paternal Involvement with Adolescents in Intact Families: The Influence of Fathers Over the Life Course" (paper presented at the annual meeting of the American Sociological Association, New York, New York, August 16-20, 1996), 28.

17. LouAnne Johnson, "My Posse Don't Do Homework," *Reader's Digest,* September 1992, 207.

18. National Center for Fathering/Gallup Poll, 1996. Total agreement with statements (based on those responding who said mostly or somewhat true):

Statement	Fathers	Mothers (about fathers)
Most fathers do things with children often.	89 percent	77 percent
Most fathers have consistent relationship with children.	97 percent	78 percent
Most fathers express affection toward children.	96 percent	81 percent
Most fathers know what a child needs in order to grow into a mature, responsible person.	92 percent	76 percent
Most fathers have a good handle on how a child's needs change as he or she grows up.	92 percent	73 percent

The lack of awareness was further highlighted by a question asked of all respondents: Only 43 percent agreed "Most fathers know what is going on in their children's lives."

19. David Popenoe, *Life Without Father* (New York: Free Press, 1996), 50.

20. Cited in Carla Cantor, "The Father Factor," *Working Mother,* June 1992, 39-42.

21. Popenoe, *Life Without Father,* 50.

22. One classic definition of what it means to be a legitimate child, as opposed to illegitimate child, is that a father disciplines the legitimate child because he loves him. See the New Testament, Hebrews 12:5-9.

23. The 1994 National Center for Fathering National Men's Survey (n = 1621) found 62 percent agreed with the statement, "I tend to hide my emotions." Only 52 percent could agree with "People are not afraid of my anger." Sixteen percent agreed that "I tend to express my anger physically."

24. Tom Bates and Mark O'Keefe, "Jesus Steals the Men's Movement," *Portland Oregonian,* August 2, 1996, E2. The article gave these numbers of followers for four

different men's movements: Promise Keepers, 2 million; Mythopoetic, about 100,000; Men's issues/fathers' rights, about 70,000; and Profeminist, about 2,000.

25. In the 1990 National Survey of Fathering Practices, the greatest area of dissonance—difference between perceived importance by fathers and their own performance—was in the area of moral and spiritual development. Role modeling, which also involves this area, was third highest in dissonance. See Canfield, *The Heart of a Father,* 235-36.

26. Ralph Smith, "Putting Fathers into Families," *Georgia Academy Journal* (winter 1993/1994): 3.

27. "The Father of the Year" essay contest is a program of the National Center for Fathering, as is the "Fathering Hall of Fame." Details may be obtained from the center.

28. The author first heard this idea proposed by Governor Pete Wilson at his historic "Focus on Fathers Summit" in California on June 13, 1995.

29. The Ms. Foundation has been pursuing two separate days as the next step beyond their original "Take Your Daughters to Work Day."

30. Popenoe, *Life Without Father,* 225-28.

31. In 1995, 81 percent of men 18-24 years of age agreed,"When making important family decisions, consideration of children should come first," compared to 1986 figures of 66 percent. These figures are from the DDB Needham Chicago office's annual Lifestyle survey. See signs of "Hope for a Rebirth of Commitment to Fathering," *Today's Father* 3, no. 4 (n.d.): 8.

Chapter Six

The Importance of Being Married

Maggie Gallagher

In the beginning was the single mother. In the interests of expanding women's sexual liberty and equality, she was to be remade into a self-sufficient choice-making and rights-bearing individual. "Can we stop defining [the female-headed family] as a scourge and view it for what it is," Judy Mann asked in a 1987 *Washington Post* column, "a demographic group that has particular needs, much the same as the elderly or two-parent families with children?"

But recently, the limits of valorizing single motherhood have become apparent. For one thing, our children stubbornly long for their absent fathers. They refuse to accept adult attempts to redefine the great enduring crisis of their young life, the moment when Dad leaves, as a mere transition to "just another family form."

For another, many women now recognize that the single-parent model of family life is not fair to women and certainly not a more gender neutral way of life. Instead of encouraging a new androgynous, egalitarian family, our cultural retreat from fatherhood has more or less let more and more men off the hook when it comes to raising children.

Now we are engaged in a great civil struggle over the role and meaning of marriage, family, and fatherhood. The father has reappeared with vigor in our public discourse, but not yet in our private homes. Even as we rhetorically rediscover the importance of fatherhood as a cultural ideal, flesh-and-blood fathers are becoming each year a scarcer commodity.

How do we acquire fathers for our children? How do men get to be good fathers, and how does society help them get there?

Marriage Attaches Fathers to Their Children

Through most of human history the answer has been obvious: Society helps men to be good fathers through marriage. From an anthropological perspective, marriage is the institution by which societies have attached fathers to children. The "legitimacy principle" says in a nutshell that the children born of this woman are the responsibility of that man, her husband. Through most of human history, the "biological father" was a very tenuous idea. Without DNA testing, it would not even be possible to know for certain that one man, and not some other, was the father. Moreover, as a matter of mere biology, men can sire a virtually unlimited number of children. Meanwhile, it is an almost universally understood truth that one man can provide care, protection, and nurture for a limited number of children.

Marriage is the institution that closes this shocking biological gap between a man's sexual and fathering capacities. It makes a sexual union with one woman a matter of public record. It obligates not just the man but his kin to acknowledge the children of this sexual union as family. In our society, marriage in theory confines him to one woman and commits him to care for his children. Out of two biologically unrelated individuals, it makes one family.

Recently, this cultural understanding of the role marriage plays has broken down. Marriage has come to be seen and discussed primarily as an emotional relationship between two adults for the purpose of furthering their own happiness. So as the data on the high costs of fatherlessness mounts, cultural elites respond by aspiring to rebuild fatherhood outside of marriage.

Enter the single father. After 20 years of futilely attempting to remake the single mother into a competent substitute for an intact family, policymakers and social workers have discovered a new object for their concern. "People are only starting to recognize the importance of including teen fathers," Beth Grube, dean of social work at Fordham's Tarrytown campus, which runs programs for young unwed fathers, told the *Citizen-Register* in 1994. "It's not only good for the father, but for the mother and child."

Hopes run high. Now, it is not just the unwed father, but the divorced father upon whom our hopes center. Joint custody, divorce mediation, the "good" divorce—these are various legal and cultural efforts to re-create and restore fatherhood outside of marriage. So far, in spite of repeated failure, we remain weirdly optimistic that through exhortation and proper legal procedures, we can create a real, committed, post-marital "family." In this new utopia, men and women who have severed ties to each other will nonetheless cheerfully and reliably cooperate to build each other's ties to children. The good-enough marriage, these new voices argue, is beyond the reach of half of our population. But the good divorce remains a real possibility.

Behind this new effort to remake fatherhood outside of marriage lies a stunted conception of what families are, or how fatherhood operates. For in the model that dominates our current debate, the family is a collection of roles, tasks performed, and goods supplied. Parents in this view are simply two people who take care of children too young to help themselves. Children may benefit from the material and emotional support of both mother and father, but in theory, there is no particular reason why mother and father have to be married to each other. In theory, parents could cooperatively raise their children in separate households.

In theory. But before we lose another generation of kids to theory, before we waste the next 20 years on a perhaps equally futile attempt to remake single fatherhood, we need to take a hard look at the realistic prospects for success. What happens to fatherhood when marriage collapses and why?

Marriage Holds Fathers to Their Children

The evidence is strikingly clear: Outside of marriage, fatherhood withers away. When the union between mother and father collapses, fathers diminish, disappear, or become strangely ineffective.

The first way fathers are lost is physically; therapists may reassure children that "though Mommy and Daddy don't love each other anymore, they will always love you," but children of divorce know better. For most, domicile is destiny: Perhaps only one-third of all children living apart from their fathers get to see their dads as often as once a week.

For the first year or so, fathers make a special effort to see their children. As time goes on, as they or their children move inconvenient distances away or as they acquire additional emotional obligations to new wives, or girlfriends or stepchildren or new babies, or as the crisis subsides and the children seem to be getting on fine or as men grow weary of facing continual hostility from ex-wives, fathers' contact with their children dwindles rapidly. Ten years down the road, almost two-thirds of all children of divorce have virtually no contact with their fathers.[1]

Children whose parents fail to marry in the first place have an even more tenuous connection to their fathers. On average, the child born outside of marriage spends just six months living with his dad. As time passes, the same pattern of the disappearing dad emerges, but more strongly. In one rare study of unwed fathers, almost three-fifths of unwed fathers whose children are two or younger saw their kids more than once a week. But by the time kids reach age seven and a half, less than a quarter of unwed fathers still saw their children frequently.[2]

Marriage Creates a Unity of Interests

The second loss children face outside of marriage is the loss of the union between mother and father. Marriage attempts to unify the interests of adults and children. When that bond breaks, a mother has little incentive and indeed faces great difficulties emotionally in helping sustain the bond between her child and the man who is her former lover.

Consider Bonnie. At 45, she is the never-married mother of eight-year-old Michael. Michael's dad lives in Germany. His father pays no support, but tells Bonnie he will send money for airplane tickets "any time." In the past, Bonnie has taken Michael to Germany to visit his dad. Because she has little money, they both have to stay in his dad's apartment. When they are there, Michael tries to make his mom and dad hold hands.

This year, Bonnie's not going to Germany. "It's too painful," she says.

Therapists tell mothers like Bonnie they shouldn't interfere with their son's adoration of his father. In the light of reason and the best interests of the child, they are right. But whose blood is that cold? Certainly not Bonnie's. Michael is not just her child, but her whole family, her great love, and her ruling passion. She is not a particularly angry person. But still the man Michael loves and longs for is the man who desperately pressured her to have an abortion, who never helped her as she struggled in a foreign land to take care of a baby. He is the man who didn't want her and worse, didn't want the greatest treasure she could offer—Michael. And her son loves him.

In a good-enough marriage, the mother helps the child idealize the father. She, like the child, has every interest in dwelling on his virtues, and minimizing his flaws. When a family breaks apart, this union of interest collapses not just economically but emotionally.

Fathers face similar difficulties. When marriage collapses, their role as husbands (or lovers) and fathers often conflict. Consider the case of Hassan Lemons, a 17-year-old unmarried father of a baby girl. When he and his girlfriend broke up, he dropped out of sight. Hassan told a reporter, "The people from [the National Institute for Responsible Fatherhood] kept saying, 'Where's your child? That's really taking it out on her.'" So Hassan made contact again. Now that he's found work as a handyman, he says he'll pay child support. There is one complication, however. He recently fathered another child, and now he says he needs to spend more time and presumably money with his new girlfriend and their baby.[3]

Hassan may mean well. But outside of marriage, he finds it almost impossible to be a committed father. Marriage unites the sexual and financial interests of the family. In marriage, a man and woman create a sexual union that includes the promise to care for each other and for their children. Outside of marriage, this unity of interests collapses.

Fathers have their own complaints. Many are doing the best they can in a difficult situation. Maybe they did not want the divorce (the majority of divorces are at least formally initiated by women); maybe they wanted to be real fathers in whole families and resent being thrust into this fractured position, each visit with the kids a reminder of what has been lost. The financial squeeze is tight, and of course a guy resents helping support a woman who wants his money but not him. If having a father was so important, why didn't she stick around and stay married, as she promised?

Under these circumstances, the man who stays in touch and pays his child support is likely to feel quite good about his performance as a father. His kids may feel differently.

The middle-class divorced fathers in Judith Wallerstein's sample were an unusually committed group. Very few had ceased visiting their children.

> Most fathers in our study thought they had done reasonably well in fulfilling their obligations, whereas three out of four of the children felt rejected by their fathers. . . . I find it startling that the sense of loss the children experience is unrelated to how often they are visited. Most of the young people regularly visit their fathers, yet most feel that they have lost them. Contrary to what many parents expect, frequency of visiting is not related to outcome; the few children in our study who have been visited by their fathers once or twice a week over the ten-year period still feel rejected.[4]

What mattered to the children, in Wallerstein's experience, was not necessarily the raw amount of time Dad spent with his kids, but the quality of the relation between father and child.

> [W]here the father is regarded as moral and competent and the boy feels wanted and accepted by his father, then the boy's psychological health is likely to be good. The psychological adjustment of teenage boys within divorced families is greatly eased by the perception that "my dad is a good man, my dad cares for me, encourages me, respects me."

Boys who saw their father as moral and competent and felt valued by him did fairly well. But when the father was seen as bad, weak, or unconcerned, the boys were likely to suffer "low-esteem, poor grades, weak aspirations."[5]

Unfortunately a mother who has been abandoned by or who has left her children's father is not generally in a very good position to help the children see their father as good, strong, and concerned. If the father left the household, it is hard for the mother to see him as loving and dependable. Conversely, if the mother left the household, she can only justify that decision by seeing the father as an ineffectual, unconcerned, or even abusive father.

In the divorce culture, both children and fathers feel the loss of the mother's love for the father. To a considerable and still unrecognized extent, the father's role is sustained through and by women.

This may be one reason why the father, so important inside an intact marriage, is so ineffective when marriage collapses. It explains as well one of the great puzzles in social science literature: the difference between orphans and divorce orphans.

Marriage Satisfies Father Hunger

Children, it turns out, have very different reactions to parental death than to parental divorce. Of the two ways to lose a father, death may be better. Robert Emery, surveying the evidence, concludes that compared to children from homes disrupted by death, children from divorced homes have more psychological problems.[6]

Children may experience a father's death as a form of abandonment, but at some deep level they know, or come to understand, that this is not true. Death, unlike divorce, is not a failure of love. Moreover in death, unlike in divorce, the mother who remains still loves and admires the father. She may even idealize him more in death than in life. Death may deprive children of their father's presence but the story of the father—of the man who made, loved, and protected them—remains intact.

The epidemic of fatherlessness we face is something strikingly new. What children must deal with today is not just fatherlessness but father abandonment. Previous generations lost fathers to the grave, but this is the first generation of Americans for whom paternal abandonment has become the norm. This is the first generation of American kids who must face not just the sad loss of their fathers, but the far more brutal knowledge that to their fathers, many other things are more important than they are.

Even joint custody or frequent visiting is no balm for father hunger. Overall, children of divorce who frequently see their fathers don't seem to do any better than children of divorce who never or seldom see their fathers. In one large scale national survey, "teenagers who saw their fathers regularly were just as likely as those with infrequent contact to have problems in school or engage in delinquent acts and precocious sexual behavior," note Frank Furstenberg and Andrew Cherlin.[7] So while inside of marriage the presence of an active father makes a great difference for children, outside of marriage the presence of the same father seems not to have the same benefits.

There is much other evidence that the father's role is particularly fragile and vulnerable to disruption outside of marriage. Children who do not live with their mothers are almost as likely as children who do live with their mothers to report they have a good relationship with Mom. Not so with fathers. Sixty-nine percent of children living with fathers report a good relationship, compared to just 36 percent of kids who do not live with Dad.

More than half of kids who don't live with their fathers say they don't get all the paternal affection they need. Again, those who saw their fathers frequently did not evaluate their relationships more favorably than those who saw them infrequently. Overall, only half of nonresidential fathers are considered "family" by their kids, compared to all fathers living with their children, and even 70 percent of stepfathers living with their kids.[8]

We have begun to emphasize the importance of fathering. What we have not yet done is come to grips with the reality men face: The only reliable way to be an effective father is inside marriage to the mother of one's children.

What does it mean to be a good father? At a basic level, a father puts his family's needs first. His sexuality is (in theory) at his wife's disposal and not any other woman's—and therefore cannot threaten the well-being of his children. His income is their income.

But what if there are two mothers and two children to care for? His commitment to both cannot be supreme. Even for men who wish to be responsible fathers, for all practical purposes one set of children must be subordinated to another. As is often the case in families fractured by divorce or failure to marry, when the father is a man of very limited resources, struggling to get by in a world where the wages of less-educated men are falling, the difficulties of being a good dad to two or more sets of children intensify. But for all fathers, time, energy, and money are limited commodities.

Marriage is the vehicle by which society creates firm, reliable ties between men and their children—transforms lovers into fathers. In marriage, men make a commitment to care for the children their sexual acts may produce. In marriage, men have a reasonable certainty that the children produced are in fact their own.

Marriage creates a unity of interests between fathers, mothers, and children. When marriage collapses, the crucial tie between fathers and children is not just weakened, it is transformed in ways that are hostile to the interests of children and to their profound desire for union with both their parents.

It is not biology, but law, custom, and mores that make fathers out of men. The fact that the tie between father and child is less "natural," more fragile, more a product of culture, than the tie between mother and child does not mean it is less important. The relative fragility of fatherhood does mean that attaching men to their children, creating a tie so firm a child's heart can rely on it, is a social problem in the way that creating attachments between women and their children is not.

How do we give children the fathers they need and long for? Marriage is the tried and true answer. None of our current fumbling attempts to re-create these ties outside of marriage are likely to succeed in anything but diverting us from the critical task: restoring marriage as the normal, usual, and generally reliable way of bringing up baby.

Notes

1. Frank F. Furstenberg Jr. and Andrew J. Cherlin, *Divided Families: What Happens to Children When Parents Part* (Cambridge, Mass.: Harvard University Press, 1991), 35-36.

2. Susan Chira, "Novel Idea in Welfare Plan: Helping Children by Helping Their Fathers," *New York Times,* March 30, 1994.

3. Ibid.

4. Judith S. Wallerstein and Sandra Blakeslee, *Second Chances: Men, Women and Children A Decade After Divorce* (New York: Ticknor and Fields, 1990), 238.

5. Ibid.

6. Robert E. Emery, *Marriage, Divorce and Children's Adjustments* (Newbury Park, Calif.: Sage Publications, 1988).

7. Furstenberg and Cherlin, *Divided Families*, 72.

8. James L. Peterson and Nicholas Zill, "Marital Disruption, Parent-Child Relationships and Behavior Problems in Children," *Journal of Marriage and the Family* 48, no. 2 (May 1986): 295 ff.

Chapter Seven

Clueless Generation

Barbara Dafoe Whitehead

Not long ago, I spoke to a church group in Miami on the subject of divorce. During the question and answer period, a young woman in the audience stood and introduced herself as a "child of divorce." She explained that she had turned out "just fine," thanks to her mother's love, hard work, and sacrifice. At the same time, she acknowledged, her parents' divorce had created economic hardship and emotional pain. For that reason, she said, she wanted to avoid divorce when she began to raise a family of her own. Her life goal was to have a good marriage that lasted.

When it came to achieving that goal, however, the young woman said, "I don't know what a good marriage is like, because I didn't see one first-hand. A lot of my friends' parents were divorced as well, so I didn't see good marriages in their families either. I am basically clueless about how a couple resolves conflicts without breaking up or how a wife learns to trust a husband." She then posed this question to the audience of mostly middle-aged, baby boomers: "What does your generation have to say to my generation about how to make marriage work and how to make marriage last?"

Her question caught the audience by surprise, as if no one in the group had ever thought about it. The question hung in the air until someone offered a few academic observations on the institution of marriage. One or two members of the audience chimed in. But the discussion was feeble and half-hearted and quickly gave way to a more spirited (and well-worn) debate over the issue of whether or not unhappily married parents were justified in getting a divorce. The young woman left the meeting without an answer to her question.

As I reflected on the event, I was struck by two things. First of all, the young woman was changing the subject of the conversation from divorce to marriage. Her aspirations were for marriage, and she was turning to those older for some advice.

I was also struck by how discomfited the audience was by the young woman's question. Even a priest in the audience professed uneasiness and confusion over how to respond, without somehow seeming to criticize people's decision to divorce or to dishonor the hard work and sacrifice of many single mothers. Clearly, the older adults in the room were absorbed and invested in a different set of questions, shaped by their own life experiences and, quite possibly, by their own disappointments with marriage.

Without making too much of this single incident, I think it provides a useful introduction to a larger and neglected issue in our debate over the family. Much attention has been devoted to an examination of the behavior and attitudes of American adults who have already made major life decisions about marriage and parenthood: what to do about welfare moms and deadbeat dads? Far less attention has been devoted to exploring the attitudes on marriage held by younger adults, many of whom have not yet married or had children. (For the purposes of this chapter, younger adults refers to men and women between the ages of 18 and 29.)

Yet clearly the attitudes and family formation behavior of these younger Americans will play a crucial role in determining the pace and direction of the trends of divorce, unwed parenthood, and father absence. More to the point, it is important to have a sound understanding of how younger Americans think about this troubled institution if one wishes to make it less troubled.

This chapter takes a preliminary step in this direction by considering three questions: First, what do we know about the attitudes of younger Americans toward marriage? Second, how are younger adults' attitudes about marriage and parenthood influenced by the experience and attitudes of their parents? Finally, what do we know about the intergenerational transmission of a body of thought and practice on marriage? What do the cultural custodians of a marriage tradition have to say to younger people about marriage?

Attitudes toward Marriage among Younger Americans

Like the young woman in Miami, young adults seek marriage as a life goal. In recent years, the importance high school seniors say they place on marriage has increased. The annual Monitoring the Future Survey asks high school seniors to rate their life goals on a four point scale from "extremely important" to "not important." According to the Survey, the life goal of "having a good marriage and family life" has gone up for both males and females in the years between 1976 and 1992. There has also been a slight upward trend in the percent who said they would prefer to have a mate most of their lives, so the aspiration to marital permanence has also persisted over time.[1]

However, the high school seniors' lofty aspirations for marriage are not matched by similarly high expectations that they will be successful in achieving this life goal. The percent of young people who said they agree or mostly agree with the statement that "one sees so few good marriages that one questions it as a way of life" increased between 1976 and 1992 while the percent of those who said it was very likely they would stay married to the same person for life decreased over the same time period for both males and females.[2] Given the high rates of divorce, it is hardly surprising that high school students would have diminished expectations for lifelong marriage. The oft-repeated statement that half of all marriages will end in divorce (a misunderstood and often misused statistic which is a projection based on current trends, not a prophecy) probably also contributes to a more pessimistic appraisal of the chances for lasting marriage.

Other measures point to weakening support for marriage as prerequisite to parenthood, and especially motherhood. Compared to adults 60 and older, younger adults are significantly less likely to agree with the statement that "people who want to have children should get married." Slightly more than 86 percent of men and more than 90 percent of women 60 or older agree or strongly agree with this statement compared to 62 percent of men and 50 percent of women, 18-29, according to data from the 1994 General Social Survey. It is interesting to note that younger women are less likely to agree with this statement than are younger men, evidence of a pattern of disenchantment with marriage among women which I will discuss later.

Compared to Americans 60 and older, younger Americans are also far less likely to see two parents as necessary to successful childrearing.[3] For example, while slightly fewer than 15 percent of men 60 or older agree or strongly agree that "one parent can bring up a child as well as two parents," almost 35 percent of men, 18-29, agree or strongly agree with the statement. The gap is even more pronounced between older and younger women, with 22.5 percent of women, 60 and older, agreeing or strongly agreeing with the statement compared to 61.9 percent of women, 18-29.

Younger Americans also have generally positive views of cohabitation. Close to 60 percent of men and 56 percent of women agree with the statement that "it is all right for a couple to live together without intending to get married" and even higher percentage of men and women, 18-29, endorse the statement "it's a good idea for a couple who intend to get married to live together first." These attitudes are consistent with the dramatic shift toward cohabitation as the initial form of partnership among younger cohorts. For example, for more than 93 percent of women born between 1933 and 1942, marriage was the first "living together" partnership; only 36 percent of women born between 1963 and 1974 report marriage as their first partnership.[4] Since cohabiting unions do not last as long as marital unions and since cohabiting unions that eventuate in marriage are more likely to end in divorce than marriages that are not preceded by cohabitation, the shift toward cohabiting unions among younger men and women may be taken as further evidence of the weakening of marriage.

Finally, survey evidence indicates a shift away from the idea that marriage contributes to personal happiness. While roughly 63 percent of adults 60 and older agree with the statement that "married people are generally happier than unmarried people," only 33 percent of men and close to 25 percent of women, 18-29, held this view. Note, too, that although there is no difference between older men and women on this issue, a gender gap emerges within the younger group, with a lower percentage of young women than young men agreeing with the statement.

Overall, therefore, the attitudes about marriage among younger people are decidedly mixed. Evidence of high aspirations to lifelong marriage must be set alongside the evidence of declining confidence and support for marriage as the institution governing childrearing, as a relationship governing personal happiness, and as an easily achievable life goal. Young men and women alike are losing confidence in marriage, but on several key measures, young women are more disenchanted than their male counterparts.

However, it would be a mistake to conclude that younger Americans are complacent about this situation. Today's youth culture reverberates with strong themes of protest against divorce. The music, movies, and memoirs of Generation Xers suggest that these young people view divorce the way baby boomers viewed Vietnam: as a sign of the moral failure of their parents' generation. Writes one young poet: "Your summer of love has turned into our winter of despair."[5]

Parental Influences

The older generation has customarily taken the responsibility for guiding and supporting the younger generation in matters of mating and marrying. Although the choice of a marital partner is usually left to the children themselves, American parents nonetheless exert strong influence over their children's attitudes and behaviors both directly, through their own example and experience, and indirectly through the transmission of their attitudes and beliefs. And although our romantic ideology is dedicated to the proposition that people fall in love with strangers, mate selection is far more socially patterned than this ideology would suggest. For example, middle-class and upper-middle-class parents continue to exert some influence over their children's prospective marital partners by influencing their children's choice of college and, to some degree, their post-college social networks as well.

The research evidence shows that parents' marital experience directly influences their children's attitudes and behaviors toward marriage as well as divorce. For example, a number of studies indicate that parental divorce negatively influences children's attitudes toward marriage. Children's own marrying behavior is also negatively influenced: Children of divorce marry at lower rates and are more likely to get divorced than children who grow up in intact married-parent households.[6]

In an 18-year intergenerational panel study of mothers and children, William G. Axinn and Arland Thornton find that a mother's marital status strongly influences her view of marriage and divorce. Mothers whose marriages end in divorce and do not remarry have more negative views of marriage and childbearing than do continuously married, widowed, or remarried mothers. Divorced, widowed, and remarried mothers all report more positive views of divorce than mothers in nondisrupted marriages. Divorced mothers also are more accepting of premarital sex and cohabitation than are continuously married or widowed mothers. Axinn and Thornton find that children's attitudes closely resemble their mothers' attitudes. For example, children whose mothers are divorced regard divorce and cohabitation more positively and marriage more negatively than children whose mothers are continuously married. Interestingly, children whose divorced mothers remarry have equally positive views of marriage as do children in intact married-parent households. However, rates of remarriage are declining among divorced mothers, so the effect of remarriage may operate only weakly as a pro-marriage influence.

The study's authors say that one limitation of this study is that it does not examine the attitudes of fathers toward marriage and divorce, but they maintain that fathers do not exert as strong an influence on children's attitudes toward marriage and family. Certainly one would expect that maternal attitudes on marriage would dominate in a society with high levels of divorce and father-absent families.

Taken together, these findings strongly suggest that there is generational momentum behind the trends of divorce and cohabitation. Or to put it another way, there is a generational momentum behind the disillusionment with, and decline of, marriage.

Breakdown in Cultural Transmission

Although parents probably play the most important role in the intergenerational transmission of attitudes toward marriage, they are not the only influence. Historically, the task of guiding the next generation in the meaning and responsibilities of marriage has been shared with those who might be called custodians of a marriage tradition, including clergy, religious congregations, teachers, popular advice experts, and scholars. As representatives of their disciplines and institutions, these cultural custodians study, teach, write books, prescribe social rules, perform ceremonies, offer counsel, interpretation, and commentary on marriage. To be sure, their guidance often goes unheeded by the young. However, at no earlier time in American history have cultural custodians of marriage abdicated this role entirely, or avoided the subject of marriage itself. Yet in the past three decades or so, there has been a notable loss of commitment to this task, with the result that there has been a breakdown in the cultural transmission of a body of knowledge, advice, and practice about marriage and a cultural "forgetting" about the very meaning and purpose of marriage.

This cultural breakdown is most extreme in inner city communities where there has been a virtual abandonment of marriage in both thought and practice. In his study of black families in Chicago's inner city, William Julius Wilson notes that "the husband-wife relationship is only weakly supported;" poor men and women see few economic or social advantages to marriage, feel little pressure to get married, and are mistrustful and antagonistic toward each other.[7]

With the decline of marriage in inner city neighborhoods, marriage also disappears as a public and ceremonial act. In some inner city neighborhoods, where 80 percent of births to teenagers are out of wedlock, teenage girls regularly attend their girlfriends' baby showers but have never witnessed a wedding. As Kay Hymowitz, a scholar at the Manhattan Institute who has studied unwed teenage childbearing in New York City, observes, "For these teenagers, marriage is dead, gone, a nonword." Since the marriage ceremony is one of the principal means of dramatizing the public and institutional features of marriage, the disappearance of brides and grooms from inner city churches is as significant as the loss of husband and wives from inner city housing projects. Both contribute to the cluelessness about marriage among the young and poor.

However, the cultural neglect of marriage is hardly limited to the inner city. Mainstream American culture has largely abandoned marriage as a topic suitable for the young. Consider, for example, contemporary children's literature. Books represent one of the most traditional cultural resources for transmitting knowledge and shaping values. Since the 1970s, a huge amount of children's literature has been dedicated to teaching children about divorce and fatherlessness and to helping parents explain "why we are getting a divorce." Yet remarkably few children's books portray contemporary marriage or parents in intact marriages as anything but dangerously dysfunctional. Some children's books offer sensitive portraits of remarriage and stepfamily life, but such stories are frequently set in the distant past. In nonfiction juvenile literature, discussions of marriage are more likely to be found in books on divorce, where the authors stress the contingency and dissolubility of marital bonds. One such book tells children that "everyone who gets married hopes and truly believes that it will last forever," but then goes on to explain that marriages fall apart because parents fall out of love as easily as they fall in love, "Everyone changes in different ways and at different times. Some married people can adjust to the changes that are going on. But sometimes they come along so suddenly or seem so big that it's like living with someone you hardly know. Two people who used to be in love have turned into strangers."[8]

This portrait of marriage can hardly inspire confidence in the durability of marital bonds, especially among children who yearn for security and the promise of "forever-and-ever" bonds in their primary family relationships. Indeed, if one looks at marriage from a child's perspective, it is difficult to imagine a crueler message about marital commitment than the one sympathetically tendered in this book.

Popular childrearing advice literature similarly overlooks marriage. Many of the popular books on childrearing, including those devoted to virtue and character building, avoid the subject of marital commitment entirely.[9] One book entitled *How To Talk To Children About Really Important Things,* includes chapters on divorce, remarriage, sexual abuse, war, drinking, prejudice, and homosexuality but devotes not a word to marriage.[10]

Within the public schools, there is broad support for teaching children about sexuality and parenthood but a great deal of reticence and resistance to teaching children about marriage as the social institution regulating sexuality and childbearing. Sex education curricula commonly avoid the word marriage or marital commitment and talk instead of "committed relationships" as the preferred context for sex, intimacy, and parenthood.

As young people approach late adolescence and early adulthood, they receive little in the way of formal or informal instruction about marriage. Even college textbooks on marriage and the family do not provide an adequate or balanced introduction to marriage. In a careful study of 20 college textbooks on marriage and the family published from 1994 to early 1996, Norval D. Glenn reports that though not explicitly anti-marriage, the textbook literature gives a generally negative portrait of the institution.[11] Glenn also notes that the textbooks emphasize the negative effects of marriage for women, despite research evidence that consistently shows married women are better off than never-married, divorced, separated, and widowed women in happiness, satisfaction, physical health, longevity, and most aspects of emotional health. They also neglect the huge research literature on the positive relationship between marriage and physical and psychological well-being, even though, in Glenn's words, "it would be hard to imagine a topic of greater relevance to the lives of the students."

Moreover, the textbooks ignore the institutional and historical role of marriage in society. Glenn writes that none of the textbooks under review includes "a systematic treatment of the social functions of marriage or of the part it plays and has played historically in the biological and cultural reproduction of populations and societies." This approach not only misrepresents but also minimizes and trivializes the function of marriage in family and social life.

The textbook literature is similarly silent on the economic benefits of marriage, even though studies consistently demonstrate that married people have more income, assets, and wealth than the separated, divorced, widowed, and never-married. Married couples also save more at the same income level than do singles.[12] Given today's students' fears about their economic futures, it seems irresponsible not to provide young people with such evidence and not to inform them that the organization of their future family lives will have major consequences for their economic lives.

When it comes to sex, another topic that preoccupies youth, my own, more casual, survey of textbook literature fails to turn up any discussion of the positive relationship between marriage and emotional satisfaction with sex. Yet the most recent and comprehensive survey of American sexuality shows that a higher proportion of both married men and women report extreme emotional satisfaction from sex than those who are not married.

As Glenn's study suggests, the textbook literature fails to present available social scientific evidence about marriage in an adequate and balanced way. This failure is all the more striking because it comes from a discipline that once concerned itself with developing and disseminating knowledge about the institution. But the neglect of marriage is not limited to the secular world of the social sciences. It is also evident within many denominations in the religious community.

Next to the family itself, the religious community has long had major responsibility for transmitting a body of thought and practice on marriage to its young. Yet in the past three decades, many denominations have shifted attention away from practical, mainstream concerns of family life such as marriage preparation and enrichment toward two intensely polarizing issues: abortion and homosexuality. To some degree, parachurch organizations such as the nondenominational Focus on the Family, led by Christian psychologist James Dobson, have replaced the denominations as sources of advice and education on marriage. And to some degree, lay marriage and family movements such as Marriage Encounter in the Roman Catholic Church and the Family Home Evening Program in the Church of Latter Day Saints have continued the work of marriage preparation and preservation. However, the retreat from teaching and preaching about marriage, especially among liberal denominations, has been one of the more remarkable and generally unremarked-upon changes in American religious life in recent years.[14]

Why the Breakdown in Transmission?

There are several possible explanations for the breakdown in the transmission of knowledge, precept, and example on marriage. Let me mention two. The first has to do with the impact of the divorce revolution.

As we have seen from the survey evidence, the experience of marital dissolution has a negative influence on attitudes about marriage. It is reasonable to think that when many individuals go through the personal trauma of divorce over a relatively short period of time, individual disappointment can create a collective sense of disappointment and even a culture of disappointment and grievance about marriage. At the same time, as the survey research also indicates, the personal experience of divorce, however distressing, contributes to a more positive view of divorce. It is similarly reasonable, therefore, to assume that a society in the throes of a divorce revolution would begin to look more favorably on divorce and even to embrace divorce as a way of life.

With marriage devalued as the source of personal and social goods at the same time that divorce has been invested with positive value, I would argue that this cultural shift in the relative valuation of marriage and divorce has been a major force in the weakening of the transmission of a marriage tradition. Specifically, it has contributed to a disillusionment with marriage as a source of personal or social well-being; it has weakened the interest and sense of obligation among older Americans to guide younger Americans in marriage; and it has fostered a loss of commitment to marriage among the custodians of its meaning and traditions.

A second possible reason for the breakdown in the intergenerational transmission of a marriage tradition has to do with women's growing disenchantment with marriage. More than men, women are the bearers of a marriage tradition and the norm-setters in the marriage relationship. (To test this proposition, simply compare the amount of space devoted to marriage in women's magazines to that in magazines aimed at men.) Yet in recent years, women's attachment to and positive appraisal of marriage has eroded. One of the clearest signs of this erosion has been the sharp rise in unmarried motherhood among college-educated women.

Contrary to the predictions of first-stage feminists, the relaxation of social pressures on women to marry and have children has not led to a revolt against motherhood among American women. Fertility is increasing at both ends of the age spectrum, among 14 year olds and 40 year olds. Some women are so desperate to become biological mothers today that they will endure expensive and physically grueling fertility treatments in order to conceive. However, as the survey evidence demonstrates, there is weakening commitment among women to the idea that marriage and motherhood must go together. Women want to be mothers, but they are increasingly ambivalent about whether they want to be wives.

One might anticipate that the decline in women's pro-marriage sentiments would be reflected in the popular culture. And, indeed, a sourness and sometimes outright spitefulness about men and marriage pervades the novels, soap operas, magazines, television docudramas and talk shows targeted at women. Fresh examples appear almost every day. Even as I write, the *New York Times* carries a feature story on the screening of *The First Wives Club*, a movie about three divorced wives who take revenge on their ex-spouses. Watching the movie, a select group of socialite ex-wives "hooted in laughter, snorted in recognition and . . . nodded in approval as the ex-wives in the movie emerged stronger, more in control, and better dressed . . ." after their divorces.

The *Times* predicts that the movie will be a huge success: "[E]x-wives everywhere will for the first time have a movie that may change their image, and will certainly give them courage. . . ."[14]

Implications for the Fatherhood Movement

What does the "cultural forgetting" about marriage have to do with the effort to revitalize fatherhood? Let me suggest some implications for the fatherhood movement. First of all and most obviously, anyone who wishes to strengthen married fatherhood will have to swim against powerful cultural currents.

Our recent experience reminds us how quickly an institution can fall apart when it loses support and sponsorship within the culture. The historical records suggest that marriage can survive sharp increases in divorce, as it did in the post-World War II period. However, the historical record of that period also indicates that marriage was able to survive the post-war surge in divorce largely as the result of a broad-based and well-executed strategy to protect and preserve it against the economic, social, and cultural forces that threatened its stability. The body of inherited tradition, revised practice, and new knowledge which shapes our thinking about marriage is not a surplus commodity, to be stored away for years and dipped into later if we decide we need it. It is highly perishable and must be used, practiced, enriched, nourished, passed on, and then used again by the next generation if it is to endure.

When it comes to marriage, the cultural storehouse is depleted, its shelves almost bare. Our marriage culture has become so thin and meager, the cluelessness about the meaning and purpose of marriage so broadly diffused, that there is very little to transmit or inherit.

Second, a culture of divorce has entrenched itself in middle-class American society. Mainstream America sees the nation's harmful family trends as problems of welfare or teenagers or the underclass, but looks upon divorce as an individual entitlement to be protected and defended against criticism or incursion. As a consequence, there is a strong consensus in favor of strengthening fatherhood within a divorce culture by helping fathers and mothers work cooperatively outside of marriage to raise their children, but there is no equally strong consensus about strengthening and preserving marriage as the basis of the childrearing partnership. Absent such support, it is likely that we will move in the direction of institutionalizing a system of fatherhood that is inferior in its levels of support, supervision, and father-child contact than is one institutionally established through marriage.

Third, the effort to strengthen marriage as the institutional basis for responsible fatherhood must also contend with the generational currents moving away from marriage. Younger men and women are increasingly uncertain that they can achieve lasting marriage and increasingly less well-encultured in the meaning and responsibilities of marriage. Today, the cultural messages to young people emphasize the need to keep options open and to invest in oneself as a "hedge" against the unreliability of intimate partnerships, a tendency that surely works against marital commitment itself, not to mention the likelihood of marital permanence.

Finally, there is also a gender gap between younger men and women with women less supportive of marriage than men on several key measures. The fatherhood movement has not yet acknowledged the degree to which a pro-marriage strategy must address women's disenchantment with marriage. Yet if it is to be successful, I believe it must do so.

Notes

1. Norval D. Glenn, "Values, Attitudes and the State of American Marriage," in *Promises To Keep: Decline and Renewal of Marriage in America,* ed. David Popenoe, Jean Bethke Elshtain, and David Blankenhorn (Lanham, Md.: Rowman and Littlefield, 1996), 21.

2. Ibid., 26-27.

3. I am indebted to Norval D. Glenn for providing me with the survey data from the General Social Survey.

4. Edward O. Laumann et al., *The Social Organization of Sexuality: Sexual Practices in the United States* (Chicago: University of Chicago Press, 1994), 602.

5. Cited in Neil Howe and Bill Strauss, *Thirteenth Generation: Abort, Retry, Ignore, Fail?* (New York: Vintage Books, 1993), 47.

6. William G. Axinn and Arland Thornton, "The Influence of Parents' Marital Dissolutions on Children's Attitudes Toward Family Formation," *Demography* 33, no. 1 (February 1996): 67.

7. William Julius Wilson, *When Work Disappears: The World of the New Urban Poor* (New York: Knopf, 1996), 98-99.

8. Peter Mayle, *Why Are We Getting A Divorce?* (New York: Harmony Books, 1988), 13.

9. A notable exception is William Bennett's book *The Moral Compass,* which includes a section on husbands and wives.

10. Charles E. Schaefer, *How To Talk To Children About Really Important Things* (New York: Harper and Row, 1984), 67-80, passim.

11. My discussion of textbook literature is based on a report by Norval D. Glenn, *Closed Hearts, Closed Minds: The Textbook Story of Marriage* (New York: Institute for American Values, 1997).

12. Linda Waite, "Does Marriage Matter?" *Demography* 32, no. 4 (November 1995): 492-93.

13. For an illuminating discussion of these tendencies within individual denominations, see *Faith Traditions & the Family,* ed. Phyllis D. Airhart and Margaret Lamberts Bendroth (Louisville: Westminster John Knox Press, 1996). This volume is one of the first in a multivolume series entitled *The Family, Religion and Culture,* edited by Don S. Browning and Ian S. Evison.

14. Judith H. Dobryzynski, "Ex-Wives of the Rich and Famous See a Film and Pronounce It Fact," *New York Times,* September 18, 1996, C1.

Chapter Eight

Clues

Judith S. Wallerstein

My disappointment with the leadership of the fatherhood movement is in their failure to acknowledge that the father-child relationship is created and sustained by the close enduring bond between both parents. Most men and women understand this connection intuitively, although many in today's world have never actually seen a man and woman in a loving relationship that was lasting. They come to adulthood with a clouded vision and without the requisite understanding of how to build a new family. To use Barbara Dafoe Whitehead's phrase, they are clueless in the face of the major challenge of adult life.

Marriage reform must focus on restoring confidence, especially among young people, in marriage as a rewarding relationship that is well worth the sacrifices it entails. The task is complex and far-reaching because the institution of marriage does not stand alone. Recent changes in the state of marriage reflect a complex interplay of powerful economic and social forces as well as significant differences in the aspirations and values of today's young people. Modern men and women expect more of each other as individuals, but they expect less of marriage. Programs for marriage reform, therefore, must address a generation that poses an unprecedented challenge.

The Loss of Clues

Young people today have been raised amidst widespread disappointment in marriage, as they have seen it fail in their own families and in the lives of their teachers and their political and religious leaders. Many anticipate that their own relationships will similarly end in heartbreak. They approach adulthood with the high hopes of the young, but with the uneasy sense that marriage is fragile and probably flawed, and commitment almost impossible to find. A related concern is that many young people regard not only marriage but also parenthood with grave misgivings. There is a vital connection between the child's growing up in a stable, harmonious marriage and his subsequent capacity to become a sensitive, responsible parent. Marriage reform and active fatherhood are inseparable in any plans to improve the lives of children, because ultimately parents' relationships with their children depend on their own experiences within the families in which they are raised.

Neither the wish to be a parent nor the ability to parent well are givens. Both mature gradually within the rich soil of the well-functioning family. Lacking some of the powerful biological and psychological bonds that tie mother and infant, fatherhood especially draws on deep wells of feeling and a continuity of experience that extends far back into childhood and adolescence. The love of the father for his child and his willingness to make sacrifices to provide for the long-term needs of that child are both built on the father's complex internal images of his own nurturant and protective mother and father and their partnership on his behalf. Tragically, young men who suffer emotional or physical abandonment by their own fathers during their growing-up years have a difficult time understanding or taking on the responsibilities that parenting entails. Their conscious efforts to parent are often thwarted by their own reawakened yearnings and resentment as their efforts bring them into close touch with their early deprivations. As a result of sustained and near heroic efforts, any one individual may overcome an unhappy childhood and set a new course successfully. But society as a whole requires a stable base in order to assure the well-being of future generations.

Clues through Policy Reform

Restoring society's confidence in marriage and the two-parent family cannot succeed if we simply issue a call for return to marriage as it used to be. On the contrary, the success of such a venture depends on the sympathetic understanding of a contemporary vision of man-woman relationships. Marriage reform also depends on an accurate reading of the difficulties couples confront and how overwhelmed they feel in today's world. It is important to recognize how much the modern young family needs support along with protection from the economic and social forces that encroach on its borders. Finally, intervention strategies should acknowledge that 80 percent of divorces occur within the first nine years of marriage.[1] Effective reform must target these critical early years.

Public policy cannot create good marriages, but it can surely buffer the most common stresses associated with divorce. The lack of balance between the demands of the workplace and the needs of family life is a serious threat to marriage. When young people cannot find stable jobs with adequate incomes, they will not marry. This is the plight of many in our minority communities. Among those who do marry, studies have shown that divorce, domestic violence, and marital strife rise steeply with unemployment.[2] Yet in the recent downsizing policies of industry, by which millions of people in the 25-to-54-year age group lost their jobs, and the great majority of those who found replacement jobs were not able to match their earlier earnings, there was scarcely any public concern expressed about the high risk in this social upheaval to American marriages.

There are many measures in which both industry and government can participate that can protect the integrity of marriage and family life during periods of economic retrenchment. These include maintaining health insurance for affected workers and their families, allocating adequate unemployment insurance, good severance pay, vocational training and counseling, and other measures that will maintain an individual's employability and self-esteem during the crisis. People also need to feel reasonably certain that layoffs are the last option that will be considered. Few workers think so in the present social climate.

With a few notable exceptions, the corporate workplace does not consider the impact of personnel policies on the families of its employees. Although there has been some belated public recognition that long working hours leave little time for parents to spend with their children, there is no comparable acknowledgment that the workplace exerts a major influence on the quality and stability of marriage. Heavy work schedules seriously erode married life. Men and women in our country typically work many more hours each week than do their counterparts in Western Europe.[3] As a result, working people don't have time for their children or for each other. Families with young children are especially likely to postpone intimate talk, sex, and friendship. Yet these are the ties that replenish the marital relationship. Unfortunately, layoffs and the greater job insecurity of recent years have increased working hours of many to the breaking point. A priority in marital reform would be to limit the excessive work demands which have become routine in many industries.

Many personnel policies, such as unpaid family leave, burden the family precisely when the young couple most needs support. New health policies allow a woman only 24 hours in the hospital for childbirth, and take little note of who will take care of the new mother and child during the early days at home. The several-month period after the birth of the baby is a difficult adjustment time in young marriages. Studies have shown that the stability of the marriage hangs in the balance at this time.[4] Policies of unpaid leave that young families cannot afford add to the stress which the young couple is already experiencing.

A program to support marriage would enable the mother or father who wishes to do so to stay home to raise the children. Government policy should provide the homemaker with social security protection, as is the case in many European countries such as Germany. Legislation and changes in school and workplace structure are needed to provide opportunities for reentry as well as for retraining and employment when the children are grown. A wide range of measures is necessary in order to assure the parent who wishes to be a full-time homemaker that taking a several-year leave of absence from the workplace will not marginalize that person for life.

Marital reform should realign the priority that the business world currently enjoys in an individual's life and assert the equal importance of the family. There are many programs which could redress the balance and create a family-friendly workplace. A beginning list of suggested remedies would include tax breaks for companies that establish family-friendly policies; jobs for young adults at salaries that will support a family based on a reasonable time-limited work week; opportunities for workers to reduce workloads in response to temporary family needs, with the option to return to full-time work; jobs that combine work at home with work on-site; and industry-wide adoption of paid family leave. Other policies that have been on the table for many years have included tax breaks for married couples and allowances for children. Many of these kinds of programs have been implemented in the countries of Western Europe. These policies do impose costs on employers and the government, which must be offset by some combination of lower wages and dividend payments, higher taxes, or less government spending in other areas. Nevertheless, if we are serious about supporting families, we must be willing to allocate resources towards that goal.[5]

Clues through Education

Reshaping relationships within marriage in ways that promote greater stability and commitment depends on changing the hearts and minds of young people. Time was that children's experiences within the family were expected to prepare them for adult life including marriage and parenting. The current crisis in family stability has led to a growing interest in educational programs that can make up for the lacunae in the child's experience of family life. The critical question is, how much can educational programs at their best be expected to achieve in meeting the needs of young people for knowledge and moral guidelines to family life? The answer to this question is not known. But the argument that young people today are bewildered because many have never seen a harmonious marriage, and that society has an obligation to intervene on their behalf, is a compelling one.

Educational programs for marriage are on the increase. To date, courses have primarily been offered within religious settings to already engaged couples. Many of these programs may indeed be helpful in ways that need to be studied. Nevertheless, I would argue that existing programs being offered or mandated by religious institutions just before marriage provide too little and arrive too late to influence young adults' core attitudes or values. Such attitudes evolve over many years and come together at key points in an individual's development long before marriage. I would propose, therefore, a multilevel curriculum which would be offered to young people at various developmental stages en route to marriage.

While it is true that education about relationships begins in early childhood and continues throughout life, it is in adolescence that attitudes toward self and relationships with the opposite sex, along with moral concepts of right and wrong, become consolidated. Accordingly, adolescence represents the critical time to intervene with educational programs. Ideally, such programs should provide adolescents with the opportunity to think about a range of relationships including friendship, love, and marriage. Related courses should provide opportunities to learn simple principles of infant and child care and to acquire hands-on experience.

More advanced courses could follow at the college level, when the range of subjects would be expanded but the emphasis on the students' concerns would remain; so that, for example, the question of how to combine family with career plans—a major concern to college women—would be included. Premarital courses for engaged couples would also be broadened to focus on the tasks of building the marriage. These premarital courses could be continued during the first year or two of the marriage itself to provide mutual support during this critical time. Finally, at the predictable stress points of marriage, expert guidance should be available to tide couples over crises.

Clues from Us All

There is no one profession that stands ready to assume responsibility for these multitiered educational programs. Nor is there a preferred venue. Some could surely meet under the auspices of churches or synagogues. Courses in family life, including simple child care, could and should be part of the high school curriculum. Courses in family sociology in community colleges and universities could be expanded to involve students in exploring the serious concerns they confront in planning their future. A first step would be to establish intensive training for faculty drawn from a range of disciplines, encouraging them to design several models of curricula that would be piloted and evaluated in different social groups throughout the society.

In sum, marriage reform needs first and foremost to provide the family with greater protection from the disruptive forces of the workplace. Public policies should support full-time parenting and buffer chronic and acute stresses on young families. These changes will require legislative action, educational programs, and major reorientation in the business community with widespread restructuring of career lines to enable worker entry, or reentry, into the workplace after children have been raised. Additionally, the upcoming generation would likely benefit from a community wide, multitiered educational effort designed to strengthen the confidence of young people in their future roles as marital partners and parents.

Notes

1. Norval Glenn and Kathryn Kramer, "The Marriages and Divorces of Children of Divorce," *Journal of Marriage and the Family* 49 (November 1987): 811-25.

2. D. J. Hernandez, "Study in Household and Family Formation," U.S. Bureau of the Census, *Current Population Reports*, series P23-179 (Washington, D.C.: U.S. Government Printing Office, 1992).

3. Juliet B. Schor, *The Overworked American: The Unexpected Decline of Leisure* (New York: Basic Books, 1993).

4. Carolyn Cowan and Philip Cowan, *When Partners Become Parents* (New York: Basic Books, 1992).

5. Rebecca Blank, ed., *Social Protection vs. Economic Flexibility* (Chicago: University of Chicago Press, 1994).

Chapter Nine

There Must Be 50 Ways to Start a Family

Ronald B. Mincy and Hillard Pouncy

When Congress enacted the 1996 Personal Responsibility and Work Opportunity Reconciliation Act, it joined with many of the authors in this volume and declared marriage and responsible fatherhood the foundations of a successful society. While we agree that strong, functional families are vital to poor and nonpoor communities alike, we also note that in neighborhoods where low-income fatherlessness is concentrated, leaders and practitioners now look for policies and practices that help them respond to current realities. In these neighborhoods, the majority of children are born out of wedlock and the majority of children who receive Temporary Assistance to Needy Families (TANF, the new term for welfare) have not had their paternity established. Their fathers have not legally declared themselves to be their fathers. In short, fatherlessness manifests itself differently at different income levels.

In an earlier chapter, Maggie Gallagher missed this point about the diversity of fatherlessness. When she discussed, for example, the case of Hassan Lemons, the 17-year-old father of a baby girl, she cited Lemons as a case illustrating what happens when a marriage collapses and a man's husband/lover role conflicts with his father role. However, Lemons was never married, and he is in a very different situation from men who were married and then divorce their wives. As we point out in the following pages, under certain circumstances, fathers like Lemons are able to join with the mother of their children to become team parents and form what we term a *fragile family*—a family formed by out-of-wedlock birth(s) to disadvantaged parents.[1]

There is no one-size-fits-all strategy for promoting responsible fatherhood. We believe the responsible fatherhood movement must broaden its messages and strategies to promote responsible fatherhood within fragile families.

Since race and income are highly correlated and interracial marriage is still rare, fatherlessness manifests itself differently by race. A majority of white children, 80 percent, live in two-parent families (including stepparents). A minority of black children, 37 percent, live with two parents (including stepparents). For other minorities—American Indians, different Latino groups— the percent of children living in two-parent households vary between the rates for whites and blacks.[2]

Many believe the increase in single-parent households for all racial groups is a change for the worse. Some in the responsible fatherhood movement want to see a fundamental change in the culture of American society, one that champions the restoration of the traditional marriage as the first line of defense for children, families, and civil society. Proponents have developed specific strategies designed to use marriage to increase the role of fathers in the lives of children. We call these marriage-first strategies.

Marriage-first strategists base their views on an incomplete analysis and a false consensus within the responsible fatherhood movement about the problem of fatherlessness in American society. When middle- and high-income fathers leave middle- and high-income families, for example, they primarily leave as a result of divorce or separation. For this population, cultural reform and other strategies intended to save, sustain, strengthen, or develop stable marriages perhaps make sense.

Many low-income fathers, however, leave their families after out-of-wedlock births, without first establishing legal paternity or getting married. This, the predominant pattern of forming a fatherless family among low-income blacks, is now spreading to low-income families among whites and other ethnic groups. Even if young, low-income, minority and nonminority fathers marry after an out-of-wedlock pregnancy or birth, many cannot sustain the marriage, primarily because of stresses and strains associated with working poverty. Taken together, the above examples show that a cultural reform makes little sense with fragile families. Instead, it makes more sense to rethink how public welfare systems can help both the low-income mother and father become more functional parents.

Economic Explanations of Fatherlessness

Declining marriage rates play a fundamental role in the overall growth of fatherlessness in America, and this decline affects racial groups differently. Although marriage rates have been falling since the 1940s, they dropped most sharply from the 1960s on, and more sharply for black than for white Americans.[3] In the late 1940s, for example, among women between the ages of 25 and 44, the marriage rate was 80 percent for white women and 67 percent for black women.[4] By 1980, 75 percent of white women and 44 percent of black women were married.

At the same time, there has been a growing divergence in fatherlessness by race. In 1950, for example, 8 percent of white families and 17 percent of black families were fatherless. By 1990, this figure had grown to 13 percent of white families and 50 percent of black families. And since most fatherless black families form after an out-of-wedlock birth, economic factors are likely to result in a persistent gap between black and white fatherless families, even though out-of-wedlock births are rising faster among whites than among blacks.

Daniel Patrick Moynihan played a prominent role in shaping the debate over whether cultural or economic forces best explained the divergence in fatherlessness among blacks and whites.[5] Moynihan argued that black men's economic prospects were the paramount explanation. On average, black men have lower employment rates and lower earnings than white men, which reduce their ability, relative to whites, to fulfill the provider role. Among blacks, the advantages in earnings and employment rates of men over women are smaller than among whites. As a result, black men are less likely to marry or be sought as marriage partners than white men and more likely than white men to divorce or separate after marriage.

Moynihan observed that a quarter of black families were fatherless, and described his findings as a national crisis. In response he called for broad-based efforts to combat the underlying economic cause, employment discrimination against black men. Almost two decades later, economists William Darity and Samuel Myers also argued that high rates of joblessness among black men contribute to the decline in black marriage rates.[6] They have since been joined by a chorus of other researchers and advocates.

Other leaders believe the link between the economic prospects of black men and marriage is part of the story, but it is an incomplete explanation for declines in fatherlessness among blacks. If black men's economic prospects were the dominant factor in black fatherlessness, one might expect declines in marriage rates among unemployed black men to be higher than among employed black men. However, Robert Lerman and others have pointed out that the reverse is true.[7] And Saul Hoffman, Greg Duncan, and Ronald B. Mincy found that only about one-quarter of the decline in marriage among young black women can be accounted for by the decline in income of young black men.[8]

William Julius Wilson, in his recent book, *When Work Disappears*, re-affirms the link between family and economic factors with data from his Chicago-based 1987-88 Urban Poverty and Family Life Study. He concludes that joblessness is unrelated to the chance that a young man will become an unmarried father. However, for younger black men who do become unmarried fathers, job status is strongly associated with "his entry into marriage after the birth of his child."[9] That is, joblessness is a determining factor in the creation of fragile families.

Finally, women's earnings and employment prospects are a third part of the story. They too are linked to declines in marriage and the rise in fatherless families among blacks and whites.[10] "Perhaps good job opportunities for women might actually encourage non-marital births."[11] As the barriers keeping women from employment and high wages have diminished, their dependence upon male earnings has declined. In consequence, women are marrying at a later age, or are remaining single, and those involved in unsatisfying marriages are more likely to initiate a divorce. Thus women are far from passive actors in the trend toward fatherlessness. This means that any attempt to increase the role of fathers must not only encourage fathers to assume a more active role, but must also persuade women to allow them to do so. This counsel is important for private interventions and public policy.

What is also still unclear about the link between economic factors and marriage is the direction of causality. For example, in a recent paper examining the consequences of changes in fatherhood status, marital status, and earnings, Lerman noted a rise in earnings among residential fathers:

> Even after holding constant for initial age, race, education, test scores and prior earnings, a change from being an unwed and absent father to being a residential father was associated with a gain of over $3,300 per year. Moving to a married state was associated with a higher rise in earnings. . . . [T]hose who married between 1988 and 1993 and were still married in 1993 earned nearly $5,000 more than those who were not married in 1993 but who had the same age, race, schooling, test scores and prior earnings.[12]

However, the relationships among economic forces, marriage, and responsible fatherhood can work in either direction. It may be that young men who are more responsible and mature are more likely to marry and work. Or perhaps, once young men take on the responsibilities of marriage and fatherhood, they change their behavior with respect to work. A third possibility is that the workplace responds differently to married men than to unwed, noncustodial fathers, as some studies have speculated.[13]

Public Welfare Issues

This discussion illustrates how salient economic factors can be to marriage and fatherlessness. But it does little to endorse marriage-first strategies for families in which economic constraints are prominent, as they are in fragile families— families formed after out-of-wedlock births to parents who are both disadvantaged and who do not immediately marry or establish legal paternity. Because the mother is disadvantaged, the fragile family is by definition dependent, and therefore is almost immediately engaged in public family support and income security systems. Such systems can become influential in the relationship between the parents, thus determining the relationship between father and child. Those who want to promote the involvement of fathers in such families must understand how the systems influence relationships between unwed parents, and therefore family formation. Only then will they be equipped to recommend changes in the systems that encourage father involvement.

Female professionals dominate the maternal and child health, family support, and income security systems on which fragile families depend. These professionals react to the marriage-first message with suspicion at best. One reason for their suspicion is that some marriage-first strategists do not qualify their belief in marriage as the ideal circumstance in which to promote children's well-being. The professionals have witnessed too many wives and children who have been harmed by abusive and oppressive husbands and fathers. Without qualification, marriage-first strategists may appear to be saying that these children are better off than children reared in fatherless families. Most members of the responsible fatherhood movement focus on middle- and upper-income people who have minimal contact with the public welfare system and can afford to ignore the way welfare professionals react to the marriage-first message. Those of us who are trying to promote responsible fatherhood among unwed and disadvantaged parents and children, however, must obtain the trust of these professionals. If we do not learn to articulate a message about male/female roles and relationships that these professionals can hear, we will be unable to strengthen the fragile families we serve. Therefore, a broader coalition intended to make fathers central to the future of American civil society, if it is to be successful, requires a reformulation of rhetoric and strategies. Since we believe, as do the marriage-first strategists, that fathers are essential, we hope to work with them to develop mutually accommodating rhetoric and strategies.

Diversity in Patterns of Family Formation

Studies of family formation and family structure have documented a significant departure from the traditional American marriage pattern, which includes the following events: dating, relationship, marriage, and childbirth, leading to a traditional family. As a result, researchers are asking, "When does the process of family formation begin and end?" For example, several decades ago, divorce was clearly the final event in family formation. Now, as Larry Bumpass and his colleagues noted in 1989, divorce is a poor indicator of the final event.[14] Its timing and occurrence "is often a legal artifact"[15] out of sync with the moment of real marital dissolution. Separation, or the end of cohabitation, is now considered a better indicator of the end of marital union than divorce.

Although Bumpass and his colleagues are reluctant to accept cohabitation as a proxy for the first event in family formation, they do conclude:

> It is clear that marriage marks a significant transition, especially in the onset of planned childbearing. In terms of family experience, however, we are being forced increasingly toward treating living arrangements as the primary criterion, and the timing (and occurrence) of marriage as an important variable.[16]

Contemporary family formation encompasses several patterns in which cohabitation and other events critical to childbearing occur outside marriage. Of the events involved in these patterns, cohabitation is the one researchers have studied most. Using data from the National Survey of Families and Households, Larry Bumpass and James Sweet first documented significant increases in American cohabitation rates. They found that almost half the population under 35 had cohabited at some point. This percentage remained about the same at the beginning of the 1990s.[17] By the mid-1990s, Bumpass and R. Kelly Raley concluded, "we can no longer discuss family structure or family transitions sensibly when using only marital statuses and transitions."[18]

Cohabitation is also increasingly associated with marriage, fertility, and family formation. For example, 1984 data from the National Survey of Families and Households show that the number of persons entering marriage who had previously cohabited rose from 11 percent in the early 1970s to 44 percent by the early 1980s.[19] By the late 1980s, 45 percent of cohabiting households included children and 5 percent of all births from 1970 to 1984 were to cohabiting parents. "This represents 27 percent of all births to unmarried women."[20]

Despite the steep rise in cohabitation and other alternative family structures documented over the last two decades, the United States collects data and makes social policy as though the traditional family—the intact, two-parent household formed by marriage—were our only family form. We do not, for example, treat cohabiting couples and traditional families as legal equivalents, as happens sometimes in France, Denmark, Sweden, and Canada.[21]

Although cohabitation plays a role in family formation in all racial or ethnic groups, this role is more significant in some groups than in others. For example, 40 percent of Mexican-American nonmarital births were to cohabiting women, as were 30 percent of non-Hispanic white nonmarital births.[22] Among blacks, 18 percent of nonmarital births were to cohabiting women. In fact, this difference in nonmarital cohabitation rates helps account for black-white difference in the proportion of children living in two-parent families.[23]

This research casts doubt on the salience of the framework we currently use to guide public policy toward children and families. This framework recognizes only two kinds of families: (1) those formed through a process that includes marriage, and (2) those formed as a result of a birth to an unmarried mother. While policymakers understand and acknowledge the process through which the first kind of family forms, they treat the second kind of family as static and perceive no developmental process leading to the formation of such a family. The data, however, suggest that more and more families fall somewhere between traditional and never-married families, a group that this framework ignores. The result is a widening gap between policy and a growing number of American families. Fragile families are a unique, critical, and separate part of this "between" category.

Traditional Family Formation

In traditional family formation, young couples move through a series of linear events toward the traditional family consisting of father, mother, and children. Chart 1 depicts this process, in which the couple dates, forms a relationship, marries, and begins their family. In this pattern, cohabitation, intercourse, conception, and childbirth all occur after marriage. Of course, the traditional family is not always the end of the process of family formation. That process sometimes ends in divorce, separation, or the death of a spouse, leaving a type-1 fatherless family.

As a framework for designing interventions and policies to strengthen contemporary American families, the traditional pattern of family formation has three important shortcomings. First, this pattern treats families consisting of a never-married mother and her child(ren) as outliers, exceptions, or discrete events. These are the type-2 fatherless families depicted in Chart 9.1. The traditional pattern does not provide a way to think about the process by which type-2 fatherless families form. It also ignores actual or potential relationships involving unwed parents and their children and the effects of government policies on these relationships.

Second, the traditional model encourages the application of policies and interventions designed for type-1 fatherless families to type-2 fatherless families. Differences between these families, however, may make policies designed for one inappropriate for the other. For example, type-1 fatherless families usually involve men and women who are at least in their mid-20s. Children in these families also tend to be older. The relationships that created these families have formalized, soured, and died. In most cases, the parents have already tried to reconcile. They may even have had the benefit of professional marriage counseling. Despite these efforts, one or both parents have thought things through and decided that it would be better to end the relationship. At this point, policies and interventions can have only limited objectives: severing legal and property ties between the parents and ensuring that the child's needs can be met by setting and enforcing custody, child support, and visitation orders.

By contrast, type-2 fatherless families often involve parents who are disadvantaged young adults with young children. In many cases, the relationships between the parents are not well developed and have not had the benefit of counseling of any kind. Indeed, the pregnancy may be the event that causes the parents to think seriously, for the first time, about the nature of their relationship. In these cases, there is no reason to restrict the work of policies or interventions to questions of custody, child support, and visitation. This, however, is exactly what occurs.

The third shortcoming of the traditional pattern of family formation is how it complicates incorporating poverty among men. Suppose a man earned less than

CHART 9.1: Traditional Family Formation

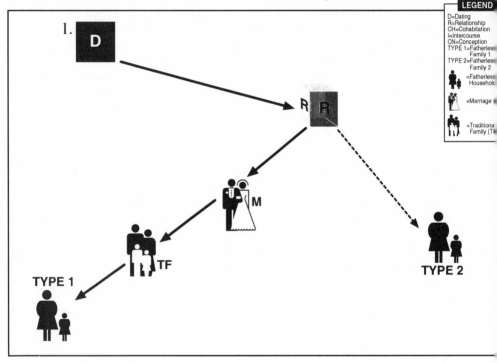

$6,000 in 1990, the poverty threshold for a single person household in that year, and was the father of a child with a young woman to whom he was not married and who had no earnings during the year. This father could hardly afford to live alone, because he would be ineligible for most forms of housing assistance and his income would be too low to afford housing in most private markets. If this father lived with his parents, he would owe child support. However, his parents' income would affect his eligibility for means-tested benefits such as employment training. This has prevented many young men from getting the assistance they need to increase their earnings and thereby contribute more to the support of children living elsewhere.[24] If this father lived with friends, he would also owe child support, but he would be treated as a single individual when he applied for means-tested benefits. Few public benefits are available for single individuals. Finally, if this father lived with the mother of his child and their baby, he would not owe child support. However, his income would play a dominant role in determining the mother and child's eligibility for other means-tested benefits such as Medicaid, food stamps, cash assistance, and housing assistance. This has discouraged many unwed parents from marrying or cohabiting.

These shortcomings make traditional family formation a poor guide for problem solving and policy making with type-2 fatherless families. Although policy options exist that would help low-income fathers to contribute more to the financial, emotional, and developmental needs of their children, these options are hidden by the very conceptual framework most observers use to critique or design income security policy, family support policy, and family support interventions.

Contemporary Family Formation

Chart 9.2 presents contemporary patterns of family formation that provide guides for problem solving with segments of the population disposed to the marriage-first strategies. In this chart, families begin with dating and relationships, as before, but the next steps are nonlinear and complex. The complexity arises because intercourse, cohabitation, and conception can occur outside marriage. Recognizing this does not mean one must condone it. But even if one believes that mothers, fathers, children, and American civil society would all be better off if the traditional linear pattern prevailed and resulted in strong, equitable, and stable marriages, thousands of American young people are involved in premarital intercourse, conception, and cohabitation. When these young people botch or reject contraception and abortion, perhaps because they have previously contemplated marriage, options must be available to continue to nurture their relationship until it results in marriage and the traditional family. Successful nurturing of this sort would reduce the number of children living in type-2 fatherless families. We also need strategies to help

CHART 9.2: Contemporary Family Formation

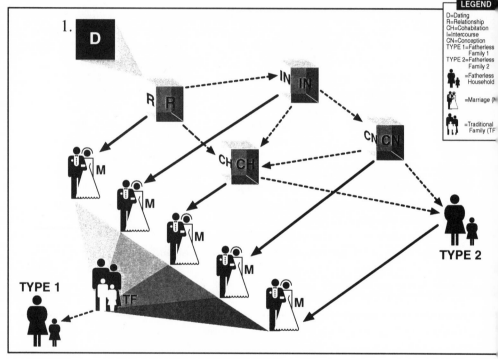

LEGEND

D=Dating
R=Relationship
CH=Cohabitation
I=Intercourse
CN=Conception
TYPE 1=Fatherless
Family 1
TYPE 2=Fatherless
Family 2
=Fatherless
Household
=Marriage (M
=Traditional
Family (TF

married couples sustain, improve, and strengthen their marriages, which would reduce the number of children in type-1 fatherless families. Finally, we need strategies to help fathers maintain relationships with children after divorce or separation.

The responsible fatherhood movement has been quietly developing such strategies. Its work includes the broad-based cultural reforms of the National Fatherhood Initiative. Premarital inventories and marriage encounters have been developed by "marriage savers" such as Michael McManus. Fathers' rights advocates, for example, Ron Henry and David Levy, have been pushing for joint-custody orders in divorce settlements, stronger enforcement of custody and visitation orders, and neutral dropoff points following divorce. While much work lies ahead, the broad framework for the responsible fatherhood movement has already been developed.

Fragile Family Formation

The responsible fatherhood movement, however, has paid little attention to population groups for whom marriage-first strategies have little relevance. Parents in these groups usually cannot afford to maintain families because they are poorly educated and experience high rates of unemployment and underemployment. They also live in communities where few young people marry. When they form intimate relationships, therefore, they may not plan to marry. These couples cannot afford to give children what they need to compete in the American mainstream; they would be better off if they practiced abstinence or contraception. But some do not, and when they conceive many reject abortion or adoption as options.

Chart 9.3 illustrates three patterns that can lead to the formation of fragile families. We consider these patterns after the conception of the child, reading from left to right in the chart. In the first pattern, the couple cohabits after the conception of the child, so that co-residence facilitates the fathers' continued involvement in the lives of mother and child. In the next pattern, the father remains involved, even though the parents never cohabit. In the third pattern, something occurs in the relationship between the mother and father so that the father withdraws, and a type-2 fatherless family forms. Subsequently, the parents restore their relationship, and through this, the father restores the relationship with his child. In each case the father remains involved in the life of the child with the mother's consent and cooperation.

As the chart suggests, these patterns have several possible terminal events. Some disadvantaged unwed parents and children remain in fragile families. This does not require that the mother and father remain romantically involved, but does require that they get the skills and support they need to work as a team to provide for their child's financial, emotional, and developmental needs. In some instances, marriages result from fragile families, although this is rare because

CHART 9.3: Fragile Family Formation

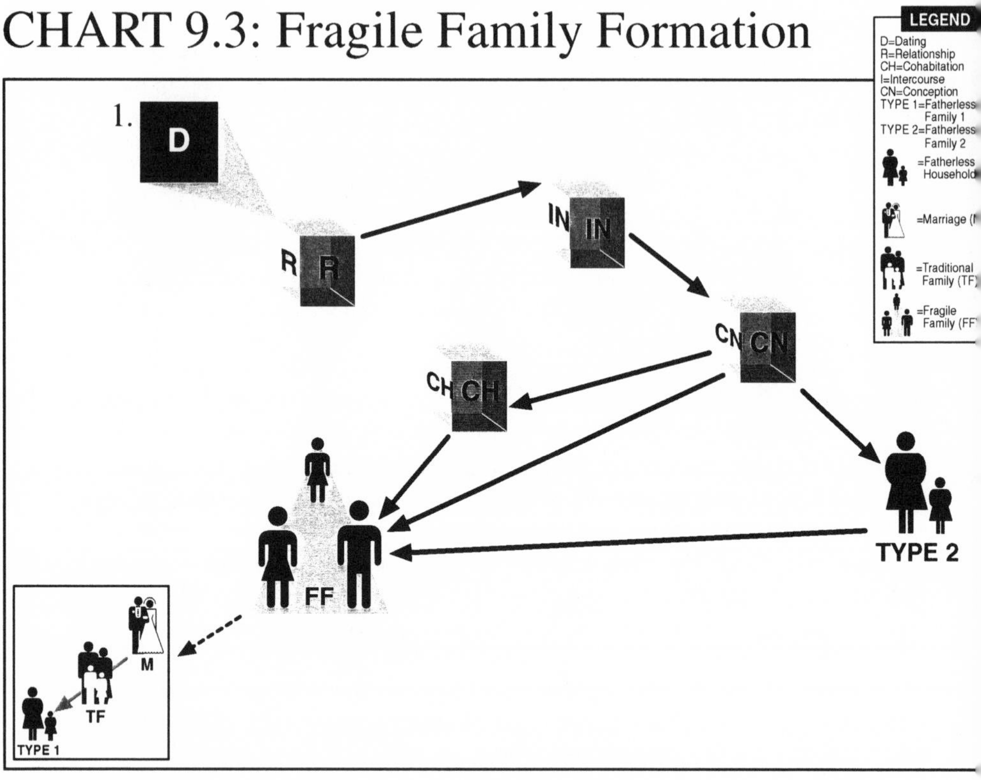

1.

D

R

IN

CN

CH

FF

TYPE 2

M

TF

TYPE 1

the obstacles are many, as we shall see. Even if the parents marry, the traditional family that emerges from a fragile family is still at risk of becoming a type-1 fatherless family through marital dissolution. Nonetheless, children who were once involved in a fragile family will, one hopes, be more likely to receive support from both parents than children reared entirely in type-2 fatherless families.

All too often, however, none of the requisite strategies or supports are available to enable low-income fathers to maintain relationships with their children and partners. Moreover, once responsibility for a child becomes an additional barrier, the young woman is even less likely to marry than she was before. Unless these scenarios—or the declining economic and marriage prospects of less-skilled young men and women—change, the unbridled growth of type-2 fatherless families will continue.

Community-based responsible fatherhood programs have been developed to help unwed and disadvantaged parents move along the path to fragile family formation and, in some cases, marriage. Except for a few demonstration projects, however, this work has received modest public and private support over the last 15 years.[25] However, a national forum called the National Practitioners Network on Fathers and Families (NPNFF) is forming to develop and disseminate the best practices in this field.[26] NPNFF could provide a vehicle by which the responsible fatherhood movement could effectively extend concern for fatherlessness in America to populations for whom marriage-first strategies are not viable.

Social Policy and Fragile Families

Social welfare policy plays a critical role in the pattern adopted by families formed as a result of out-of-wedlock births to young disadvantaged parents. The reasons are basic and compelling. Resource-strapped school systems in low-income communities are unable to overcome the multiple disadvantages experienced by their male and female students. Thus young women and, especially, men who grow up in these communities are unprepared to enter the mainstream American economy.[27] When premarital intercourse leads to pregnancy, these young people conceive children in poverty. Therefore, income security and family support systems are almost immediately involved, whether the conception is the result of an abusive, sexually exploitive relationship or a relationship between a couple who wants a future together. In our view, only the latter case is a fragile family.

Public welfare systems can engage fragile families in ways that support and maintain the relationship between the parents or push them apart. Since policymakers continue to develop these systems with traditional family formation in mind, they do not perceive the father as partner in the case of an unwed conception. Income security and family support systems bring resources, however meager, to the mother and child, leaving the father as destitute as he was before the conception. He brings nothing to his fragile family and may even threaten its eligibility for needed public benefits. Because of their focus on the traditional family, policymakers focus on events following marital dissolution, such as child support, access, and visitation. The policies that emerge create additional hurdles for the fragile family. As a result, fatherlessness among groups that conceive in poverty dwarfs fatherlessness among other groups.

Because disadvantaged unwed mothers, fathers, and children become caught in systems that do not meet their needs, the systems themselves ultimately push disadvantaged unwed parents toward becoming type-2 fatherless families and away from being fragile families. This obscures the reality: Many policy options exist to help these families before marital dissolution is reached.

Fragile Families and Welfare Policy

To receive cash assistance, an unwed mother must show that her income is below the eligibility standard for cash assistance in her state. Unless the combined incomes of a mother and the father of her child outweigh the sum of the Medicaid benefits, child care, food stamps, and cash assistance she and the child would receive, she loses money if the father remains involved in the family. When the father's income is low and unstable, this provides a strong incentive to push him away, which places many fragile families in an income/benefits trap. If the father remains with the family and takes a job, he may initially manage to lift his fragile family above the eligibility standard, but not to the level of all the benefits for which mother and child are eligible. Eventually, this job might lead to a higher paying job, but in the meantime, the mother and child are financially better off without him.[28] If he avoids taking a low-paying job in the formal economy, precisely because he and his partner are afraid of this income/benefits trap, he is less likely to acquire the experience he needs to find a job that will eventually produce enough income for the fragile family to escape poverty.

The benefit provisions of the new welfare law, called the Personal Responsibility and Work Opportunities Reconciliation Act, may exacerbate this problem or alleviate it. The new law provides federal grants to states under a new grant program called Temporary Assistance to Needy Families. States can use the federal grants to provide assistance to individuals who belong to families with children, and it is now easier for states to make grants to two-parent families than it was under the old law. Therefore, if a state wants to provide employment training services to unwed and disadvantaged fathers, it may do so as long as the father lives with his child and the child's mother. However, states cannot use federal funds to make grants to families for more than five years, and the amount of federal funds a state receives to assist individual families is limited. If federal funds are used to provide such services to fathers, the period of the grant is deducted from the five years of their families' eligibility.

Parent's Fair Share, the most recent of a series of demonstration projects serving low-income fathers and their families, suggests a strategy to help fragile families out of this income/benefits trap. The demonstration enabled fathers to receive job training assistance similar to the assistance available to mothers enrolled in the employment and training (JOBS) component of the 1988 Family Support Act. The demonstration also provided parents with enhanced child support enforcement, peer support, instruction in parenting skills, and mediation services. In its preliminary evaluation of the demonstration, the Manpower Demonstration Research Corporation noted these benefits:

> More than one interviewee said that the communication skills he had learned or refined in peer support, coupled with his newly-developed ability to think problems through calmly, had improved his relationship with a spouse or girlfriend. Facilitators report that several peer support participants have reconciled with the custodial parent after a long hiatus.[29]

Other programs offering similar services have also reported success in strengthening the involvement of noncustodial fathers with their fragile families. Programs focusing services on the fragile family unit rather than the mother only serve as a pattern for policy reform in this area.

Paternity and Child Support Policies

During pregnancy and shortly after childbirth many young unwed couples are open to a discussion of their options, including paternity establishment and marriage.[30] However, few people who advise young parents from disadvantaged communities encourage the couple to keep the father involved. These young people usually get advice from peers and family members. Given their experience with the welfare system, the poor prospects of so many men, and the preponderance of fatherless families in the community, friends and family usually advise the couple to let the mother go it alone. When the expectant mother receives prenatal care or applies for welfare, she also receives counseling from professionals, but counseling services are seldom available to the father. At best, counselors persuade the parents to establish paternity. Often counselors take sides, focusing only on the mother and the child, and they reinforce schisms.[31] Of course, when the father is "bad," predatory, or irresponsible, a service provider has to take such a position. But in most cases service providers ignore the window of opportunity between the pregnancy and early childhood period to help fragile families establish paternity and develop their relationships.

The effects that the paternity establishment and child support provisions of the Personal Responsibility and Work Opportunities Reconciliation Act will have on this problem are still unclear. One provision requires states to reduce a mother's cash assistance benefits by at least 25 percent if she does not cooperate in identifying the father of her child for the purpose of establishing paternity and helping the state collect child support. Another provision enables child support agencies to impose penalties on welfare agencies if the latter do not use standards of cooperation developed by the former. These provisions may put additional pressure on welfare workers to pit the mother and child's financial security against the father's child support obligation.

After the parents establish paternity, child support enforcement further discourages family formation. In many states a family court sets a child support order immediately following paternity establishment. If the father's income is low or unstable, or if he is unable to document a consistent pattern of earnings, the family court can impose a child support order that is above the father's ability to pay. If he is unable to maintain the payments—for whatever reason—the system does not forgive past due payments. The payments accrue, becoming heavy debts. If the mother is on welfare, this is a debt to the state, which can also include the value of medical expenses associated with the child's birth. Moreover, the father's failure to pay his debt places him in contempt of the family court, which can lead to incarceration. Thus, if a low-income father does not believe his earnings are high or stable enough to meet financial obligations related to his child, the parents may avoid establishing paternity and moving toward family formation.

Again, the child support provisions of the new law may aggravate these problems. The provisions make it easier for child support enforcement agencies to garnish wages, suspend driver's licenses, intercept tax refunds, record delinquent child support payments on credit and bank reports, and when the father gets a new job, place address and other vital information in a data file available to child support agencies throughout the country. Although child support enforcement agencies often need such provisions to collect payments from divorced fathers with stable jobs and income, the provisions will prevent low-income fathers from getting or maintaining jobs they need to support their families.

Nevertheless, the new law may provide welfare and child support agencies with opportunities to rethink child support enforcement policy in ways that strengthen fragile families. Such rethinking would be consistent with one of the four purposes of the new law: to encourage the formation and maintenance of two-parent households. Although Congress provided specific goals and timetables for states to achieve the other three purposes (providing temporary cash assistance, encouraging work, and reducing teen pregnancies), the new law includes no specific goals, timetables, or strategies for encouraging the formation and maintenance of two-parent families.

More than a decade of demonstration research and community-based practice suggests that community-based responsible fatherhood programs can help achieve this goal. The Personal Responsibility and Work Opportunities Reconciliation Act requires states to develop community outreach strategies to increase paternity establishment rates. To meet these requirements, child support enforcement agencies might enter cooperative agreements with community-based responsible fatherhood programs. Under the agreements, the programs would encourage unwed parents to establish paternity for their children in a nonadversarial environment. Birthing clinics now provide such services, but these have limited potential because few birthing clinics use male staff or other features that make them "father friendly."

In exchange for helping child support enforcement agencies meet their paternity establishment goals, community-based responsible fatherhood program workers might be trained to assist fragile families. Program workers could help fathers document their earnings before child support hearings occur, for example, so courts could set child support orders that are within the father's means. In lieu of cash child support payments, community-based responsible fatherhood programs might monitor in-kind services rendered by fathers who lack stable sources of income. Services could include child care and/or participation in employment training programs, leading to stable employment. After these fathers obtain jobs, program staff could work with the fragile family and the court to structure child support orders, so that delinquent payments do not pile up. Later, as the earnings of the low-income fathers increase—a likely outcome given the results in Healthy Start's pilot programs—payments could rise as well. Programs might also help families and courts modify child support orders if the father experienced a spell of unemployment—a common experience of many disadvantaged workers who receive such services.[32] Judge David Grey Ross, the deputy director of the federal Office of Child Support Enforcement, is encouraging child support agencies to develop partnerships with community-based responsible fatherhood programs. With his leadership, we hope to see progress during the early implementation of the new law.

New child support provisions can also strengthen fragile families in other ways. For example, one provision requires states to develop the capacity to require fathers who are delinquent in their payments to participate in work activities, but at present it is unclear if federal child support funds will be used to support such activities. If they are, child support agencies could contract with community-based responsible fatherhood programs, especially those affiliated with employment training agencies, to provide such services. Another provision provides funds for visitation and access programs for fathers who are paying child support. With these funds, community-based responsible fatherhood programs might aid fragile families having relationship problems that interfere with visitation. These efforts would build on the experience of demonstration projects involving formal mediation and team parenting, a concept being developed by members of the National Practitioners Network for Fathers and Families. Finally, programs might assist unwed parents to find co-residential housing, so that they could avoid the child support system altogether. This, however, would involve major changes in housing policy.

Public Housing Policy

Residency in federally funded public housing authorities blocks noncustodial fathers from living with their families. Housing subsidies currently benefit 45 percent of poor single-parent families with children. For this reason, many welfare recipients rely heavily on public housing, and fragile families must add housing subsidies to the list of public benefits when they calculate the income/benefits trap associated with welfare. Rent for a fatherless family may be quite low, while the rent for a two-parent family may be more than the family can afford. Also, many public housing agencies have strict rules forbidding families from letting anyone with a criminal record live with them. This is a particularly useful rule that prohibits families from renting space to drug dealers and gangs. However, a significant number of low-income minority men have criminal records.[33] When these young men have served their prison terms and are attempting to rebuild their lives, their ability to reunite with their children and families can reduce recidivism. Thus public housing rules that absolutely prohibit association with ex-offenders discourage fragile family formation.

Under the leadership of its former secretary, Henry Cisneros, the U.S. Department of Housing and Urban Development was considering efforts to remove some of these barriers. For example, some housing authorities had been developing pilot projects that would have allowed nonresident fathers of welfare families to live in public housing with their families without a rental surcharge for up to 18 months. This is an example of a housing policy change that helps strengthen fragile families.

Policies to Prevent Teenage Pregnancies

There is anecdotal evidence that when young people who are at risk of becoming early unwed parents are given activities that generate pride and satisfaction in accomplishing concrete tasks, the value of becoming a parent is displaced as a source of pride and accomplishment. "When systems link young people to natural mentors and thus move them more toward constructive adult peer groups . . . young people gain a realistic hope that working hard will allow them and their potential marriage partners to achieve a middle-class income and a satisfying career."[34] However, such opportunities are rare for poor youth. Available opportunities primarily target girls through life skills training that is specifically attached to pregnancy prevention programs. The chance to help even more poor youth think realistically of sexual partners also as marriage and family partners is too often lost. Such efforts as apprenticeships and school-to-career programs that link teenage boys and girls to high-wage careers in growth industries are examples of the types of strategies that may be most effective in preventing pregnancy.

The Fragile Family

Strategies to increase father involvement in the lives of children born to disadvantaged unwed parents cannot use the traditional pattern of family formation as a guide. Such a pattern ignores opportunities to strengthen relationships between parents during critical events, such as conception and cohabitation, that occur outside marriage.

Unfortunately, welfare policy, child support laws, public housing policies, and even the social environment of disadvantaged young people push unwed and disadvantaged fathers away from their families. Community-based responsible fatherhood programs may be the only places where low-skilled young people can go to build hope in their partners and get support in their relationships.

Marriage-first cultural reforms will help some low-skilled young people delay childbearing until they can marry and raise a traditional family. However, such reform messages represent a hollow promise for many others, unless there is increased support for education, job creation, and workforce development programs for which childless adults are eligible. The most pragmatic message we hear in this area is President Clinton's call upon the private sector to create new entry-level jobs for welfare recipients, most of whom are mothers. Without a simultaneous effort to increase employment of fathers, marriage and fragile family formation will diminish.

In addition to its stand on cultural reform, the responsible fatherhood movement must pay much closer attention to the economic and policy forces that are really affecting family formation among disadvantaged young people. If the movement does this, it will broaden its messages and its strategies to strengthen the fragile family. We expect the number of children born to unwed and disadvantaged parents to increase in the near future, and we want no part of a responsible fatherhood movement that ignores their needs.

Notes

1. Ronald B. Mincy, "Strengthening Fragile Families: A Proposed Strategy for the Ford Foundation" (New York: The Ford Foundation, 1994).

2. Dennis P. Hogan and Daniel T. Lichter, "Children and Youth: Living Arrangements and Welfare," in *State of the Union: America in the 1990s,* ed. Reynolds Farley (New York: Russell Sage Foundation, 1995).

3. Many of the arguments about the role of economic forces in the withdrawal of low-income African American fathers apply to some groups of Latino fathers as well. These arguments best explain the withdrawal of fathers from Latino families in ethnic groups, such as Dominicans, Puerto Ricans, and Mexican Americans, with poverty rates and average incomes close to those of African Americans. Unfortunately, data on the determinants of family formation among Latinos has not been readily available, and what is available often does not separate ethnic groups. Therefore, researchers have not been

able to test hypotheses about the determinants of African Americans. These groups have vastly different average incomes, and in most cases marriage and childbearing occur among members of the same race.

4. William Julius Wilson, *The Truly Disadvantaged: The Inner City, The Underclass, and Public Policy* (Chicago: University of Chicago Press, 1987), 69.

5. Daniel Patrick Moynihan, *The Negro Family: The Case for National Action* (Washington, D.C.: Office of Policy Planning and Research, U.S. Department of Labor, 1965).

6. William A. Darity Jr., and Samuel Myers Jr., "Changes in Black Family Structure: Implication for Welfare Dependency," *American Economic Review* 73 (May 1983): 59-64.

7. Robert I. Lerman, "Employment Opportunities of Young Men and Family Formation," *American Economic Review* 79 (May 1989): 62-66; David Ellwood and Jonathan Crane, "Family Change Among Black Americans: What Do We Know," *Journal of Economic Perspectives* 4, no. 4 (1990): 65-84.

8. Saul Hoffman, Gregory J. Duncan, and Ronald B. Mincy, "Marriage and Welfare Use Among Young Women: Do Labor Market, Welfare and Neighborhood Factors Account for Declining Rates of Marriage Among Black and White Women?" (paper presented at the annual meeting of the American Economics Association, New Orleans, December 1991).

9. William Julius Wilson, *When Work Disappears: The World of the New Urban Poor* (New York: Knopf, 1996), 95.

10. Lynn Burbridge, "Policy Implications of a Declining Marriage Rate among African Americans," in *The Decline in Marriages Among African Americans: Causes, Consequences and Policy Implications,* eds. M. Belinda Tucker and Claudia Mitchell-Kernan (New York: Russell Sage Foundation, 1995); Sara McLanahan and Lynne Casper, "Growing Diversity and Inequality in the American Family," in *State of the Union: America in the 1990s,* ed. Reynolds Farley (New York: Russell Sage Foundation, 1995).

11. Robert I. Lerman, "Earnings Opportunities and Fatherhood: Patterns, Causes, and Effects" (paper prepared for a meeting of the National Center on Fathers and Families [NCOFF], April 1996).

12. Ibid.

13. Robert A. Nakosteen and Michael A. Zimmer, "Marital Status and Earnings of Young Men: A Model with Endogenous Selection," *Journal of Human Resources* 22, no. 2 (spring 1987): 248-68.

14. Larry L. Bumpass and James A. Sweet, "Children's Experience in Single-Parent Families: Implications of Cohabitation and Marital Transitions," *Family Planning Perspectives* 21 (1989): 256-60.

15. Larry L. Bumpass and R. Kelly Raley, "Redefining Single-Parent Families: Cohabitation and Changing Family Reality," *Demography* 32, no. 1 (February 1995): 107.

16. Ibid.

17. U.S. Department of Health and Human Services, "Report to Congress on Out-of-Wedlock Childbearing," DHHS Pub. no. (PGHS) 95-1257 (Washington, D.C.: U.S. Government Printing Office, 1995), 32-33. This section of the report is based on data from Larry L. Bumpass and James A. Sweet, "Cohabitation, Marriage and Union

Stability: Preliminary Findings from NSFH2," working paper 65 (Madison: Center for Demography and Ecology, University of Wisconsin, 1995).

18. Bumpass and Raley, "Redefining Single-Parent Families," 107.

19. Bumpass and Sweet, "Children's Experience," 258.

20. Ibid.

21. McLanahan and Casper, "Growing Diversity and Inequality."

22. Bumpass and Sweet, "Children's Experience," 258.

23. Ibid.

24. Mary Achatz and Crystal A. MacAllum, *Young Unwed Fathers: Report from the Field* (Philadelphia: Public/Private Ventures, 1994).

25. Note, for example, the effort carried out by The Strengthening Fragile Families Initiative, Washington, D.C., Jeff Johnson, Executive Director. See reports on the Parent's Fair Share demonstration funded by a consortium of federal and state agencies and private foundations, including Fred Doolittle and Suzanne Lynn, "What Happens with Increased Enforcement of the Child Support Obligations of Poor Men" (paper presented at the 18th Annual Research Conference of the Association for Public Policy Analysis and Management, Pittsburgh, Pa., October 31-November 2, 1996); and Manpower Demonstration Research Corporation, "Report on the Parents' Fair Share Pilot Phase" (October 1993). See also Achatz and MacAllum, *Young Unwed Fathers,* on the Public/Private Ventures Young Unwed Fathers Demonstration; and for a summary of these and other current efforts, Ronald B. Mincy and Hillard Pouncy, "Delivering Dads: Toward an Administrative Structure for Strengthening Fragile Families," in *The New Paternalism: Supervisory Approaches to Poverty,* ed. Lawrence M. Mead (Washington, D.C.: Brookings Institution Press, 1997).

26. Edward Pitt, "It's Official! NPNFF Incorporates," *The Collaborator* 3, no. 1 (winter 1997).

27. Ronald B. Mincy, ed., introduction to *Nurturing Young Black Males: Challenges to Agencies, Programs and Social Policy* (Washington, D.C.: Urban Institute Press, 1994).

28. Daniel R. Meyer, "Can Fathers Support Children Born Outside of Marriage? Data on Fathers' Incomes over Time," in *Studies of the Circumstance of Mothers and Fathers,* vol. 2 of *Paternity Establishment: A Public Policy Conference,* ed. Daniel R. Meyer (Madison, Wis.: Institute for Research on Poverty, 1992), 223-61.

29. Manpower Demonstration Research Corporation, 4-24.

30. Mary Achatz, Crystal A. MacAllum, and Daniel O. Ash, *Face to Face With Fathers: A Report on Low-Income Fathers and Their Experience with Child Support Enforcement* (Chicago: Center on Fathers, Families, and Public Policy, 1997).

31. Esther Wattenberg, "Paternity Actions and Young Fathers," in *Young Unwed Fathers: Changing Roles and Emerging Policies,* ed. Robert I. Lerman and Theodora J. Ooms (Philadelphia: Temple University Press, 1993).

32. Kirk Harris and Daniel Ash, "What Are Low-Income Noncustodial Father's Experiences with the Child Support Enforcement System?" Toby Herr, Suzanne L. Wagner, and Robert Halpern, "Making the Shoe Fit: Creating a Work-Prep System for a Large and Diverse Welfare Population" (papers prepared for the 18th Annual Research Conference of the Association for Public Policy Analysis and Management, Pittsburgh, Pa., October 31-November 2, 1996).

33. Mark Maurer, *Young Black Men and the Criminal Justice System: A Growing*

National Problem (Washington, D.C.: The Sentencing Project, 1990).

34. Lerman, "Earnings Opportunities and Fatherhood."

Chapter Ten

After the Divorce

Ronald K. Henry

After World War II, the rise of divorce as a mass phenomenon created a new social category—the "thrown-away" or "driven-away" father. For the first time in history outside the institution of slavery, large numbers of fit, loving parents were involuntarily separated from their children by force of law.

To the legal system, children became just one more marital asset to be granted to a winner and denied to a loser. In keeping with the social thinking of those times, courts felt themselves perfectly justified in picking a "custodian" and a "visitor" for the child. The notion in the 1950s and 1960s was that mothers were inherently superior parents and that fathers should "manfully" withdraw except to send regular support checks. Out of this environment, the divorce reform component of the fathers movement arose to offer hope to men who refused to "just fade away" unlike General MacArthur's famous old soldier.

The divorce reform movement today consists of married and divorced men and women, grandparents, children's advocates, and grown-up children who endured their own parents' divorce. The divorce reform movement is founded on and animated by an unshakable belief in one simple principle: Children are born with, want, love, and need two parents.

Some of the men who have gone through the divorce process and become involved in the divorce reform movement have been labeled "angry." But stop and think for a moment whether angry might be too weak a description for your own feelings if the judge who controlled access to your children had said:

> You have never seen a bigger pain in the ass than the father who wants to get involved; he can be repulsive. He wants to meet the kid after school at 3:00, take the kid out to dinner during the week, have the kid on his own birthday, talk to the kid on the phone every evening, go to every open school

night, take the kid away for whole weekends so they can be alone together. This type of involved father is pathological.[1]

For myself, married with children, never divorced, the pain and destruction of divorce can only be understood vicariously. My wife's parents were divorced when she was only five years old. She couldn't understand why Daddy didn't love her anymore and why Daddy rarely saw her. Daddy, of course, still loved her, but was kept away by a "standard visitation order" that made almost no accommodation for the travels and duties of an active military officer. It took Connie and her father nearly 30 years to recover from the pain and re-establish what I take for granted as a normal father-daughter relationship. Many children never recover what the courts have taken from them.

Regardless of the social pathology under consideration, whether it is teenage pregnancy, drug abuse, suicide, poor academic achievement, low self-esteem, or any of the other ills upon which our society spends tens of billions of dollars every year, social science research has identified family breakdown and father absence as a primary causal factor. While society will always have the tragedy of "runaway" parents, we can and must change a legal system that needlessly creates thrown-away and driven-away parents. That system is contrary to the best interests of children and every day creates more old soldiers who will not fade away from the battle for divorce reform.

The Pendulum of Public Prejudice

Throughout most of our nation's history and in much of the world today, the law contained a strong or conclusive presumption that sole custody would be awarded to the father in the event of family dissolution. For example, in 1848, the early feminist meeting in Seneca Falls, New York, included the fact that fathers automatically received custody as a principal complaint in its Declaration of Sentiments.

Prior to the industrial revolution, most parents worked side-by-side with the children on the family farm or in the family trade. Children were nurtured and educated through almost continuous contact with both parents, and childrearing books through the 18th and mid-19th centuries emphasized the father's centrality in raising the children and preparing them for the adult world. As the industrial revolution accelerated through the 19th century by pushing more fathers out of the family enterprise and into the factories, social theorists began to exalt rigid sex role separations with father as external wage earner and with mother as home-bound nurturer. Still, the pendulum swung slowly, and the pro-feminist philosopher, John Stewart Mill, observed that while the idea was interesting, the public was insufficiently prepared to discuss mother custody.

Continued industrialization, coupled with the then-perceived virtue of getting women out of the paid workforce in order to create jobs for returning servicemen at the end of World War I, culminated in a full-blown "cult of motherhood" and the establishment of the "tender-years doctrine" in most states. The pendulum of public prejudice, having swung from one extreme to the other, then enforced automatic mother custody with the same rigidity as the earlier enforcement of automatic father custody.

In approximately the last 20 years, the pendulum has begun swinging toward a more centered position[2], and most states have abrogated the tender-years doctrine through statute or court decision as a violation of equal protection. Virtually all states now give at least lip service to the principle that custody decisions should be made in accordance with the "best interests" of the children rather than by reference to the parents' gender. Although the legal regimes vary, it is now recognized in all states that either the mother or the father can "win" the battle for custody of the child.

Children's Needs

While the law was advancing to the point of recognizing that either mother or father could be the better parent, social science research confirmed that the best parent is both parents. Ten years ago, it was considered impolite to suggest that two-parent families were functionally superior to single-parent families. Today, the notions that two-parent families are unimportant and that government can provide an effective substitute have been repudiated. In their place is a broad political and scientific consensus that children need two parents.

The view from the Left by groups like the Progressive Policy Institute is this:

> Traditional liberals' unwillingness to acknowledge that two-parent families are the most effective units for raising children has led them into a series of policy cul-de-sacs. . . . Our point is that at the level of statistical aggregates and society-wide phenomena, significant differences do emerge between one-parent and two-parent families, differences that can and should shape our understanding of social policy.[3]

The view from the Right by groups like the American Legislative Exchange Council is this:

> With an unanimity of view that is virtually unparalleled, social science researchers have documented the fact that children of divorce or unwed birth fair poorly in comparison to children from intact families. Regardless of the social problem which is under consideration, whether it be drug abuse, juvenile delinquency, teenage pregnancy, low self-esteem, poor academic achievement, or even suicide, research points to family breakdown as a primary cause.[4]

In accordance with the resurrected understanding that two-parent families are important for children, liberals and conservatives have reached common ground on the importance of encouraging family formation and family preservation. But what about children of divorce?

Winner/Loser Legal Structures

Courts are most accustomed to adversarial presentations that are resolved by the selection of a winner and a loser. The system works well in commercial disputes. The court picks a winner and a loser; the loser is ordered to pay the winner; then we move on to the next case. The difference in domestic relations cases is that it is immoral and destructive to treat children as prizes to be awarded to a winner and denied to a loser.

Children are born with two parents. Children want, love, and need two parents. The fact that mother and father no longer live under the same roof does nothing to diminish the child's need for both parents. The only thing that is assured by a winner-take-all domestic relations system is that the child will necessarily lose because the child walked into court with two parents and walks out with only one.

If we are honestly concerned with preserving the best interests of the child, we must examine unflinchingly the procedures by which we purport to identify those best interests. The key is in understanding the nature of a custody decree.

The Custody Decree As an Injunction

From birth and throughout the marriage, the law recognizes that the child has two parents. Both of these parents have unrestricted access and equal custodial rights with respect to the child. A custody decree is an order which restricts parents' access and custodial rights with respect to the child and, like any other injunction, enjoins the parents from the exercise of their former, unrestricted rights.

While a custody decree is an injunctive order, the courts too often fail to apply the principles that are applicable to all other injunctions. In all other situations, the guiding principle is that injunctive relief should be carefully crafted to impose only such minimum restrictions upon the parties' prior freedom as is required to resolve the present dispute. In contrast and largely because of the past swings of the pendulum (automatic father sole custody, automatic mother sole custody), the most common custody decrees issued by the courts today impose maximum rather than minimum change upon the parent-child relationship.

Domestic relations courts receive litigants at the time of greatest emotional stress. By encouraging winner/loser resolutions, they exacerbate the tension and magnify the trauma for the children who are the prize of the contest. Divorce court becomes an opportunity to win or get even for real or imagined past abuses. It also creates the terror of losing. All of these magnify and intensify the adversarial nature of the process.

The Real Legal Task

Legal procedures and presumptions have consequences beyond the cases that are actually litigated. The rules that determine how individual cases will be litigated also shape the negotiations for the settlements that are reached in the vast majority of cases. Indeed, one of the principal claims made on behalf of the so-called "primary caretaker" doctrine is that it will force settlements by making the winner easily identifiable in advance.

There is no doubt that the choice of any set of procedures and presumptions will shape the negotiations and litigation postures of the parties to a custody dispute. The question is whether a particular set of procedures and presumptions will enhance the "best interests" of the child. Predictability and simplicity cannot be goals in themselves. A preference for the tallest parent is certainly simple and no more nor less rational than our earlier assumptions that all fathers or all mothers were automatically the better parents. The real task is to ascertain the best interests of the child in a manner that encourages rational decisions by the court and encourages child-oriented negotiations.

The Best Parent Is Both Parents

The broad political and scientific consensus that children do better when they have two actively involved parents should shape our approach to custody determinations. We devote massive attention to the need for family formation and family preservation precisely because we know that children need two parents. It is damaging to children when we allow that knowledge to be submerged or forgotten upon the filing of a divorce petition.

Domestic relations law should not be focused upon developing easier ways to pick the winner and loser. Asking who will be the winner and who will be the loser is the wrong question because we know that the child will be the loser in either event. In the vast bulk of all cases, both mother and father are good parents who genuinely love their children and who wish to function as parents, not visitors, to those children. Our inquiry should not be addressed to the question of which parent is marginally better than the other. Instead, the courts should seek to preserve for the child as much as possible the benefits that we unambiguously know come from full, active, emotional, and physical relationships between the child and both parents.

It is at this point that the nature of a custody decree as an injunction becomes important. The courts should strive to impose as little change from the intact two-parent family as necessary to accommodate the changed circumstances of the litigants.

In cases of mature, cooperative parents, the court will need to do little more than bless the parties saying, "Go, ye, and co-parent in peace." Other cases, however, involve conflict between the parents which arises on a continuum from the mundane (who takes little Billy home for Christmas dinner) to the horrific (child sex abuse allegations, whether true or false). The key to preserving the best interests of the child lies in recognizing that is not necessary to conduct a "parentectomy,"[5] the cutting out of one parent, in order to resolve the conflict. As with any injunction, the judge should impose only such restrictions on the child's relationship with both parents as are necessary to resolve the existing and foreseeable disputes.

Encouraging Shared Parenting after Divorce

Lawyers, like most mortals, take comfort from their ability to place matters into pigeonholes. Historically, the choices were seen as father custody or mother custody. More recently, a legal pigeonhole for joint custody has been acknowledged. Joint custody is often further subdivided into joint legal custody (meaning shared decision making) and joint physical custody (meaning residence in each parent's household beyond whatever amount of time is meant by "visitation").

An examination of actual custody decrees, however, reveals a continuum rather than three discrete categories. In all but a tiny minority of the most pathological cases, the custody order contains explicit provisions for continuing contact between the child and both parents, including overnight residence. Except for a tiny minority, then, all custody decrees preserve at least a portion of the shared parenting which existed prior to the divorce. Father custody, mother custody, and joint custody are merely points on the continuum of shared parenting.

By understanding that all custody decrees represent discrete points on the continuum of shared parenting,[6] it is possible to acknowledge some of the realities that we have always known but have not always remembered while fashioning those decrees.

First, most parents are normal. In most marriages, both spouses are good parents who love and wish to be an active part of their children's lives. Policies should be based upon the norm of human response rather than upon the pathological extremes. The winner-take-all approach to custody encourages a bifurcation into good parent and bad parent categories. The bad parent is then more easily relegated to a marginal role in the child's life. All losers, all bad parents, are then more easily painted with the same brush of a "standard visitation schedule" encompassing alternate weekends and scattered holidays. All losers, ranging from those who were almost winners to those who barely avoided termination of parental rights, are thus lumped together by the presumption of pathology. Abolition of the presumption of pathology is the first step toward protection of the child's best interests.

Second, effective parenting takes time. Disneyland Daddies, Marginal Mommies, and their noncustodial children have a common complaint: "Visitation" just doesn't feel like a real parent-child relationship. Parent to child teaching occurs in the quiet moments, the shared tasks, the talks at the end of the day. School-night sleep-overs are every bit as important as Saturday extravaganzas, especially for older children who see weekends as a time of conflict between the attractions of parents and peers.

Third, stereotypes damage children. Stereotypes about fathers seeking custody to avoid child support and mothers grasping children as meal tickets do not help to resolve custody disputes. Both stereotypes ignore the simple human fact that parents love their children and want to be with them. Stereotypes have become so ingrained that the U.S. Department of Health and Human Services was actually surprised to learn that young fathers care about their children:

> Research to date has produced a new and significant insight about the fathers of children born to teens: They typically are motivated to support their families, even when they are not married to their partners, and even though they earn disproportionately little and suffer from high unemployment. This finding contradicts the widely held notion that young fathers are able but unwilling to support their children.[7]

Other fathers also desire contact with their children. In August 1990, a Los Angeles Times survey reported that 39 percent of fathers would quit their jobs to stay home with their children if that option were available to them.

The bureaucracy is not alone in its surprise. David Gilmore tells how his beliefs were redirected while researching *Manhood in the Making:*

> When I first started researching this book, I was prepared to rediscover the old saw that conventional femininity is nurturing and passive and that masculinity is self-serving, egotistical, and uncaring. But I did not find this. One of my findings here is that manhood ideologies always include a criterion of selfless generosity, even to the point of sacrifice. Again and again we find that "real" men are those who give more than they take; they serve others. Real men are generous, even to a fault. . . . Manhood is therefore a nurturing concept, if we define that term as giving, subventing, or other-directed.[8]

Maintaining the stereotype that fathers do not care about their children requires a special compartmentalization of the mind. Fathers' devotion to and sacrifice on behalf of their children is so naturally expected that it is hardly noticed. The coal miner who continues to work while dying of black lung disease may look like "the patriarchy" to some, but he is just a devoted father as far as I can see. In the popular movie *The Little Mermaid* no one is surprised that King Triton sacrifices everything to save his daughter yet, upon divorce, we would expect him to walk quietly away.

Stereotypes about men create the catch-22 claims that fathers don't care enough to seek custody and that if they really cared, they would not put the children through the trauma of a custody battle. Stereotypes about women and perceptions of gender bias favoring mother custody in the courts create pressure for mothers to seek sole custody even when they recognize that it is not in the child's best interests. Organizations like Mothers Without Custody report that one of the greatest problems encountered by the more than one million noncustodial mothers in the United States is the ostracism they suffer after being pressed to explain why they do not have sole custody. Stereotypes of men and women damage children by indiscriminately ascribing fixed characteristics to large groups of individual human beings. Surely there are some fathers who are uncaring deadbeats and some mothers who are uncaring gold diggers. Lest I be accused of my own sexual stereotyping, note that the roles are sometimes reversed. When noncustodial mothers are ordered to pay child support, their compliance rate is lower than that of fathers.[9] Each child, however, has one specific father and one specific mother, not a caricature from a class.

Fourth, accept no substitutes. Since we know that children of divorce fare poorly in comparison to children from intact marriages, the defenders of the winner-take-all system have developed something of a cottage industry in seeking out factors other than parent loss to explain the deficit. The most commonly asserted rationale is poverty. Single-parent custody would be just fine, we are told, if only we could increase the government subsidies and the income transfers from noncustodians. If increased income is the salvation, we should expect children in stepfamilies to be doing quite nicely since such families have two adults plus an income transfer from the noncustodian, resulting in an economic level at or above that of intact two-parent families. Instead, children in stepfamilies show every bit as much pathology as children in single-parent homes.[10]

Many children have grown up economically impoverished and thrived as adults. The emotional and psychological impoverishment that comes from parent loss is far harder to overcome. Lawrence Meade, professor at New York University, says, "The inequalities that stem from the work place are now trivial in comparison to those stemming from family structure. What matters for success is not whether your father was rich or poor but whether you had a father at all."[11]

Divorce Reform Recommendations

Parent loss through family breakup is a disaster for children. The legal system through which divorcing families must travel can be structured to have positive or negative effects on parent-child bonds. The task is to identify and encourage structures that preserve and enhance the child's bond with both parents.

Giving legal recognition to the child's need for the continued, active physical and emotional involvement of both parents after divorce is neither new nor radical. The pieces necessary for a child-centered custody determination process are already well established throughout the states. Political realities being what they are, no state currently has in place a comprehensive and consistent program for achieving the goals set forth here. The following paragraphs propose such a program.

First, continued shared parenting should be presumed and encouraged. Joint custody was essentially nonexistent 15 years ago but its growing acceptance across the nation has been more rapid than the progress of any prior custody law reform. Every state except South Carolina now acknowledges the availability of joint custody by statute or appellate case law. The strength of the new joint custody statutes and appellate decisions varies from the presumptive to the permissive. While these statutes give helpful recognition to the virtue of continued shared parenting, they often jump to the simple creation of new custody pigeonholes without discussion of their purpose in preserving the parent-child bond. In keeping with the understanding that a custody order is an injunction, the courts should begin with the unrestricted shared parenting that existed during the marriage and back away from the child's entitlement to its continuation only reluctantly and as necessary to accommodate the needs of the specific parties.

Second, encourage cooperative behavior between parents. The structure of the law shapes behavior. If you want combat, enact laws that reward parents for attacking one another. If you want cooperation and conciliation, enact laws that reward it. California has taken a brilliant step. In cases where the distance separating the parents or other factors make equal residential time impractical, California states that its courts are to give a preference to that parent who shows the greater willingness and ability to cooperate in keeping the other parent involved in the child's life. As with any other aspect of human endeavor, you get more of the behavior you choose to reward and less of the behavior that is penalized.

Third, require parenting plans. A growing number of states and localities recognize that divorce procedures are often commenced with little or no thought given to the consequences for the children or for the practical relationships that will emerge after the divorce is granted. As a result, these states and localities encourage or require parents to attend training sessions which describe the needs of the children and the realities of the parental interactions that will be required after divorce regardless of the exact terms of the custody decree.

Many of the states report that these training sessions result in an increased number of reconciliations and voluntary agreements of shared parenting. In one small survey, the Children's Rights Council found that a majority of respondents would not have gotten divorced if they had realized the extent to which they would remain tied together by their common responsibilities to the children even in winner/loser sole custody cases. Although the survey was too small to be statistically meaningful, it identifies an area of tremendous positive potential for family preservation and the demilitarization of divorce.

For those couples who elect to proceed with the divorce, all states should require the submission of a "parenting plan" prior to the entry of the divorce decree. The program currently enforced in the state of Washington is among the most highly developed. At the outset of the divorce proceeding, each couple is required to work out a detailed parenting plan covering the full range of the child's physical, emotional, and financial needs. If the parties are able to agree upon a single-parenting plan, no custody trial is required. If the parents are unable to agree upon a single plan, each parent submits a plan and both plans are available for the court's review in determining the custody arrangement that will serve the best interests of the child.

The exercise of preparing the parenting plan forces both parents to be more realistic about their respective capabilities to provide for the needs of the child and to realize that each will benefit from sharing the burden with the other. The fact that both parenting plans will be available to the judge in contested cases provides vital information regarding the parties' actual capabilities and acts as a deterrent to manipulations in which the child is used as a weapon against the other spouse.

Fourth, establish minimum access guidelines. In the same way that states have enacted child support guidelines in an effort to restrict idiosyncracies and assure the adequacy of awards, minimum access guidelines have also been enacted. Like child support guidelines, the access guidelines have presumptive effect and stem from a recognition that historical awards were often inadequate to permit the preservation of a parent-child bond. Such guidelines may never eliminate the prejudice of the still-sitting Georgia judge who is reputed to have said, "I always award custody to the mamas 'cause I ain't never seen the calf follow the bull, they always follow the heifer," but a guideline can provide a basis for resisting prejudice both in the courtroom and on appeal.

Urgent Work Remains

In the United States today, too many children are fatherless. While fatherlessness has many causes, the portion of it that is caused by law and government requires our particularly urgent attention precisely because laws can be changed when the unnecessary damage they cause is understood. Welfare is one example of a place where laws have been recognized as harmful to fatherhood and changes are being made.

The divorce reform component of the father's movement knows that much work is needed to reverse the anti-father policies of the divorce courts. Fathers are slowly coming to be seen as more than anonymous cash donors but much more remains to be done. Too many judges do not understand children's father-hunger. Too many judges do not hear the child's voice saying that more time with Dad is a higher priority than more money from Dad. Until every child's physical and emotional needs for the father receive the same respect as the child's financial needs, the work of divorce reform will continue.

Children are born with two parents. Children want love, and need two parents. In all but the vanishing small number of pathological cases, the courts should strive to maximize the involvement of both parents. If distance or other factors prevent a substantially equal relationship with both parents, the preference should go to that parent who shows the greater willingness and ability to cooperate and nurture the other parent's relationship with the child. That's what being a caretaker is all about.

Notes

1. Former Chief Judge Richard Huttner, Kings County (Brooklyn) Family Court and member of the New York State Commission on Child Support quoted in "The Fathers Also Rise," *New York Magazine,* Nov. 18, 1985.

2. For example, the American Psychological Association adopted the following resolution at its 1977 meeting:

> Be it resolved that the Council of Representatives recognizes officially and makes suitable promulgation of the fact that it is scientifically and psychologically baseless, as well as a violation of human rights, to discriminate against men because of their sex in assignment of children's custody, in adoption, in the staffing of child-care services, and personnel practices providing for parental leave in relation to childbirth and emergencies involving children and in similar laws and procedures.

3. Progressive Policy Institute, *Putting Children First: A Progressive Family Policy for the 1990s* (Washington, D.C.: Progressive Policy Institute, September 1990).

4. American Legislative Exchange Council, *Children, Family, Neighborhood, Community: An Empowerment Agenda* (Washington D.C.: American Legislative Exchange Council, 1991).

5. Frank S. Williams, "Preventing Parentectomy After Divorce" (paper presented at the annual conference of the Children's Rights Council, Washington, D.C., 1990). Dr. Williams is Director of Family and Child Psychiatry and Director of Programs for Children and Families of Divorce at Cedars-Sinai Medical Center in Los Angeles.

6. The tiny minority of pathological cases in which one parent is purposely excluded from the child's life represents the "exception that proves the rule" and is not further considered in this analysis.

7. Office of Child Support Enforcement, *The Changing Face of Child Support Enforcement: Incentives to Work with Young Parents* (Washington, D.C.: United States Department of Health and Human Services, December 1990), xix.

8. David D. Gilmore, *Manhood in the Making: Cultural Concepts of Masculinity* (New Haven, Conn.: Yale University Press, 1990), 229.

9. See, for example, "1991 Statistics of Child Support Compliance," Office of Child Support Recovery, State of Georgia.

10. See National Commission on Children, "Speaking of Kids: A National Survey" (Washington, D.C.: U.S. Government Printing Office, 1991); and Nicholas Zill of Child Trends, Inc.

11. Lawrence Meade, "The New Politics of the New Poverty," *The Public Interest,* no. 103 (spring 1991):10.

Chapter Eleven

Beyond Government

Dan Coats

A young teaching assistant in a Midwestern city recently saw the sad, disturbing evidence of an American generation raised without fathers. One day, a second-grader climbed onto the volunteer's lap and touched his fingers against the teacher's five o'clock shadow. "What are those?" the boy asked. The child was mystified by the little stubs growing out of the teacher's cheek. "Do they hurt?" the boy asked. The teacher was shocked. This student and many of his classmates had never been close enough to an adult male to see him shave.

A generation of Americans is being raised without fathers. The ill-effects are exacerbated when not only individuals but entire communities lack fathers. A responsible, adult male in a neighborhood is often an example and source of discipline for children who are not his own. Yet some neighborhoods and public housing projects are almost completely devoid of males who are more than visitors. Without the restraining influence of fathers and male role models, these communities often become "juvenilocracies," in which power is exercised by immature, violent adolescents. Charles Ballard of the Institute for Responsible Fatherhood and Family Revitalization tells of meeting young adults in these areas who have attended several funerals of their friends, but not one wedding.

Liberal ideology dictates that our society should be neutral to these trends. A preference for intact families is dismissed as nostalgia, or even oppression. But as Alan Ehrenhalt notes, "Too many of the things we do in our lives, large and small, have come to resemble channel surfing, marked by a numbing and seemingly endless progression from one option to the next, all without the benefit of a chart, logistical or moral."[1]

In the context of caring for children, channel surfing will not suffice. The abandonment of children, particularly by fathers, is not simply a "lifestyle choice." It is a form of adult behavior with profoundly destructive consequences for children and for society. The "liberation" of adults from traditional family commitments is the most direct cause of suffering for children—more than hunger, lead paint, or failed schools. In reality, then, an emphasis on intact families is a particularly practical form of compassion.

Not long ago, the importance of fathers was a matter of debate. Now, however, the suffering of children caused by absent and irresponsible fathers is so obvious and so overwhelming that the debate has advanced to a point of widespread agreement. Senator Daniel Patrick Moynihan has said that a society of unattached males "asks for and gets chaos." The converse also is true. When the role of fathers is respected and restored, a neighborhood and a society become better places to live.

This does not, in any way, diminish the importance or minimize the contribution of millions of single mothers who raise their children in hard circumstances. They often are examples of sacrifice and commitment—models of what a parent should be.

So what can we do? What can the government do, through effective and responsive public policy, to address the critical void the absence of fathers has created in hearts, homes, and neighborhoods across the country?

Government has a definite role, but this role often is misunderstood. Striving to reduce the financial strain on single-parent families, government prescriptions often focus on economic solutions to absentee fatherhood. Economics, however, is not enough. Despite the booming economy, in the 1980s the number of single-parent households increased by 40 percent. We have found that economic indicators cannot measure the values held by our children, or the suffering felt by broken families. Our growing gross national product is accompanied by massive prison construction to house a lost generation, drug counseling in elementary schools, suicide hotlines, teen pregnancy centers, and clinics for battered children. The government also attempts to help by trying to enforce child support. This, too, is an important goal, but the financial role of fathers is just one role among many, and it clearly is not as important to children as the emotional support, love, and discipline fathers provide.

Ultimately, our problem is not a failure of political will or imagination, but a failure of love and commitment. Our worst crisis is not the budget deficit, but a deficit of time and attention given by fathers to their children. Even in families where Dad is present, children often see less of their fathers than if they had grown up in an earlier era. Parents today spend roughly 40 percent less time with their children than parents did a generation ago, and fewer than 25 percent of all children experience an average of at least one hour a day of individualized contact with their fathers.[2]

Our greatest challenge is not a lack of resources but a lack of conscience and character and integrity. These problems persist, no matter who has a temporary hold on political power—Right or Left, Republican or Democrat. We have discovered that no amount of political tinkering will restore our social order while there is moral disorder in our souls.

Cultural problems demand cultural solutions. Responsible fathers are essential to the health and survival of civil society. Government must encourage the private, religious, and nonprofit organizations that deliver and enforce this cultural message of the importance of fatherhood.

Public Policy and the American Family

Of all the institutions that comprise civil society, the institution of the family is the most essential and the most endangered. Here we need to be specific: The most serious problem is absent, irresponsible fathers. It should not be controversial, though it often is, to say that fathers are not expendable and families are not optional.

In the words of Edmund Burke, the family is the origin of "the little platoon we belong to in society" and it is "the germ of public affections."[3] Families are the seedbed of our skills and attitudes. They teach us the principles of economics, the value of relationships, and the importance of moral truths. They define our view of work, responsibility, and authority. They teach us the meaning of trust, the value of honesty. They are the wellspring of every individual's strength against alienation, failure, and despair.

Families are the source not only of our personal values and security, but of our political, economic, and social order, as well. Any nation whose families are weak will eventually find itself without strong institutions of any kind.

There was a time in our country when we believed in the axiom: What strengthens the family, strengthens society. This was also true about local neighborhoods and communities. Michael Joyce and William Schambra state it this way:

> Before the modern age, American life had been organized around what historian Robert Wiebe described as "island communities." As this phrase suggests, civic life was characterized by both its self-containment and its cohesiveness. Individuals were closely bound one to another by strong families, tightly knit neighborhoods, and active voluntary and fraternal groups. Through these small, local, "human-scale" associations, Americans not only achieved a sense of belonging and connectedness but also tackled the full range of social and human problems that today have largely become the province of government.[4]

The government gained this province, according to Joyce and Schambra, when the Progressive elites of the early 20th century decided to replace local institutions with the paradigm of a "national community." Progressive leader Herbert Croly stated that the desire of the individual would be subordinate "to the demand of a dominant and constructive national purpose," as each citizen would "think first of the State and next of himself."

Families, churches, and community groups no longer would be needed to solve social problems. In fact, as Joyce and Schambra write, they were the enemy, "actively hostile to such intermediate associations." In the end, "[t]he triumph of progressive structural reform would mean, in essence, that citizen involvement in public affairs was reduced from active, intense, face-to-face problem solving on a daily basis to passively casting a lonely, solitary ballot once in a great while for a handful of offices."[5]

As a result, where the family was once the dominant force—in educating our children, in caring for the aged, in providing for the infirm and the needy—its role has been significantly weakened and often subordinated to that of the state. In fact, the family has been under withering attack, often by government policy. Yet, by every measurable standard, the state has failed to assume adequately the role of the family. Nowhere is this more apparent than in the policies that govern welfare and poverty.

In a special message to Congress on public welfare programs in 1962, President John F. Kennedy laid down the first principle of a sound welfare policy:

> The goals of our public welfare programs must be positive and constructive. . . . It must stress the integrity and preservation of the family unit. It must contribute to the attack on dependency, juvenile delinquency, family breakdown, illegitimacy, ill health, and disability. It must replace the incidence of these problems, prevent their occurrence and recurrence, and strengthen and protect the vulnerable in a highly competitive world.[6]

The *New York Times* described Kennedy's message as a recognition that no lasting solution to the problem of welfare could be bought with a government check, and that while the initial financial cost would be higher than the continuation of handouts, the dividends would come in the restoration of individual dignity and the long-term reduction in the need for government help.

President Kennedy and the *New York Times* were right. Welfare subsidies alone are never enough to lift individuals and families out of poverty. They can, and often do, subsidize habits and pathologies that lead to self-destructive behavior.

Our nation's welfare programs have served to make unmarried women dependent upon the state. While well-intentioned, they destroy the incentive young men might have for taking responsibility for their own offspring. As George Gilder once observed, we have persuaded poor fathers that they are dispensable. They believe it, and so do the mothers of their children.

For six decades, men and women who wanted to improve their world came to Washington, D.C., to affirm their faith in government. Faith in the government's ability to raise the poor. Faith in its power to drain an ocean of human misery. But that faith is dying before our eyes. Violence fills graveyards with fatherless boys not old enough to shave. The decay of sexual standards leaves countless women and children exploited and abused. Poverty grows wild among the ruins of single-parent families.

The welfare reform bill passed by the 104th Congress sought to reverse some of these debilitating and pernicious incentives by emphasizing work and imposing time limits. Requiring work for welfare and setting time limits for benefits make entry-level jobs more attractive and discourage many from entering the welfare system in the first place. Work is one of our nation's highest values. No child should be without the moral example of parents, especially fathers, who work.

The recent welfare reform legislation also has removed government-imposed incentives to fail. Government has been gravely mistaken in paying cash to teenage girls on the condition that they have children out of wedlock and never marry the father. Public policies that penalize marriage and promote illegitimacy can never be justified. Government violates its most fundamental responsibilities when it tempts people into self-destructive behavior, especially behaviors that devalue the importance of fatherhood.

Beyond Government

While these lifesaving welfare reforms are long overdue, the destructive incentives that have existed in our nation's welfare system are only part of the problem. The decline of marriage, the rise of illegitimacy, and the destructive growth of fatherlessness in America are rooted clearly in broader cultural trends that affect everyone, rich and poor. Without a welfare system, these trends would still exist and still threaten our society.

James Q. Wilson accepts the figure that less than 15 percent of rising illegitimacy between 1960 and 1974 was due to increased government benefits. He argues, "[S]ome significant part of what is popularly called the 'underclass problem' exists not simply because members of this group face perverse incentives but because they have been habituated in ways that weaken their self-control and their concerns for others."[7]

In other words, Wilson believes the basic problem lies in the realm of values and character, and those values are shaped, particularly in early childhood, by certain cultural standards. "I do not wish," Wilson adds, "to deny the importance of incentives, such as jobs, penalties, or opportunities, but I do wish to call attention to the fact that people facing the same incentives often behave in characteristically different ways because they have been habituated to do so."[8]

People are not purely economic beings, analyzing costs and benefits. We are moral beings. We make choices that reflect our values. Incentives are not irrelevant, but it is ultimately our beliefs and habits that determine our future. The social problems confronted by our nation, including the crisis of irresponsible fatherhood, are rooted in the breakdown in public trust in the institutions that direct and have humanized our lives throughout history—institutions of family, neighborhood, community associations, charities, and religious-based groups.

Sociologists talk about "mediating structures." They say that these institutions build "social capital" and "positive externalities." These academic phrases can be presented in simple terms. A child will never find an adequate substitute for a father who loves him or her. The mantle of government, the assistance of government, will never replace the warm hand of a loving parent. The impersonal directions of a government bureaucrat can never replace the wise counsel of a dedicated dad.

This is precisely the reason Nathan Glazer warns of the unintended consequences of social policy:

> Aside from these problems of expectations, cost, competency and limitations of knowledge, there is the simple reality that every piece of social policy substitutes for some traditional arrangement, a new arrangement in which public authorities take over, at least in part, the role of the family, of the ethnic and neighborhood group, of voluntary associations. In doing so, social policy weakens the position of these traditional agents and further encourages needy people to depend on the government for help rather than on the traditional structures.[9]

This concern is real and ought to reorient our thinking and our efforts. Public policy ought to be centered on a respect and reinvigoration of these traditional structures—families, schools, neighborhoods, and voluntary associations—that provide training in citizenship and pass on morality and civility to future generations. Only then will government policy truly encourage responsible fatherhood.

Wilson agrees. Since government programs tend *not* to produce self-reliance,

> ...then our policy ought to be to identify, evaluate, and encourage those local private efforts that seem to do the best job at reducing drug abuse, inducing people to marry, persuading parents, especially fathers, to take responsibility for their children, and exercising informal social control over neighborhood streets.[10]

Many of our worst social problems, including irresponsible fatherhood, will never be solved until the hearts of parents are turned toward their children; until respect is restored for human life and property; until a commitment is renewed to care about our neighbor. Government cannot reach this deep into human character. But there are people and institutions—families, churches and synagogues, private charities, grassroots community organizations—able to communicate these ideals and restore individual hope. Armed with tough love, individual responsibility, and spiritual values, they often are vehicles of life-changing miracles of renewal.

Robert Woodson, a community activist, makes the point that every social problem, including irresponsible fatherhood, is currently being defeated somewhere, by some religious or community group. This is one of America's great, untold stories. No alternative approach to our cultural crisis holds such promise, because these institutions have resources denied to government at every level—love, spiritual vitality, and true compassion. It is time to take their side—publicly, creatively, and actively—in the struggle to recivilize American society.

This reduces (though it does not necessarily eliminate) the direct role of government programs, but it also points to an active public mission: to transfer government roles and resources to the value-building institutions of our society without burdening them with intrusive regulations. Centralized, bureaucratic government control has failed, but the institutions of family, neighborhood, schools, church, charitable organizations, and voluntary associations offer hope and promise. They do not just feed and house the body; they touch the soul. They have the power to transform individuals and the power to renew our society. And as Amitai Etzioni argues, the more we rely on these private efforts the fewer demands we will make upon government. "The anchoring of individuals," Etzioni writes, "in viable families, webs of friendships, communities of faith, and neighborhoods—in short, in communities—best sustains their ability to resist the pressure of the state."[11]

While we realize that the role of government must be reduced and reoriented, we must also acknowledge that our nation will still be left with unacceptable suffering. Too many children will still grow up without a family's stability and a father's love. Too many will still enter schools through metal detectors. Too many communities will still be imprisoned by violence and fear. The fact that government programs have not worked is no excuse for those in government not to act.

Therefore, we ought to ask one question of every social policy considered by every level of government, and that question is: Does it work through these mediating, traditional, historical institutions; does it work through families, neighborhoods, or religious or community organizations; or does it simply try to replace them?

Accepting this priority would focus our attention on three areas: emphasizing the role of family, particularly the role of fathers and mentors where fathers are not present in the lives of children; rebuilding community institutions that support families; and promoting private charities and religious institutions in the work of compassion.

Private, religious, and nonprofit organizations are demonstrating how fathers can renew their commitments to their children and how mentors can transform the lives of the fatherless. In the absence of fathers and families, children need more than funding and programs, they need mentors and examples. These efforts are proving that broken trust and attachment within families can be restored.

Mentors also are needed for young fathers who are learning how to raise their families. Other young dads who have simply shirked their responsibilities and abandoned their families need mentors to reconnect them with their children. Precisely because we have a crisis in fatherhood, we need to be creative in providing models of responsible male behavior.

Private organizations, such as Promise Keepers and Big Brothers-Big Sisters, are bringing the message of responsible fatherhood and the importance of adult male role models to a broad audience, reminding fathers of their moral duties of paternity. The success and extraordinary growth of these groups are hopeful signs that many Americans sense that our nation has indeed arrived at a moment of crisis. Efforts like these show that broken trust and attachments within families can be restored. Government offers no comparable hope.

Public policy also must reestablish a preference for marriage, which does more than any other institution to encourage responsible fatherhood. Wilson observes: "Of all the institutions through which people may pass—schools, employers, the military—marriage has the largest effect. For every race and at every age, married men live longer than unmarried men and have lower rates of homicide, suicide, accidents, and mental illness. Crime rates are lower for married men and incomes are higher."[12] As a nation, our policies ought to promote, instead of serve as a disincentive to, strong, healthy marriages.

Government policy should communicate a clear, public preference for marriage and family on matters such as public housing, the tax code, family planning, and divorce law. Rewarding intact families is not, as some argue, a form of discrimination. It is a form of self-preservation. We must be more creative in this effort.

Government also can encourage the business community which is becoming more aware of creating father-friendly workplaces. A good example is the automobile factory in Springhill, Tennessee, where assembly line workers are employed on alternative schedules. Once a month, these schedules give workers five straight days at home with their families.

Turning Our Hearts toward Home

Families used to work together, extended families lived together, families were much less mobile, family size was larger, schools were smaller and located nearby, and technological and informational overload were terms not yet coined. Family members were more directly dependent upon each other—for income, for care for both younger and older family members—and conveniences to ease household chores were minimal, which meant that all family members derived significant self-worth from being critical to the functioning of their families.

With the decline of extended families, with fewer brothers and sisters, with frequent changes in schools, neighborhoods, and churches, children thus became more dependent upon interactions with their parents. At the same time, parents became caught up in the striving for material progress and the symbols of success, without stopping to treasure the more valuable things in life and without giving their children the quantity or quality of time they needed.

In his best-selling book *The Road Less Traveled*, M. Scott Peck writes that children know by both the quantity and quality of time given them how much they are valued by their parents. They want "to believe that they are loved but unconsciously they know that their parents' words do not match up to their deeds."[13] Peck says that children are not deceived by "hollow words" and "mechanical actions."

As the current fatherhood movement shows, many Americans have realized this and are now turning their hearts toward home, looking for the lasting principles upon which strong homes are founded. This has led to a re-examination of values in a search for enduring truths, including spiritual truths.

Many seem to look upon this rediscovery of fatherhood and the family as a wonderful political opportunity. Children, however, do not exist so that political parties can control power by pretending to be able to solve the problems facing families. Children are not an opportunity to re-package an economic and social agenda so people can be persuaded into supporting what they have heretofore rejected. Children are human beings to be loved, nurtured, and developed.

What America needs most at this moment is not a new political leader. Our nation needs parents, especially fathers, who will bend to hear a child's voice and care for a child's soul. What America needs most is not a set of new programs or policies. Our country needs people of conviction and tenacity who will say, "This is my family, this is my home, this is my community. I must do what I can to reclaim it, rebuild it, restore it."

When the NBA's Philadelphia 76ers won the top choice in the NBA's 1996 draft lottery, something more significant occurred than Philadelphia's simple luck of the draw. The team's general manager, Brad Greenberg, decided not to attend the league's draft lottery, thus missing a chance to talk about his team's success on national television. Instead, Brad Greenberg decided to stay home with his son Cory and celebrate Cory's 10th birthday—a decision encouraged by team owner Pat Croce. The rest of America will forget this story almost immediately. Cory, however, will remember it for his entire life, and it may even shape the kind of father that he becomes.

It has been said, "Character is what you are in the dark."[14] Almost all of the decisions necessary to be a good father are made in the dark, out of the control of government. Uncle Sam cannot fabricate fatherhood. But government can and, indeed, should actively take the side of private, religious, and nonprofit organizations that themselves are shining light on the indispensable role of fathers. This is the positive, hopeful, and limited role government can play.

Notes

1. Alan Ehrenhalt, *The Lost City* (New York: Basic Books, 1995), 272.

2. William Mattox, "Parent Trap: So Many Bills, So Little Time," *Policy Review* 55 (winter 1991): 6-13.

3. Edmund Burke, *Reflections on the French Revolution,* Everyman ed. (London: J. M. Dent and Sons, Ltd., 1955), 44.

4. Michael Joyce and William Schambra, "A New Civic Life," in Peter L. Berger and Richard John Neuhaus, *To Empower People: From State to Civil Society,* ed. Michael Novak (Washington, D.C.: AEI Press, 1996), 11-12.

5. Ibid., 16.

6. John F. Kennedy, *Public Papers of the Presidents of the United States, 1962* (Washington, D.C.: U.S. Government Printing Office, 1963), 102-3.

7. Henry J. Aaron, Thomas E. Mann, and Timothy Taylor, eds., *Values and Public Policy* (Washington, D.C.: Brookings Institution, 1994), 55.

8. Ibid., 55-56.

9. Nathan Glazer, *The Limits of Social Policy* (Cambridge, Mass.: Harvard University Press, 1988), 7.

10. Aaron, Mann, and Taylor, eds., *Values and Public Policy,* 7.

11. Amitai Etzioni, "Robbing Our Moral Voice," *The Public Interest* 116 (summer 1994): 112.

12. Aaron, Mann, and Taylor, eds., *Values and Public Policy,* 74.

13. M. Scott Peck, *The Road Less Travelled* (New York: Simon and Schuster, 1978), 23-24.

14. Attributed to D. L. Moody by his son in William R. Moody, *D. L. Moody* (New York: Macmillan, 1930), 503.

Chapter Twelve

Fatherhood and Language

Mitchell B. Pearlstein

How can we most effectively—which is to say frankly but graciously—talk about the importance of fatherhood and the calamity of fatherlessness?

Let me start with two quick stories from my own public speaking.

About a half-dozen years ago, in remarks to a diverse group of people in Duluth about the unlikelihood of the United States making real educational progress as long as so many children were brought into this world out of wedlock, a woman in the small room began to cry. It wasn't difficult to imagine why, as she was visibly pregnant and (as I correctly assumed) not married. A few moments later she explained to the now painfully uncomfortable audience that while she had been brought up to believe that it was wrong to have children outside of marriage, she was desperate to have a baby. But since there had been no potential marriage partner in her life, and since her "biological clock" was running down, she decided to conceive.

If I do say so, both of us handled the situation well. She was brave and open, and I talked about how I understood that life was complicated and messy and that I very much regretted hurting her. But I also said that widespread fatherlessness was such an immense problem that we had no choice as a national community but to discuss it head on—albeit with as much grace and fellow-feeling as we could muster.

The episode ended as well as one could hope, though it reinforced my assumption that, given such perpetual risks, most politicians and other leaders would continue working hard at not publicly addressing questions of father absence. Just imagine if cameras from the evening news had been running that day in Duluth.

More recently, I was once again talking about fatherlessness, this time in Minneapolis to a group of public-sector finance officers from several midwestern states, when a woman in the audience essentially asked how I had the nerve to frame such issues in "moral" terms. My doing so, she suggested, was highly suspect insofar as my own first marriage had ended in divorce, a fact I had acknowledged in my prepared remarks, as I almost always do when talking about families.

I responded that if only unflawed people were entitled to talk "judgmentally" about the toughest problems confronting us as a state and nation, little useful would ever be spoken. This, I said, would be a disaster compounded. Still, in the same way that most speakers are not enthused about causing expectant mothers to cry, they are equally hesitant about provoking questions in large congregations about their effrontery.

All of which is to say that productive debates and discussions about families and fathers are contingent on substantial backbones, certainly. But they also depend on a keener appreciation than is usually demonstrated about how language can either modestly cool or radically heat such an inherently flammable cluster of issues.

Without in any way suggesting a prefabricated formula or voice, let me describe what has come to work best for me. This is the case both in terms of getting my argument across as persuasively as possible, as well as, in allowing me to talk to single moms and other women with as little anger as feasible on their part and with as little squirming as possible on mine.

Opening with Qualifiers

I generally start by making it as clear as I can that my aim is not to bash single mothers, millions of whom, I say, are raising their children heroically and successfully with little help from men. I report that, along with sociologist and theologian Michael Novak, I prefer talking about the masculinization of irresponsibility rather than the feminization of poverty. One important aside: I've learned not to make this latter point with too much gusto, as not only are some men honorable and responsible and at least a few women not, but every once in a while I hear agitated and believable stories about men who really have been worked over by ex-partners and the "system" when it comes to visitation and similar issues. These occasional stories come not just from irate men themselves, but also from their angry mothers and other female relatives and friends.

It's at this point that I usually make certain to acknowledge that life does not always work out as scripted and that, indeed, I'm in my second marriage, as is my wife, who was a single mom for a long time after her first marriage ended.

Yet having said all this, I begin to make the case that while literally millions of children growing up in single-parent homes may be doing very well, and while millions of other children growing up in intact, two-parent families may be doing poorly, that generally speaking, in the main, in the aggregate, children who are forced to grow up without their biological or adoptive fathers at home tend to do worse than other children when it comes to education, crime, and every other measure we know.

I have found this three-pronged qualifier—"generally speaking, in the main, in the aggregate"—to be an essential caveat, as it is remarkable how many people have a hard time distinguishing between what is true about father absence in large settings (such as neighborhoods and nations) versus what may very well be true about it in their own homes. With great energy, many single moms want me to know that not only are their kids doing just fine, but that they're doing appreciably better than when they lived with their invariably abusive father.

In response to such testimonials, I genuinely congratulate them on their devotion and good fortune, but once again note the lesser fortune of a disproportionate number of other similarly situated families. In sum, I repeat that fatherlessness is the overwhelming social disaster of our time, as it is implicated in virtually every problem we face as a nation. I then go on to substantiate this claim in two ways.

First, I ask a hypothetical question which I readily concede at the time to be too bulky to be scientific, but which is telling nonetheless.

About 45 percent of children born in Minneapolis, I announce, are now born out of wedlock. Given these numbers, I continue, and not even beginning to take into account the additional effects of divorce and separation, is there anyone in the room who is confident that public education in Minnesota's largest city can get adequately better by the year 2000, or perhaps 2005, regardless of how much more money we might reasonably spend, and regardless of how talented and devoted teachers and administrators might become over and above current levels of talent and devotion?

I've asked this question of at least 3,000 people in Minnesota over the last few years. No more than two percent have raised their hands. I mentioned a moment ago that I recently spoke to about 75 state budget officials, men and women who deal professionally with public education. How many of these practiced observers do you think raised their hands, signaling their confidence about educational advancement? Not one. In light of this, I asked the group why there is so little public talk about what just about everyone, evidently, believes really matters? No one jumped to answer.

A second way I reinforce the assertion that fatherlessness is America's most serious social problem is by drawing from an ever-growing store of empirical research on the very personal effects, reciting the findings in rapid order for dramatic effect. Rarely do I not hear muffled gasps in the audience, or see eyebrows literally rise, when I go through these data.

All of the above is more prologue than full speech. But I have found these substantive and stylistic rudiments to set the right context and tone, not just for speeches about fatherhood, but also for broader treatments of related topics, including education, welfare, crime, and so on.

Avoiding Needless Abrasions

I suspect that most readers already have detected that I rarely use the word "illegitimacy" or its variants, relying instead on terms such as "out-of-wedlock births." This is very much a conscious decision based on the fact that "illegitimate" mightily hurts many women who hurt enough already. It's also grounded in the fact that I see much more needless pain than profit in informing youngsters that while they may indeed be children of God, they nevertheless are less than "legitimate" or "real" in the eyes of other mortals.

In this spirit, and while I found his essay on the end of courtship to be insightful, even brilliant, I would not recommend a public repetition anytime soon of a University of Chicago scholar's recent use of the acutely harsh "bastardy."

Yet having said this, I have little fondness for language that beclouds. Such politically correct straitjackets, aimed at protecting every possible sensibility, ultimately disserve everyone. In a similar vein, there is no question that a prerequisite to whittling down nonmarital births is a yet-to-be recaptured shared sense of personal stigma and shame. I'm not unmindful, for instance, of the importance of reaffirming the principle of legitimacy. Still, on balance, I think it wisest and more decent to avoid words such as illegitimate under most circumstances.

I recognize that some will interpret this interest in staying clear of words that needlessly rile as reflecting too much sensitivity on my part. Is my voice too cautious when talking about fatherhood and fatherlessness? Are my words too carefully chosen? Am I, when you get right down to it, intimidated when dealing with these issues in the presence of women—especially single mothers— because, if truth be told, I'm a man?

I would never claim that my heart always beats steadily, or that my voice never betrays tension, when talking to a demographically mixed audience about abandoned kids. But what else is new?

The subjects raised in this brief essay, and more comprehensively in this anthology, are viscerally powerful, and I see little profit in not choosing one's words prudently. Likewise, I see nothing necessarily timorous about a man demonstrating an extra measure of caution—call it manners, if you prefer— when entering this fray. I'm more than willing to make such a concession given that women generally do have more leeway when talking about the various drawbacks of "AWOL" and missing men.

Two final points in closing.

It's accurate to charge that middle-class (formerly divorced) observers like myself are generally keener to focus on out-of-wedlock births, rather than divorce and separation, when writing and speaking about absent fathers. This is not really fair, and we need to do better.

This short chapter also has dwelled on the sadness of fatherlessness and has had little if anything to say about the pleasures of engaged fatherhood itself. Yet good presentations and conversations about fatherhood do not dwell on pathologies and catastrophes alone. They also celebrate its sacred joys and obligations.

Chapter Thirteen

The Species Narrative

David L. Gutmann

Fathers are not only important in the early years of a man's life; fathers are necessary to men's well-being and civility at all major transition points across the whole masculine life cycle. The versions of the father vary, depending on the season of life. Whatever their nature, fathers play a common role: They kindle in males the psychic strength that males need to accomplish vital transitions, across the life span.

Evidence for the lifelong need of fathers comes from developmental psychology, psychoanalysis, and cultural anthropology, including my own comparative field work among Amerindian, Mayan, and Middle Eastern groups.[1] Special perspectives, especially the psychoanalytic perspective on human development, are useful for highlighting the great regularities around fatherhood in these data.

Three Approaches to Understanding Fatherhood

Ralph Linton, anthropologist, remarked in 1945, "In some ways, each man is like all other men; in some ways, each man is like some other men; and in some ways, each man is like no other men."[2] Linton was referring to the major orders of human experience. Linton's first order or Level One—each man like all men—refers to common, universal ways of underwriting individual and species survival. Linton's Level Two—each man like some others—refers to shared common language, common culture, and common ways of achieving language and culture with a few socially selected members of our species. This level refers also to the ways in which we act so as to preserve society and to maintain ourselves as social beings in the eyes of our fellows. Linton's Level Three—each man like no others—refers to the ways in which we experience ourselves and maintain ourselves as unique and special, different even from those with whom we share a common culture.

The father's most crucial functions must be studied via the methods and instruments that are fitted to the universals, to Level One. However, Level One perspectives are currently out of fashion. They remind us of forces that operate beyond conscious control, even as they influence the direction and content of awareness and conscious thinking. The tectonic forces that drive Level One experience signal us that—as Bruno Bettelheim said—"We are not the masters even in our own mental house." To consider Level One phenomena is to receive a narcissistic wound, and so in our narcissistic age these levels of experience are avoided and left out of our usually orthodox behavioral science. Instead, the father's role is critiqued from the discipline and methods of Level Two, which is sociology and cultural anthropology, or from the ideology (actually, the politically correct theology) of Level Three, which is humanistic psychology. According to sociologists of the family, fathers who insist on playing a special, authoritative role, distinct from mothers, are not serving their children. They are oppressing their women. Humanistic psychologists also deplore the authoritative father: He is, they fear, expressing masculine needs to be dominant and "phallocentric" at the expense of his wife's individuality and "self-actualization."

Thus, on the best campuses (and especially the best) biological paternity—the special male role in procreation—has been split off in theory from the social condition of fatherhood. Biological paternity is admittedly a fact of nature; but *fatherhood,* as a special condition with its own scope, powers, and responsibilities, is regarded by mainstream social scientists as a purely social invention: a ploy of corrupt patriarchy, a violation of nature.

Now we find that too many men, happy to be let off the hook, have heard the liberating message from academia: They are helping to conceive more babies and more candidates for abortion than ever before, but they are too often refusing to be trustworthy, strong, and responsible fathers. According to the new dispensation, this liberation of men from bondage to the patriarchal ideal should lead to the liberation of women. It has not. As men defect from traditional versions of fatherhood, they also defect from the tested arrangements of marriage—and from marriage per se. As a consequence, too many women are left alone with the kids in single parent families. Women are more oppressed than ever. The patriarch has gone, but so are the special rations of security and companionship that he provided. Clearly then, the sociological and humanistic revisions of fatherhood are not working. Instead, it seems that the traditional phrasings of fatherhood were more than expressions of oppressive male politics; it appears that they too were an extension, rather than a refutation, of the same kinds of natural law that also governed biological paternity.

Clearly, if we are going to develop some real answers, beyond political correctitude, to the important questions—what is the father's *special* contribution to parenting, and what do men get out of *being* fathers?—we will have to forage through the data of Level One, the grammar of human universals.

Fatherhood: Closeness through Distance

Species survival—the major issue of the first level—is underwritten by adequate parenting, by the kind of parenting that raises children to be good parents in their turn, down the generations. Erik Erikson once remarked that the long dependency of the human child is the crucial agenda for human development at all ages. The unique features of human parenthood, including the distinctive features of paternal and maternal roles, are also shaped by that same great constant—the unique vulnerability of our children. A guiding idea of this chapter is that the forms of paternity and maternity are not expressions of power politics between the sexes, but are evolved adaptations to the special requirements of the weak and needy human child. Appropriately then, before we address the matter of fatherhood, we should first address its larger context: the special needs, universal across our species, of our at-risk offspring.

Different societies do aim at their own distinctive childrearing goals, but they nevertheless maintain common understandings about the basic needs that must be addressed by any child-care regime. Thus, if it is to thrive by any reasonable criteria, the vulnerable human child must be assured of two kinds of parental nurturance: It must be given some assurance of physical security and also of emotional security.

There is also a general recognition, across our species, that the same parent cannot adequately provide both kinds of security. The child's physical security ultimately depends on activities carried out far from home: warfare, hunting (including the modern version of the hunt, for business and clients), and the cultivation of distant tillage. Far from home on their lawful occasions, fathers cannot be reliable sources of emotional nurture. Men are generally assigned the task of providing physical security on the perimeter, not because they are more privileged, but because they are more expendable. Thus, in the hard calculus of species survival, there is typically an oversupply of males, in that one man can inseminate many females, but women, on the average, can gestate only one child about every two years during their relatively brief window of fertility. The surplus males, those over the number required to maintain viable population levels, can be assigned to the dangerous, high-casualty "perimeter" tasks on which physical security and survival are based. "When it comes to slaughter, you do not send your daughter" is one of our most predictable human rules; and there are unassailably good reasons for it. By the same token, the sex on whom the population level ultimately depends is less expendable. Thus women are generally assigned to secure areas, there to supply the formative experiences that give rise to emotional security in children.

George Murdoch's tables, based on ethnographic data from 224 subsistence-level societies, indicate that any productive or military activity requiring a protracted absence from the home—hunting, trapping, herding, deep-sea fishing, offensive and defensive warfare—is performed almost exclusively by males.[3] Activities carried out closer to home—dairy farming, erecting and dismantling shelters, harvesting, tending kitchen gardens and fowl—are sometimes exclusive to men, more often exclusive to women, but are in most instances carried out by both sexes. However, hearthside activities, particularly those having to do with preserving and preparing food, are almost exclusively the province of women.

Murdoch's findings cannot be adequately interpreted by Level Two thinkers; a work site by gender distribution that is so predictable, across so many different kinds of societies, cannot be explained by sociology alone. These findings can only point to a *species* regularity, an expression of our bio-psychological nature, and not to some pan-social masculine conspiracy to keep women in their place. Incontestably, in their youth and adulthood men are creatures of the perimeter; and in the remainder of this chapter we will consider the ways in which this and other central dimensions of masculinity play out in the versions of fatherhood across the life cycle of men.

This special role of the father, to be *close from a distance*, reveals itself soon after the infant's birth. Niles Newton, basing her argument on cross-cultural research, asserts that mothers are central in the experience of the infant—whether a boy or a girl—and that fathers play an auxiliary, supportive postnatal function.[4] Newton argues that coitus, birth, and lactation—the three major expressions of female sexuality—are also strikingly vulnerable, prone to shut down in the face of outer threat. In order to reach their reproductive goal, these maternal activities all require external buffering and protection, most often provided by men. Newton cites ethnographic descriptions of young mothers in South Africa, the Middle East and China, all pointing to a standard pattern of maternal engrossment with the infant, in an intense bond that can persist through the first years of the child's life. At all these sites, the infant sleeps next to the mother and is nursed at the first sign of restlessness. Nursing takes precedence over any potentially competing activity. The mother can devote herself almost exclusively to nurturing the child because she herself is being nurtured, "mothered," by her husband. The father's task is to maintain a protected zone, one in which his gratified and secure spouse can bring about the mother-child enmeshment that is so necessary to the infant's early emotional development. The father may not be on the physical periphery of his community, but he is, at this point, on the emotional periphery of his family, relatively excluded from the intense mother-infant link. At this early but crucial period, the father connects to the mother-infant dyad through intermediaries. He tends to identify, vicariously, with the mothering that his child receives from his wife—and with the "mothering" that his wife receives from him.

Achieving Distance via the Father

At the outset of life, this mother-child merger—a continuation in psychological terms of the intrauterine umbilical link—is necessary for the infant's future psychosocial development, which must be away from the mother. Assured of a stable home base, the infant can begin to explore its world and to provoke change in it. Thus, human development proceeds by paradox, in a dialectical fashion: The almost exclusive mother-child bonding that is so crucial in the first year of life prepares for its own negation, in the period of early autonomy, during which the child practices psychological and physical separation from the mother. During this pivotal exploratory period, the linear arrangement of the family—father tends the mother, and mother tends kids—begins to break down. The father, *because* he is different from the mother, *because* he betokens the desired distance from mom, and because in his own way he *also* nurtures, becomes a psychological "object," a *presence* in the emotional life of the separating child. The linear arrangement gives way to the family triangle: Daughters fall in love with their daddies, and sons—even while they love and revere him—take the father as a kind of rival for the mother's affection. In either case, in step with the child's development, the father's role in the family has taken on a new and special meaning. As an alternate, less proximal figure of strength and provision, one who matches the child's growing need for distance, the father becomes a magnet, a way-station on the child's road outward to the world, and away from the mother. The father is still responsible for providing physical security, but at this point—even under conditions of affluence and assured supplies—he can become a vital agent in the child's emotional life. If the father can maintain a vivid and distinctive presence, then at this time of early mother-child separation, he will support the maturation of daughters as well as sons.

On the whole, sons have a more pressing need to separate psychologically from the mother. There are good reasons for this gender difference. If the species is to continue, daughters are much more likely than sons to follow—at least for some significant period—the mother's domestic and biological destiny; the daughter can continue to know herself as the mother's daughter without significantly prejudicing her future adult role as a mother in her own right. But sons are pointed toward a different fate, toward a life on some version of the perimeter, beyond the edge of the mother's domestic world. From here on, we will concentrate on the male narrative and on how he fares.

Like daughters, boys start out as creatures of the domestic world, as sons of their mothers. But early on, they must diminish their ties to her and prepare for the extra-domestic paternal role, in large part among men. At some point, the son has to redefine himself, from being the son of his mother to being the son of his father. This crucial baptism can only come about if the father is strong in his own right, and *different* from the mother. Because he is strong, because he has exclusive sexual rights with the mother, because he is invested in the son, then he is worthy of the son's love but also of his envy. Eventually, realizing that he cannot defeat the father and that it is too dangerous to even try, the son will abandon the Oedipal rivalry and will attempt instead to acquire the father's envied strength in more realistic ways: through identification, imitation, and apprenticeship, rather than by conquest. He comes to terms with the paradox of male power: By submitting to the father's discipline and authority, the son can eventually inherit his power. Given some assurance via his internal "father," the superego, that he is in touch with the father's powers, the son begins to feel the glow of strength and resource in himself. Given this assurance that he could survive—psychologically, at least—on his own, the son can begin to accomplish the necessary detachment from the mother. He will still love and respect her, but he will no longer desperately *need* her.

Summing up, in order to separate from the mother, in order to eventually be a provider to others, the son needs a father whose strengths distinguish him from the mother's, and in spheres that are socially separate, and often physically distant, from the mother's domain.

An important study by Margaret Huyck, based on in-depth data from older, stable families in a Chicago suburb, supports the argument: Fathers who are absent in the emotional sense, fathers who are "maternal" rather than distinctively paternal, fathers who are the mother's androgynous twin cannot foster the boy's developmental transition from being mother's son to being father's son.[5] Sons of physically or psychologically absent fathers do separate from the mother in the physical and social sense. They leave home; they find girlfriends or wives; but because they have not separated in the psychological sense, they bring the maternal transference with them into the marriage and turn their spouse into another "mom."

This special arrangement can stabilize these dependent men, but only if the wife cooperates and only as long as the supply of maternal surrogates lasts. These mother's sons are put at risk in the post-parental years when their now older wives—having raised their kids—begin to defect from the mothering way. They still share the husband's bed, they still get the meals out, but their feelings toward their husbands have changed. They are still willing to be the wife but not the husband's mother. They have established psychological distance while still retaining physical closeness. In so doing, the older wife has imposed, on the needy husband, a separation from the maternal presence that he himself has never before encountered, expected, or initiated. This belated separation from mom can precipitate the much-debated "mid-life crisis" in vulnerable men. In order to hold the wife's attention and keep her in a nurturing way, predisposed men can develop significant somatic symptoms. Through them, they say to the wife, "If you don't want to take care of *me*, at least be caring toward my liver or toward my heart."

Their symptoms also bring them to the attention of clinic personnel, internists, and nurses. For such men, nurses can be the final mother surrogates of the life cycle. In short, failures of early separation can—via a nurturing wife—be compensated for a long time, but they eventually declare themselves, often quite catastrophically, in response to the "normal" distancing and separations of the post-parental family.

But in the normal course of development, the son who has closed out the rivalry with his father still conserves love and respect for him. He can go on to learn from his father and from other authoritative figures: uncles, older brothers, teachers, coaches. This is the so-called "latency period"—the time when the child, no longer distracted by powerful appetites or fears, can devote himself to the rapid acquisition of new learning, new skills. The school, stocked with fellow students and teachers, becomes a society in its own right, alternate to the family.

Fathers and the Rites of Passage

The preteen period represents the calm before the storm. The onset of puberty shakes up the psychological status quo of latency: The personality is subject to tectonic shocks as the body moves toward sexual maturity and adult physical powers. Human psychology recognizes no mind-body dichotomy; the expanding, surgent body sends hormone-driven shock waves through the whole psychological system. Boys are suddenly thrust into adult bodies, even as their emotional life regresses to a more primitive form. The Oedipal struggle with the father is revived, but now in a more dangerous form: The pubertal boy's challenge to the father is no longer the grandiose delusion of a physical and mental midget; now it is backed up by a body that can be more powerful and a mind that can be quicker than the father's. In effect, the growing boy's future commitment to destiny on the perimeter is put at risk by puberty: He is prone to challenge the father, to reject the father's way, to turn again toward the mother and her ways.

This pubertal transition is universal, and most viable cultures have developed fairly predictable ways to ensure that the biological transition to puberty does not lead to social crisis, in the form of aggravated adolescent rebellion. Particularly in traditional societies, the whole age-grade of male elders is mobilized to back up the father's threatened authority, to help the boy complete the migration away from the mother, and to turn him back toward the perimeter and toward the ways of men. The biological father helps the son achieve the first vital separation: from the mother. The collective fathers are required to bring about the second great separation: from the family as a whole and even from the physical precincts of the home community.

Now the pubertal son deals not only with his own father but with his father's colleagues, the elders and fathers of his community, and ultimately, through them, with the ancestral fathers of his people. The collective fathers arrange an ordeal, a rite of passage, through which the pubertal son is consecrated to these various forms of paternity. The rite of passage takes as many forms as there are distinct cultures; it can range from penile subincision with cowry shells as practiced by Papuan natives to the bar mitzvah ceremonial of Orthodox Jews.

In all cases, the young candidates are exposed to a trial, usually under the attentive, critical gaze of the assembled senior men, who watch for signs of weakness. John Whiting and Irving Child found that the severity of the ordeal varied, across cultures, with the length of the breast-feeding period.[6] Because the ritual is a passage away from the mother, and since late weaning implies a strong maternal bond, then a stringent ordeal is required to break it. By the same token, if the boy is too visibly frightened or tearful, then he has not passed the test: He has cried for his mother, he still belongs to her world, and he has not been reborn—as a father's son and junior colleague—into the company of men. But if the lad endures with some grace and fortitude, then he has begun to make it as a man: He is one of the "twice born," adopted as a son of the collective fathers and as an age-grade brother of the initiates who have endured with him. Success in the passage ritual demonstrates that the young man has the fortitude necessary for risky assignments beyond the boundaries of the community.

Besides testing his fitness, the rite of passage provides the initiate with "brothers": the age class of young men who are bonded to him through the ritual. These brothers represent the piece of the community that will go with him on his journeys beyond its borders.

But even more important, the ritual begins the attachment to some totemic sponsor, whose supernatural powers—his "medicine" or his *mana*—will also provide the initiate with luck and protection on the road. In other words, the rite of passage extends the idea of paternity beyond the biological father, into the collectivity of community elders, and finally beyond them to the ultimate fathers—the spiritualized ancestors and the mythic fathers of the people and their world. Through such dramatic rituals, the boy experiences the essential unity of the biological and spiritual fathers, the connection that Glenn Stanton celebrates in chapter 14.

Typically, a culture is rooted in an origin myth: a story of how the People, at a time of trial and supreme danger were sponsored, rescued, and rendered special by the intervention of unordinary—usually supernatural—beings. The typical puberty ritual recapitulates this drama. Like his people in the origin myth, the candidate is in a liminal condition, a state of emergency; and if he survives the ordeal, it is because he—like his folk in the founding myth—has found favor with a totemic sponsor. As a young child, he became for a time the son of his natural father; now, as a youth, he becomes—via the ritual—the protégé of some favoring deity. The earlier, post-Oedipal alliance with the biological father endowed the son with some sense of inner resource, allowing him to separate from the protective mother. This later affiliation with the spiritual fathers gives the son the courage that he needs to separate, physically, from the community as a whole: from the nurturing mothers again, from the biological fathers, and from the community foster fathers as well. More importantly, the cosmic connection refreshes the candidate's sense of inner resource—the conviction of having captured some substance of the totemic fathers—that will help him to become, with confidence, a father in his own right. Knowing that he can leave the home and the community, knowing that he can live off his own psychic substance and even be a source of security for others, the son can look toward mating, marriage, and fatherhood. Like his father before him, he can court a woman; he can attempt the frightening but exciting voyage into her body; and—secure in his manhood—he can return to the domestic world, the world of women, of the mothers, not as a needy child, but as a mate and as a providing father.

Erik Erikson said deprivation per se is not psychologically destructive; it is only deprivation without meaning, without redeeming significance, that is psychologically destructive. Human cultures, whatever particular forms they might take, have a great and universal function: to endow the routine sacrifices of human parenthood with high significance and dignity. Without culture—as we can see all around us—children are at risk, and too often from their own resentful parents. But when the young man has been linked—through his father and through the rituals managed by the fathers—to some part of the myth on which his culture is founded, then he too can become an adequate father. Rather than seeming to limit his freedoms, the state of fatherhood will grant him a special dignity, an *identity*, precisely *because* of the significant sacrifices that this condition demands.

The World without Fathers

What happens when—as in our American case—this transmission belt of the father's substance into the son's breaks down?

There appear to be four major outcomes; and minor qualifications aside, none of them are good. Thus, poorly fathered sons are less likely to separate from their mothers; as a consequence, fearing entrapment, young men become so vulnerable to women that they end by avoiding them, brutalizing them, or both. Inadequately fathered young men inseminate women but avoid *fatherhood*. Lacking a good superego, these men find strength not in the law but in criminality, and much of their violence is pointed at women. Father's sons may patronize women, but they also protect them. "Mama's boys" are most likely to prove their manhood—as in the "fatherless" inner city—by savaging women. They violate those who represent, outwardly, the shameful, feminine part of themselves.

Finally, in ever increasing numbers, young men stay home with their mothers, but they do not—by becoming fathers in their own right—help daughters in their turn to become mothers.

The deconstruction of fatherhood in our own society can lead to abortive, often destructive attempts to achieve separation from the mother and to gain— without fathers—the sense of inner resource usually provided by adequate sires. When sons cannot achieve psychological distance from the mother, they will either cling to her and her surrogates or they will in compensation amplify, often violently, their physical and social distance from her. They may become vagrants and swell the ranks of the homeless; through delinquency, they may shock and provoke the mother to the point where she drives them out of the home; or they might find impersonal replacements for the mothers in the form of addicting substances. Booze and drugs can provide, at least temporarily, the sense of inner resource, of "high," that makes it possible for sons—at least temporarily—to tolerate the sense of separation from the mother. When there is no strong father to aid the son in this developmental task, then he will too often turn to the kinds of "righteous" substances which—temporarily at least—fill him with the sense of strength and goodness.

Men who have not separated psychologically from their mothers find it hard to enter into closeness with women. Such intimacy always carries the risk of losing the intimate other, the unique one who cannot be replaced. They believe it is better to look for good feelings in impersonal substances—booze and drugs—that cannot be used up, that can always be replaced.

Multitudes of young men have recently discovered another, more drastic means for achieving social distance from their mothers, while at the same time avoiding fatherhood: the homosexual community. Again, like liquor bottles or drug vials, homosexual sex tends to be impersonal and its participants tend to be replaceable to each other. In the gay community, as with other centers of addiction, one can find pleasure without risking intimacy and the possibility of irreplaceable loss. At the same time, distance has been gained from the mothers. The homosexual world is a camp of men that excludes—even mocks and caricatures—the "breeders," the dangerous mothers.

Finally, in the absence of reliable fathers and elders, young men try to create their own puberty rituals and administer to each other their own initiations. In the parental society, the tests of manhood are administered by the male elders and are in the service of lawfulness, order, and male productivity. But when the tests are conducted by unsupervised gangs of adolescent males, the candidates must prove courage, usually through their defiance of the law; their passage is not into responsible manhood but too often into the world of the criminal. Instead of curbing antisocial rebellion, the puberty rites of teenage gangs too often augment it.

The Ultimate Fathers and the Final Passage

Fatherly beings, spiritual in nature, stationed in their own realm beyond the pragmatic community, are necessary to endorse the final passage of the male life cycle: from vigorous manhood to old age, and finally from life into the farthest country of death.

In the traditional community, senior post-parental men can achieve great status, not because of their physical strength and ferocity but, paradoxically, because of their relative mildness. Typically, *they*, rather than young men, are interlocutors between the community and its gods. If your community is in trouble, you do not send young Prometheus to ask for God's mercy. He will steal God's fire and make matters worse; but old men, instead of offending, will humbly pray for divine grace and—as in the founding myth—the weak elders become recipients and vessels of the healing powers.

There exists, then, a generational rule of some universality that compensates the traditional aged for their losses of physical power by the acquisition of supernatural power. Young men kill with edged weapons, but older men can kill with a curse. Lucien Levy-Bruhl observed that in the preliterate folk society the old man is "encircled by a kind of mystic halo," an essence so pervasive that his body parts and even his excrement can become the residence of *tabu* power.[7]

Leo Simmons, ethnogerontologist, provides this observation:

> It was not strength or brawn alone that won in battle or staved off bad luck or healed the dreaded disease; it was a special power, mysterious and most potent in the hands of old men and old women who have survived all these dangers . . . Not *all* magicians were old, but superannuation and the supernatural were very commonly and closely linked.[8]

Simmons reports many examples of the older man's awesome *tabu* powers, the most striking coming from the Hottentot of Africa, where the old men initiate young men, who have passed their early life among women, into manhood. The climax of the rite comes when the old man urinates on the candidate, who receives the urine with joy, rubbing it vigorously into his skin. His old sponsor then tells the candidate that he will increase and multiply and that his beard will soon grow. Clearly, in this case, even the urine of the old man has heroic power, the *mana* of the patriarchal phallus through which it passed. In the most concrete sense, it "marinates" the young man with the powers of the old man, thus bringing the lad in his turn to manhood. Here we see, unequivocally, the strong face of aging, the face that is hidden from us in our own secular, contra-parental, contragerontic society.

In sum, whether by virtue of their special weakness or their special strength, traditional elders are *elected*. While young men live on the physical perimeter of the community, to contain and capture the forces of ordinary nature, the old men retreat physically to the interior, domestic zone. But once having established a secure home base, they can again move out, not to the physical borders, but to the spiritual perimeter of the community, there to fend off the bad power and to harvest the good power of the gods. The seeming withdrawal into domesticity is a stage in the developmental dialectic, the precondition for a subsequent advance—an imaginative leap outward to the supernaturals.

Older men discover in the supernatural fathers the strength that they no longer find within themselves. They use prayer to beseech, for themselves and for the people, their fire from the gods.

When older men lose—usually under conditions of secularization and urbanization—their cosmic connection, they also lose the sense of an assured center, within themselves; and they fall away from the high status of *elder,* down to their modern condition: "the aged." Aging men, by contrast to elders, lack the sense of connection to the totemic fathers. Without that inner assurance, they cannot easily decouple from tokens of prestige and vitality that originate outside of themselves, for example, in their employment and social roles. Thus, they do not suffer illness—the loss of the body—easily, and they find it difficult to retire from the power and honor of gainful work. The late life depressions that afflict many of our aged express, symptomatically, their discovery of senescent emptiness. These aged do not inspire or strengthen younger men; on the contrary, they may frighten and even disgust them.

But the elders of traditional societies, or of traditional sub-cultures within our secular society—because they are bridgeheads between the community and its father-gods—can give up the lesser potencies of youth. They can even endure, with some grace and courage, the final separation from life. As they accomplish these final transitions, senior men—elders—become the social "fathers" that young men need as they face their own life tasks and their own entry into fatherhood.

Notes

1. David L. Gutmann, *Reclaimed Powers: Towards a New Psychology of Men and Women in Later Life* (New York: Basic Books, 1987).

2. Abraham Kardiner and Ralph Linton, *The Psychological Frontiers of Society* (New York: Columbia University Press, 1945).

3. George Murdoch, "Comparative data on the division of labor by sex," *Social Forces* 15 (1935): 551-53.

4. Niles Newton, "Psycho-social aspects of the mother/father/child unit" (paper presented at meetings of the Swedish Nutrition Foundation, Uppsala, 1973).

5. Margaret H. Huyck, "Development and pathology in post-parental men" in *Older*

Men's Lives, ed. Edward Thompson Jr. (Thousand Oaks, Calif.: Sage, 1994).

6. John W. Whiting and Irving Child, *Child Training and Personality: A Cross-Cultural Study* (New Haven, Conn.: Yale University Press, 1953).

7. Lucien Levy-Bruhl, *The "Soul" of the Primitive* (London: Allen and Unwin, 1928).

8. Leo W. Simmons, *The Role of the Aged in Primitive Society* (New Haven, Conn.: Yale University Press, 1945).

Chapter Fourteen

The Core of the Universe

Glenn T. Stanton

> *For the most important thing we can know about George MacDonald is that . . . an almost perfect relationship with his father was the root of all his wisdom. From his own father, he said, he first learned that Fatherhood must be the core of the universe.*
> —C. S. Lewis
> *George MacDonald, An Anthology*

Early in 1990, two men were driving from Boulder to Pueblo along a striking span of Colorado interstate that parallels the beautiful Front Range of the Rocky Mountains, while engaged unknowingly, in a portentous conversation. As the two friends sought to pass the time, one asked the other, "What is your life dream?" Each of them, having reached a remarkably high level of success in their respective careers, knew the question was touching an issue that transcended mere professional achievement. What kind of imprint of eternal significance did they desire to leave given the time remaining in their natural lives? That man, then University of Colorado football coach Bill McCartney, told his good friend Dave Wardell that he wanted to be a part of bringing thousands of men together for the purpose of publicly renewing and committing themselves to the promises they have made to God, their wives, their children, and their fellow citizens.

The seed of this dream started to sprout when later that year 72 men gathered to pray for this effort called Promise Keepers. In 1991, the first year a

Promise Keepers event was held, more than 4,000 men gathered in the basketball arena on the University of Colorado campus to renew and declare their commitments to God and their roles as husbands and fathers. Two years later, the event attracted 50,000 men, and in 1994, events were held in seven cities attracting nearly 300,000 men. Those numbers swelled to 700,000 men in 13 different sites in 1995 which were dwarfed by the 1996 numbers of an estimated 1.5 million men attending Promise Keepers events in 27 cities.

The efforts that work from a Christian perspective to unite fathers with their children in a meaningful way are successful for a simple but important reason: They have a special and unique vibrancy to them. That vibrancy is the context they offer for fathering. They help father and son see they are each participants in a much larger story, a meta-narrative of a Father and Son which is the foundation of the Christian story.

While Promise Keepers is by far the largest and most popular work of this nature, it is certainly not the only spiritually-motivated effort to help men become better fathers and husbands. The Catholic Church has been engaged in this work for decades. Perhaps the oldest and most successful efforts of this type is the Cursillo (a Spanish word meaning "little course"). The emphasis of a Cursillo weekend for men is learning what it means to live under Christ as a man, a husband, and a father. It uses a peer-based format with laymen teaching and encouraging other men. The Catholic Church also has parish-based programs for fathers as well. One of the oldest and fastest growing of such groups is the "Men of Saint Joseph" in Manchester, New Hampshire. These are men who meet regularly to teach and inspire one another in their roles as husbands and fathers. The Men of Saint Joseph focus on enhancing five key areas of a man's life: worship of God, prayer, the sacrament of reconciliation, spending time with family, and accountability to God and other Christian men.

The Southern Baptist Convention has a vibrant program aimed at men and their family roles. This program, called Legacy Builders, is presented in the form of a weekend retreat and has impacted the lives of nearly 6,000 men in its short-15 month history. Jim Burton, director of Men's Ministries for the Southern Baptist Brotherhood Commission, explains that while they are interested in promoting the idea that dads be physically present with their children, their emphasis is specifically focused on encouraging a vibrant emotional and spiritual engagement between a father and his children.

"We teach men that the measure of manhood is not in power, position, or money," explains Burton, "but in the ability of that man to confront and shape the kind of legacy he is giving to his children." While working primarily with men in local churches, Burton says their Legacy Builders program with prison inmates is growing steadily.

The brightest spot regarding fatherhood work in the black community is, in my estimation, the brightest spot in the fatherhood movement itself. Charles Ballard and his National Institute For Responsible Fatherhood and Family

Revitalization turn the hearts of young fathers to their children. Begun in the heart of Cleveland's Hough neighborhood in 1982, his work is so successful that the Joint Center for Political and Economic Studies and the Ford Foundation have assisted Ballard in establishing his program in five major cities throughout the U.S.[1] While Ballard's work is not expressly Christian, it is strongly Christian in its motivation and essence. Whenever Charles Ballard speaks about himself and his program, he will often preface his remarks with these simple but forceful words: "To understand Charles Ballard and his work is to understand the power of the gospel of Jesus Christ."

It would be incorrect to conclude from this chapter that only Christianity can produce good fathers and that only Christianity has anything substantive or instructive to say about fatherhood. Such conclusions clearly contradict observable reality. There are many faith traditions that are wonderfully instructive about fatherhood and these faiths have and are producing excellent fathers. However, Christianity and its doctrine of the Trinity uniquely provides a practical metaphysic for fatherhood.

This effort to recover the ideal of fatherhood—the fatherhood movement—is dedicated to recovering the script of fatherhood where men are committed to and engaged in the lives of their children on a daily basis. The religious stream of the fatherhood movement, consisting of those working from the conviction of their Christian faith, is essential because it reminds us that the fatherhood script is an indispensable part of a much larger story: a "meta-narrative" that our society has practically lost and must recover. This chapter will address three main issues: (1) how our culture lost possession of the meta-narrative, (2) the significant role fatherhood plays in this story, and (3) why both need to be recovered.

This discussion is important and profitable to both Christian and non-Christian individuals and organizations of the fatherhood movement for two reasons. First, it is beneficial for those working from a faith perspective to understand that Christianity really does have something quite substantive to say about the societal importance of fatherhood because "Father" is more than merely a traditional or symbolic way of referring to God. Unpacking and understanding this truth will add philosophical breadth and depth to their work and allow them to bring more substance to the common table of the fatherhood restoring effort. Second, this discussion is helpful to the secular co-workers in the fatherhood movement because it offers them a window of understanding into the motivation and theological foundation of their faith-directed fellow laborers. This understanding is essential for genuine cooperation as well as for the cohesion and strength of a significant social movement.

Post-Modernity and the Loss of the Meta-Narrative

Few films capture the predicament of postmodern man as vividly as *Grand*

Canyon. It shows, in arresting fashion, how the chasm between what is right and what we do has grown as deep and wide as that great hole in Arizona. It communicates the same thing about our relationships with God and one another. The well-known line that captures the thesis of the film and the dilemma of postmodern man is uttered by Simon, a black tow-truck driver as he attempts to service his customer, a prosperous white immigration lawyer named Mack whose shiny Lexus has broken down late at night in a very bad section of Los Angeles. When Simon arrives on the scene, he finds five gang members have forced Mack from his car and are ready to help themselves to the vehicle and the rest of Mack's trinkets. Mack is sure he will be killed right in the middle of what was once called civilization.

Simon, anxious to do his job, is confronted by these young thugs who are unwilling to yield their new acquisition. Isolating the young, well-armed gang-leader who feels an overwhelming need to prove his manhood, Simon tries to persuade this neo-anarchist to allow him to do his job. In this, Simon experiences his neighborhood's descent into the purest state of nature Hobbes ever imagined. He protests with an even mixture of fear and frustration, "Man, the world ain't s'pposed to work like this. . . . This ain't the way it's s'pposed to be."

Simon is right, and here is why. In the beginning, God created as He willed and it was all very, very good. Humanity and the nature of things were as intended. Observing the world after the fall though, after our original parents made a conscious decision and exerted willful energies in doubt of God's goodness, we can now say with Simon, "This ain't the way it's s'pposed to be."

While the picture of humanity and the world was originally clear and distinct, it is now fuzzy. All has been affected. We, collectively, are not as we were meant to be. Our relationships have changed . . . with God, our neighbors, our spouses, our children, with everyone, even ourselves. We have become, in a very literal sense, disintegrated. We have come apart, detached from ourselves and the proper context for our lives. This abyss is as expansive as the Grand Canyon.

But as Man in the last few centuries has contemplated this divide and considered what to do about it, he has largely ended up in despair. This is "the crisis of our age" as Pitirim Sorokin, first chair and founder of Harvard's Sociology Department, posited: "It is a crisis in [our culture's] art and science, philosophy and religion, law and morals, manners and mores; in the forms of social, political, and economic organization, including the nature of the family and marriage—in brief, it is a crisis involving almost the whole way of thought and conduct of Western society."[2]

One key aspect of cultural disintegration is the disintegration of fatherhood. This disintegration of fatherhood is inextricably tied to the loss of a larger story or meta-narrative; hence, the recovery of fatherhood and the fatherhood script is impossible if the meta-narrative from which it originates is not also recovered.

To be sure, our culture's loss of any connection to a larger story has been slow but certain. This loss can be demonstrated and understood by looking at developments in two indicative disciplines: philosophy and the visual arts. They are indicative of this cultural shift in that the former impacts popular intellectual movements and the latter impacts movements in popular culture in general. We will look at a few leaders in these two disciplines, not as a survey of this trend, but merely as useful icons who mark our descent into the despair of postmodernism.

While most of these thinkers and artists would be classified as "modern," I offer another way of categorizing them. I list them as the beginning of the postmodern age because they reacted against, and initiated the move beyond, the Enlightenment which was the modern age. As Robert Jenson, theologian at St. Olaf College, has correctly pointed out, postmodernism is not a belief system in itself, but rather the death of modernism and the absence of anything substantive replacing it.[3] As we learn from these thinkers and artists, postmodernism is an empty stage that features a one-act play called despair.

In philosophy we observe despair in the works of Nietzsche, Wittgenstein, and Sartre. Nietzsche's madman in "The Gay Science" sought to shock modern man into living consistently with his worldview, which had no meaningful place for God. God was at best a symbolic fixture. As the madman entered the marketplace with his lantern trimmed, he cried, "I seek God! I seek God!" The madman was received as just that and mocked.

His audience derisively responds, "Why, did he get lost? Has he gone on vacation? Perhaps he is playing hide and seek. Or did he lose his way like a small child?"

In an instant, the madman transforms from timid seeker to self-assured prophet. Nietzsche explains, "The madman jumped into their midst and pierced them with his glances. 'Whither is God?' he cried. 'I shall tell you. We have killed him—you and I. All of us are his murderers. . . . God is dead, God remains dead. And we have killed him.'"[4]

The demeanor of the crowd is immediately transformed from one of sarcastic mocking to astonished offense. It was all right to live as if God was dead . . . as long as no one ever talked about it. Clearly, Nietzsche (if he is ever clear) is making a diagnosis more about the culture of his day than about the physical health and well-being of God. He was telling the people of his day they no longer had room for God in any significant part of their belief system. In effect they "killed" him, but were unwilling to dispose of the body. They were incapable of living consistently with the death of God and accepting the inevitable, but radical "transvaluation of values" this choice demanded.

After Nietzsche came Ludwig Wittgenstein who, with his seldom read but highly influential *Tractatus Logico-Philosophicus*, inspired the logical positivists

(who Russell Kirk says, were "suicidally bent upon establishing the impossibility of knowing anything"[5]). It appeared as if Wittgenstein had struck a serious blow to metaphysical speculation and that appearance has been long · lasting. Not only was God dead, as he related to any practical area of our lives, but any talk of him was nonsensical. In fact, according to Wittgenstein, any talk of things transcendently meaningful (beauty, truth, virtue, and ethics) is useless because these things are of a world beyond the strictly empirical domain of natural science. Wittgenstein begins his *Tractatus* with this simple proposition:
"The world is all that is the case."
Four propositions later he asserts:
"The facts in logical space are the world."
These primary observations, with others, led Wittgenstein to conclude:
"Most of the propositions and questions to be found in philosophical works are not false but nonsensical. Consequently we cannot give any answer to questions of this kind, but can only establish that they are nonsensical."
And therefore,

> The correct method in philosophy would really be the following: to say nothing except what can be said, i.e., propositions of natural science—i.e., something that has nothing to do with philosophy—and then, whenever someone else wanted to say something metaphysical, to demonstrate to him that he had failed to give a meaning to certain signs in his proposition. . . . this method would be the only strictly correct one.

Wittgenstein concludes his *Tractatus* in the simplicity with which he began:
"What we cannot speak about we must pass over in silence."[6]
The implication of this conclusion is immensely powerful. Wittgenstein taught the world that if man jumps the fence and ventures outside the yard of the empiricists, all he finds on the other side is a vast silence. There is nothing there for him. He finds no answers to his deepest and most honest questions, no meaning for his life, no direction. He finds nothing to help him deal with his disintegration . . . just silence, a vast, dark, empty, cold silence. The conclusion is despair. Postmodern man ends with despair because finite man still desires transcendence. He knows there must be meaning beyond the yard of empiricism. But what?
Enter the existentialists and Sartre as the spokesman for them. Sartre recognized that finite man's existence comes to nothing but absurdity if it has no infinite integration point, and of course, for the secular existentialists, there was no infinite reference, only silence. However, for Sartre, man creates meaning and purpose by authenticating himself by some randomly self-selected course of action. Regarding the morality or end of such a chosen action, there is silence. Therefore, the existentialist can decide to authenticate himself by building houses with Habitat for Humanity for a summer or taking a high-powered, bolt-action rifle to the nearest bell tower and unloading a few rounds

on unsuspecting passers-by. The only guide is the internal moral compass that we each set according to our own bearings. Or, as Karl Jaspers, the German existentialist, believed, man must have an ineffable "final experience" which brings, in its own way, special meaning to our lives. In *Grand Canyon* this was exactly the experience of the kitsch, blood-and-guts film-producer named Davis while he lay in the hospital. He was recovering from a serious gunshot wound to the leg obtained from a street hood in exchange for Davis' Rolex watch. As he lay in his hospital bed, he witnesses the skyline of Los Angeles transformed from shimmering darkness to iridescent orange in the beauty of a single sunrise. It was this indescribable and otherwise meaningless experience that gave "meaning" to Davis's life. It was his final experience, changing the context and direction of his life . . . at least for a while.

As ideas are known to do, this conclusion of despair didn't stay confined to the community of philosophers. It drifted over into other areas of culture. Despair manifested itself in the visual arts.

Pablo Picasso marks the beginning of what is truly postmodern art in that he really began to communicate disintegration with his presentation of human forms in unhuman, "grotesque" ways. Picasso followed logically behind and went beyond Cezanne, Gauguin, and van Gogh who painted humanity in unrealistic ways, but still discernible as humanity.

Although Picasso moved the game-piece further down the board to despair, it was the Dada school and their chief spokesperson, Marcel Duchamp, who represented the utter despair of Wittgenstein in the visual arts. His famous *Nude Descending a Staircase* was a total abandonment of the human form, while the low point of this despair was found in Marcel's "readymades" in which he took everyday objects like salvaged urinals or bicycle wheels and simply declared them art. Marcel's work really serves as a powerful bullhorn to popular culture, screaming Wittgenstein's message with great intensity that the universe is silent regarding ultimate meaning.

Implications of the Loss of Meta-Narrative

Now, what does this brief (and albeit simplistic) survey of the recent developments of philosophy and art have to do with the problem of fatherlessness, especially from a religious perspective? To understand how the man on the street in this century is thinking we must observe and learn how the intellectuals and artists thought in the last century. These cultural gatekeepers contributed to what James Davison Hunter calls "indeterminacy"—defined as "a rejection of any foundation by which coherent agreements could be reached." This indeterminacy leaves us with what Hunter labels the "aesthetization of morals."[7] This reduction of ethics to a matter of individual taste is similar to what a friend of mine calls the "absolutism of my personal experience." It is the idea that what I choose to do is objectively right for me and the only universal wrong is to offer a negative appraisal of anyone else's personal choice. When Nietzsche's madman has helped us over our initial shock and we start to live as if God really is dead, this is all we are left with: indeterminacy, the aesthetization of morals, and the absolutism of my own experience. Evidence of this is found in the classification of Duchamp's urinal as art.

These characteristics are deep in the warp and woof of the common man's moral decision-making process, and they rule the day. Although my local butcher, baker, or gun-toting gang-banger are not intellectual disciples of Wittgenstein or the Dada school, they are direct heirs of that heritage. They unwittingly live by default what those before them believed by conviction. The ideas of the previous century's intellectual elite trickle down and infiltrate the understanding and actions of today's "Joe Lunch-box." Jenson calls this phenomenon a "historical lag." He explains, "the general culture has now caught up with postmodernism, and for the experience of the fact, we should turn from the elite art to the streets of our cities and the classrooms of our suburbs. . . ."[8] We should turn to our men and their families.

How has the aesthetization of morals affected our family lives and structures? Each of us are making up our own individual stories or life narratives as we go along because we have lost sight of any larger story. For an increasing number of those in society, these self-directed narratives are not turning out to be happy stories. We see this in the epidemic of men impregnating women without any commitment to the idea of fatherhood, not to mention any commitment to their child's mother in the form of marriage. We see this in women conceiving children without any commitment to the father and in too many cases, no commitment to the child. In a society that has lost the meta-narrative for its story and thus a larger context upon which to live it, all we are left with is existentialism and random chance. Even for the virtuous postmodern, the mantra of our age is a hollow devotion to "practice random kindness and acts of senseless beauty." Beyond this, there is no overarching, metaphysical basis for ethical decision making.

The Need: A Metaphysic for Fatherhood

The fatherhood movement correctly realizes that humanity must be reconnected to a larger predefined script called fatherhood because without it, children suffer and society weakens. This view, however, is wholly pragmatic and unwittingly keeps us confined to the backyard of logical positivism. Pragmatics is not all there is. There is, there must be, more than social utility. The movement must recognize the other side of the fence with the realization that the metaphysical world is not silent, but rather, has much to tell us about the nature and importance of fatherhood. The movement must see itself in light of the meta-narrative. Only then can it realize two things: There is a metaphysic for fatherhood, and this metaphysic answers the very important question of why fatherhood is the core of the universe.

For Christians, this meta-narrative is found in the tradition of Christianity whose God is Father and the Messiah His Son. This statement presents us with two broad and foundational truths that demand our exploration. The first regards the nature of God as Father. The second is the history and nature of His relationship with the Son.

The Nature of God the Father

Regarding the nature of God as Father, it is intriguing that of all the ways the God of the universe could choose to relate to His people, He chose to come to us and identify Himself as Father. What kind of Father is He?

As we begin to address the Fatherhood of God, it should be noted that I am aware of the gender debate over God's personality and the argument for inclusive language posited by some theologians. However, the idea of God as Father is important and must be retained because it is descriptive of His character and His interaction and relationship with His children. It is wrong thinking to reject the idea of God the Father because our earthly fathers were failures. There is no causal connection here. We must instead see God as the Heavenly Father who calls our earthly fathers (and ourselves) to accountability as proper fathers. Dianne Tennis, author of *Is God the Only Reliable Father?* explains the benefits of viewing God as Father:

> Holding on to that reliable Father God can be a way of informing and challenging the status quo. For human fathers are experienced as unreliable. . . . By contrast, God as Father does not abandon. If God the Father is reliable, he surely expects reliability from earthly fathers. And so can we! A reliable Father God is a source of calling men into fathering. A reliable Father God is a source of judgment on unreliable sexual arrangements, a source of hope for women and for the fatherless, a symbol emerging out of our loss. . . .[9]

Jurgen Moltmann adds to this idea of Father God as the supreme model for fathering:

> In patriarchal societies, this experience of freedom brought about a modification in the image of God . . . [However,] [w]here God as Father was emphasized, the Christian patriarchy arose, that is, paternalism tempered by compassion and love from above. Where the compassion and unconditional love were taken as the beginning, there existed a fundamental critique of the domination of father, that is, a de-theocratization of the understanding of God and democratization of the authority of men. . . . Those who set their bearings on Jesus and call out "Abba" with him, have broken with law and the power systems of patriarchy.[10]

There are, I believe, four general conceptions most people have of God the

Father. The first one, to use an earthly analogy, is what David Blankenhorn describes as the old father. "The Old Father wields power. He controls. He decides. He tells other people what to do. He has fangs. This aspect of his character generates suspicion and resentment." This is the popular caricature of the dads of the '50s, and we are compelled to believe they were like this because, as Blankenhorn explains, "so many of their highly educated children have written books saying so."[11] Many view God this way, as the overbearing, arbitrary, power-wielding, patriarch who rules by fear and oppression.

The other extreme is to see the Heavenly Father as the new father, a kind of Alan Alda personality: highly compassionate, nonjudgmental, and intensely sensitive. This conception is similar to what J. B. Phillips calls the "heavenly bosom."[12] By earthly comparisons, this is the new dad of the '70s and '80s. This conception of God limits him to a kind and comforting, but largely impotent, grandfather. This ideal has arisen largely as a response to the previous patriarchal, dominance conception of God. Both are extreme conceptions and like most extremes, are flawed.

The third option about God is as a Father merely in the sense that he acted only procreatively and his interaction ends there. He is the Father of the deistic proposition who spread His seed in creation and has now fled the scene. He is the cosmic deadbeat dad.

The fourth view is what I would call the orthodox Christian view of God, and, I posit, is the more favorable conception. First, we should realize that when God communicates Himself as Father, this is not just a random, sentimental, or even convenient symbol, but the word carries real meaning. It communicates something profound about the very nature and character of God. It tells us He is more than the God who acts in procreation alone. He is present, engaged in our lives, and exhibits personality in this relationship.

The orthodox view of God is a middle-road between the two extreme conceptions we have just discussed. He is the Father who exhibits both strength and love. John, the Apostle, tells us in his first letter to the Church that God has bestowed upon us such a great love that "we should be called children of God" (1 John 3:1). It is God's tremendous love for us as His children that compels Him to pursue us with great passion. That pursuit and redemption is the story of the Old and New Testaments.

Redemption touches the other side of the character of the Father because it presupposes separation. According to historic Christian teaching, humanity's first parents transgressed the clear commandment of God and as a result, sin has infected the entire human race. Therefore, because of God the Father's love for humanity, He makes humankind aware of and judges wrongdoing according to Proverbs 3:12: "For whom the LORD loves He reproves, Even as a father, the son in whom he delights." For God to be a Father of love, He must necessarily be a Father of judgment, for that is what loving fathers do. They draw boundaries. They have standards. They spell out clear expectations and have real consequences when these are transgressed. God is love, but He is not only love. He is corrective, but He is not only corrective. He is both, for His love is corrective and His correction is loving. He provides the preeminent example for us as fathers. He is present in our lives and is simultaneously providing for our deepest needs: love and redemption.

But He is not a Father merely in some abstract, descriptive sense. Beyond the character of God Himself, like any father, His Fatherness is distinguished and understood by the nature of His relationship with His Son.

The Father-Son Relationship

Christianity is a tradition that gives us a cosmogony that is instructive regarding the very being of human relationships. That is because, in the Christian ideal, relationship was prior to everything else that existed. As Francis Schaeffer, Christian philosopher and author, illuminates consistently throughout his work, even though the narrative of the biblical cosmogony begins quite literally "In the beginning," there was something existing prior to "In the beginning." This something must necessarily mark the core of the universe and is found in the existence of the Trinity. This has foundational implications for us because the nature of this "primary relationship" is one between a Father and His Son.[13]

There are a number of characteristics that mark this primary relationship. Genesis 1:26 tells us that God declared, "Let Us make man in Our image, according to Our likeness. . . ." This statement teaches us a number of things about the nature of this relationship. First and foremost, He is the Father who is there with the Son. Second, they are engaged with one another. They have a relationship marked by communication and cooperative interaction in the creative process. These are the first two characteristics of this primary Father-Son relationship: presence and communicative, cooperative engagement.

This relationship between Father and Son is not one of static existence or even mere creative, cooperative energy, but marked by deep intimacy. A vivid picture of this relationship is found in John's record of Christ's conversation with the Father just before his arrest by the Roman cohort. In the midst of this very intimate and passionate interaction between the Son of God and His Father, we learn in John 17:24 the history of this most devoted of all relationships. Jesus proclaims, "Thou didst love Me before the foundation of the world." The Father loved the Son and the Son loved the Father before there was anything else, and this love was intense.

Jesus referred to God as Father 170 times in the New Testament, and in nearly all of these instances, Jesus used the word *Abba*, a very intimate Aramaic form of address. It is found in the lexicon of children's babble to signify the primary source of trust, protection, and provision. Its English counterpart is *daddy* or *papa,* a word that conveys the most intimate of all adult-child relationships.[14] This tells us two more important things about this primary relationship: It was and is intensely intimate as well as prior to everything else.

This relationship between Father and Son was of such a nature that Christ was able to assert (John 10:30) that He and the Father were one. He did not mean oneness in some undifferentiated monistic sense, but that the Father and Son were of one mind and spirit. There exists an eternal unity between them. They are eternally present with one another;[15] they are cooperating in their sacred work; they communicate; and they have love for one another. Their self-chosen identities have meaning only in relation to one another. Fatherhood means nothing without relation to a son, and the son cannot exist without a father.

The point is that while relationship was prior to "In the beginning" so were all the characteristics of that primary relationship: presence, communication, unity, cooperation, intimacy, and love. Our knowledge of the Father's existence and His relationship with Christ the Son tells us we do not have to write the fatherhood script ourselves. We have a wonderful and perfect model to follow.

The Importance of Communication and Love

The two key components to this primary relationship are communication and love. In communication is the implication of presence and cooperation. In love is the implication of affection, intimacy, and community. Schaeffer explains the impact of this: "This means that love and communication are intrinsic. And hence, when modern man screams for love and communication (as he so frequently does), Christians have an answer: There is value to love and value to communication because it is rooted into what intrinsically always has been."[16]

Fatherhood and the nature of that perfect primary Father-Son relationship must be, as MacDonald learned from his father, the core of the universe. It is this truth that solves the predicament of postmodern man and his disintegration. It not only says that we can be integrated again to ourselves and to others, but that we can be integrated to a much larger story than ourselves and the observable, sensory world. This is the larger story of God, the Father who is there, who loves us and dwells in the vastness of eternity.

This primary relationship communicates many things to us with great force. It says to Wittgenstein and his heirs that the universe is not silent. It says to Duchamp and his followers that the world is not without meaning and beauty. It says to the street thug that there is a social order. It says to the sexual profligate that there is relational accountability and consequences for irresponsibility. It says to the community reformer that there is more than just pragmatics.

Finally, it says to humanity that the longing you feel down in the deepest parts of your being for connection with a loving, caring, involved, corrective father is no fluke. You have it because you are part of a universe that has relationship as its core. You were created out of that relationship, and you will not rest until you are rejoined with it.

In the meantime, while we reside in this "shadowland" before the Great Divorce, as C. S. Lewis described it, humanity needs to live in an earthly model of the heavenly picture. We know through an absolute wealth of social science data that the well-being of children and society is intimately related to the prevalence of involved men acting as fathers. We must no longer see this as merely a sociological fact, but also as a spiritual truth. As David Popenoe mentions in chapter 2, "It is not likely that we can have permanent moral renewal without society-wide religious reawakening." The recovery of fatherhood can be the first step toward the reintegration of ourselves and our society, but only if we see it in the context of the meta-narrative.

Not only is fatherhood the foundation of this meta-narrative, but as David Gutmann informs us so eloquently in the previous chapter, fatherhood is, anthropologically speaking, the means of connecting coming generations to this larger story. "When older men lose . . . their cosmic connection," Gutmann says, "they also lose the sense of an assured center . . . and they fall away from the high status of *elder,* down to their modern condition: 'the aged.' Aging men . . . lack the sense of connection to the totemic fathers." Fathers cannot export to their children and community what they do not possess, and likewise, fathers—elders—who do possess this important connection, naturally export it through the living of their lives.

In support of Gutmann's assertion, Larry Crabb Jr., author, professor, and regular Promise Keeper speaker, addresses this intergenerational transmission and says the Christian Trinitarian message on fathering is instructive to the fatherhood movement because it tells men that by living for something more important than his children, a father gives them the most precious gift any father can give—the gift of transcendence. His ongoing involvement with them keeps them from feeling abandoned and worthless. His passion for God keeps them from thinking they are the center of life. Instead, they are drawn to join him in pressing on toward the highest goal. . . . We're not the point; none of us is. God is. There is a story bigger than ours, a story that transcends every other. And until we see our story as only a subplot in that eternal drama, we'll never see its meaning.[17]

The fatherhood movement can only succeed as it sees itself as something larger than merely a pragmatic social reform movement. It must see itself as an effort to connect men and society with what is metaphysically the core of the universe: fatherhood. Only then can men be properly motivated to become good fathers, and only then can fatherhood recover its full meaning.

Notes

1. The five cities are Nashville, San Diego, Milwaukee, Washington, D.C., and Yonkers, New York. For more information on Ballard's work see Charles Ballard,

"Prodigal Dad: How We Bring Fathers Home to Their Children," *Policy Review* (winter 1995): 66-70.

2. Pitirim A. Sorokin, *The Crisis of Our Age* (New York: E. P. Dutton and Co., Inc., 1941), 17.

3. Robert W. Jenson, "How the World Lost Its Story," *First Things* 36 (1993): 19-24.

4. Friedrich Nietzsche, "The Gay Science," in *The Portable Nietzsche,* ed. Walter Kaufmann (New York: Penguin Books, 1959), 95.

5. See Russell Kirk, *The Enemies of the Permanent Things* (Peru, Ill.: Sherwood, Sugden and Company, 1988), 97.

6. Ludwig Wittgenstein, *Tractatus Logico-Philosophicus* (London: Routledge and Kegan Paul, 1961), 7, 37, 151; see propositions 1, 1.13, 4.003, 6.53, and 7.

7. James Davison Hunter, "After Modernity, What?" *Echoes* 1 (spring 1996): 1.

8. Jenson, "How the World Lost Its Story," 20-21.

9. Dianne Tennis, *Is God the Only Reliable Father?* (Philadelphia: Westminster Press, 1985), 9.

10. Jurgen Moltmann, "I Believe in God the Father: Patriarchal or Non-Patriarchal Reference," *The Drew Gateway* 59 (1990): 3-25.

11. David Blankenhorn, *Fatherless America: Confronting Our Most Urgent Social Problem* (New York: Basic Books, 1995), 89, 105. Blankenhorn does something bold and unique by defending the '50s father as a pretty decent guy. He says he worked hard, came home every night for dinner, went to countless Little League games, and set moral boundaries and requirements for his children. In short, he was present and engaged in the lives of his children, which is more than we can say for many of his sons.

12. J. B. Phillips, *Your God Is Too Small* (New York: Macmillan, 1961), 33-37.

13. For a more thorough discussion of the Trinity and its implications in Christian thought, see Catherine Mowry LaCugna, *God for Us: The Trinity & Christian Life* (New York: HarperCollins, 1991).

14. Moltmann, "I Believe in God," *The Drew Gateway,* 3-25; Robert Hamerton-Kelly, "God the Father in the Bible and in the Experience of Jesus: The State of the Question," in *God as Father?* ed. Johannes-Baptist Betz and Edward Schillebeecks (New York: Seabury Press, 1981), 95-102.

15. The *only* time that Christ did not refer to the Father as *Abba* is, according to Psalm 22, when the Son was separated from the Father at his death on the cross. See Moltmann, "I Believe in God," 18.

16. Francis A. Schaeffer, *Genesis in Space and Time*, vol. 2 of *The Complete Works of Francis A. Schaeffer: A Christian Worldview* (Wheaton, Ill.: Crossway Books, 1982), 14.

17. Larry Crabb Jr. and Larry Crabb Sr., *God of My Father: A Son's Reflection on his Father's Walk of Faith* (Grand Rapids, Mich.: Zondervan, 1994), 9, 43. This book is a wonderful presentation from a very gifted thinker and writer on how one father has had a rich and lasting impact on his children.

Chapter Fifteen

A Few Ideas: Voices for Fatherhood

Allan Carlson

Legislators should rewrite tax policy to deliver massive tax relief to families with dependent children. Three ways to do this are below.

First, triple the value of the personal exemption to $7,500 per person, indexed to inflation. A personal exemption of this magnitude provides an appropriate adjustment to both market failure toward families and the state's socialization of children's time through mandatory school attendance and insurance value in caring for aged parents. Under today's regime where the costs of raising children are largely private, the individual logically concludes: "Let someone else go to the trouble and expense of raising the children who will pay for my retirement." Unlike welfare benefits, this exemption gain comes solely through a sheltering of earned income, thereby giving encouragement only to responsible procreation.

Second, restore income splitting, as it existed in the U.S. tax code between 1948 and 1963, within a more progressive rate structure. Income splitting treats marriage as a partnership, with each spouse holding claim to exactly one-half of the couple's community income, and half of the tax liability. Within progressive tax rates, the results are to encourage marriage, and discourage divorce. Or...

Third, create a flat tax system where the only offset is the $7,500 per person exemption, leaving marriage and the presence of children as the only tax shelters. While a pure flat income tax at rates above five percent is detrimental to family bonds, large per-capita exemptions limited to persons related by blood, marriage, or adoption eliminate most negative outcomes.

Martha Farrell Erickson

The Internet is becoming a significant tool for responding to the call for a fatherhood movement.

One of the first major websites to focus on fathers was FatherNet (http://www.cyfc.umn.edu), an information and networking system set up by the University of Minnesota's Children, Youth, and Family Consortium. FatherNet provides resources, from research articles to advice on parenting; links fathers and professionals through a directory of programs, experts, and organizations; and facilitates informal support and information sharing among fathers through on-line discussion groups. It links users to other father-focused websites, including the following:

> At Home Dad Newsletter (http://www.athomedad.com)
> Full-Time Dads (http://www.slowlane.com)
> National Center for Fathering (http://www.fathers.com)
> National Fatherhood Initiative (http://www.fatherhood.org)

Leaders and front-line workers in fatherhood programs, as well as researchers and policymakers, can benefit from the Internet by sharing findings and gleaning information. Innovative strategies for supporting fathers can spread quickly through the Web. (For example, within weeks after FatherNet announced Minnesota's Allina Health System program that gives "Daddy Kits" to new fathers, the program was adapted by a Michigan group.) Journalists who frequent the Web for story leads can seek out father-friendly organizations, increasing media coverage. Fathers from all walks of life, however, not just those well-off economically and educationally, must have access to equipment, know-how to navigate the system, and literacy skills to make effective use of the vast array of material found therein.

Chester E. Finn Jr.

Schools can strengthen fatherhood in three key areas.

First, provide effective outreach to fathers. Signal that fathers, as well as mothers, are welcome anytime. Have room "fathers" and room "mothers," or ask fathers to volunteer in the gym. Notices about school events from parent-teacher conferences to fundraisers should be sent to all parents, including noncustodial ones. Ask both parents to sign report cards. Make conference times convenient for working parents. Devise communication methods that do not depend on face-to-face contact or limited school hours.

Second, use curriculum to support fatherhood. Books and stories with pro-father content should be included as a matter of course, much as classrooms might use materials about ethnic and religious groups and other prominent social and demographic elements. Students could compose letters to dad, write essays about dad, research dad's biography, or construct maps to where dad works.

Third, use mentoring programs or activities for those students lacking involved fathers. Hire more male teachers and counselors. Use tutoring programs that engage male college or high school students, and set up Big Brother programs that match youngsters in need with willing volunteers. When organizing father-child school events, encourage children's fathers to "adopt" other students for the occasion. Invite grandfathers, uncles, and other male relatives and family friends to participate in school-related activities when dad cannot attend.

William A. Galston

Building on federal welfare legislation, state legislatures could reform welfare to promote involved fatherhood. Here are five ideas.

First, establish, with the help of the National Campaign to Prevent Teen Pregnancy, a state-level teen pregnancy coordinating council to promote partnerships between schools and community-based programs.

Second, provide substantial transitional assistance, up to age 21, for young couples who get married before the birth of their first child and stay married.

Third, experiment with conditioning some or all benefits on regular, significant paternal involvement with mother and child.

Fourth, experiment with conditioning some or all benefits on the mothers' good faith efforts, while pregnant, to identify the fathers of their children.

Fifth, encourage courts and administrative agencies to structure child support obligations to allow a father to substitute in-kind assistance (say, 20 hours of child care each week) for a portion of the money otherwise due the mother.

Stephen Goldsmith

In September of 1995, the City of Indianapolis launched a series of initiatives to confront directly and comprehensively the problem of family breakdown. The Rebuilding Families program, established with the support of Indianapolis' leading religious, nonprofit, and social service organizations, employs a wide range of strategies to reduce single parenthood and improve the support and economic opportunities available to vulnerable families.

First, we aimed to combat the "normalization" of teen pregnancy and reinforce the understanding that teen pregnancy is wrong. Through a program called *A Promise to Keep*, for example, older, self-confident teens serve as powerful messengers for promoting chastity among teens and compete with teen idols in the media who endorse premarital sex.

Second, we targeted school policies that failed to discourage teen pregnancy.

We called upon school officials to send a clear message that adult behavior nets adult consequences by precluding teen parents from participating in school athletic activities. Although school officials thus far remain firmly against the policy, we continue to apply pressure by releasing the number of births per school to spur parental and teacher concern.

Third, we attempted to balance the flood of messages in popular culture that implicitly endorse premarital sexual activity. Local sports figures appeared in advertisements encouraging abstinence than ran on local television stations, on video kiosks in malls and in movie theaters throughout the city.

Finally, we stepped up child enforcement with a program we call Job or Jail. Judges refer unemployed, noncustodial fathers to organizations such as the Father Resource Center, which teaches parenting and makes job placements. Individuals who refuse to participate are given community service jobs. If they refuse private sector employment and community service work, they go to jail. This combination of assistance and enforcement helps fathers provide for their children while demonstrating in no uncertain terms our commitment to holding them accountable.

Michael C. Laracy and Irene Skricki

Here are six ideas for expanding employment opportunities to help low-income men become better fathers and better candidates for marriage.

First, create on-the-job training programs within the private sector through the use of job-focused tax incentives like enterprise zones to expand our nation's economic growth to the inner cities.

Second, create decent-paying public sector jobs in the inner cities, perhaps along the model of the Works Progress Administration of the 1930s.

Third, provide disadvantaged young men with training in "soft skills" of appropriate workplace attitudes and behavior.

Fourth, modify the Earned Income Tax Credit to increase benefits to noncustodial parents who meet their child support obligations and to two-parent, two-worker families.

Fifth, grant noncustodial parents access to social service benefits, such as, Medicaid, Job Training Partnership Act, and food stamps, in exchange for active involvement with their children.

Sixth, social service organizations should hire male staff and institute outreach efforts to encourage young men to take advantage of the services.

David L. Levy

To help all families who experience divorce, leaders should work in two major areas.

First, the legal system should be reformed. It should encourage mediation rather than litigation. Seventy to 80 percent of parents in mediation arrive at a mutually agreeable solution on financial, property, and child issues. If a judge must be called upon, he or she should be experienced in family matters. Law schools must provide better education for judges by giving them a background in psychology or family dynamics. Judges should be taught to understand Parental Alienation Syndrome in which parent A gets the child to join in the attack on Parent B.

Second, parents of divorce need to be made aware of their children's needs. Children need to feel loved, to be given hugs and compliments, to feel safe with both parents, and to see parents treat each other with respect. Ex-spouses should treat each other as they want to be treated, looking for the face of their child each time they see each other.

Children need to have both parents actively involved in their lives. Each parent contributes something unique. As parents juggle work, home, and the other aspects of life, their children should come first. Divorced parents must be more sensitive because children's basic trust and loyalty of their parents to each other and to them have been challenged by the divorce itself. Parents should make their relationship with their children as positive as possible by spending quality time at home with them, joining in their activities, being a partner in their schooling, and taking an active role in their health.

William R. Mattox Jr.

Here are four ideas with which legislators ought to confront America's divorce problem.

First, promote justice for "no-fault" spouses. While "mutual consent" is required for the marital union to be consummated, one spouse can end the marriage without the other's consent—even if the spouse wanting out has no evidence of fault on the part of the other spouse. Legislation is needed to ensure that people who have met their public commitments are not taken advantage of in divorce and custody proceedings.

Second, end "divorce-on-demand" by lengthening waiting periods. Such waiting periods would provide couples an opportunity to cool off and gain some perspective about their relationship and provide counselors more time for various interventions to work.

Third, require couples with children to establish joint parenting plans prior to divorce. In addition to serving the needs of any involved children, this might cause some couples to rethink their decision to break up as they realize the degree to which they will continue to be connected to their child's other parent. Fourth, require "informed consent" prior to finalizing a divorce. David Larson, president of the National Institute for Healthcare Research, recently compiled an inch-thick report of more than 300 studies showing that divorce is strongly linked to a wide range of health-related problems. Just as doctors are often required to give an advance warning to patients about the possible risks of surgery or the harmful side effects of medication, Larson believes family mediators and court officials should be required to review research findings on the negative consequences of divorce with couples contemplating divorce.

Michael J. McManus

A national movement called Marriage Savers™ has been planted in 80 cities as of Febuary 14, 1998, by up to 300 pastors from 30 denominations. Divorce rates are down in at least 12 of those cities, by as much as 40 percent in Modesto, California. The core idea is this: In every church there are couples with strong marriages who really could be of help to other couples, but have never been asked, inspired, or trained to come alongside another couple and be of assistance.

Cross-sections of pastors are creating a Community Marriage Policy™, a trademarked action plan in which churches agree to do the following five things.

First, require a minimum of four months marriage preparation, including the use of a premarital inventory.

Second, provide engaged couples with older mentoring couples in solid marriages to administer the inventory and talk through the issues it brings to the surface.

Third, strengthen existing marriages by encouraging attendance at Marriage Encounter or by organizing an annual retreat using Family Life videos for inspiration.

Fourth, save troubled marriages by creating a Marriage Ministry of mentoring couples whose marriages once nearly failed due to such problems as adultery or alcoholism—to help those now threatened by divorce to make it.

Fifth, create a Stepfamily Support Group using couples who have successfully blended families with kids from a previous marriage to help those new to this family form.

To help recruit mentoring couples, 3,000 churches are using a Marriage Savers Resource Collection that includes six videos, a copy of the 342-page book *Marriage Savers* and the 112-page *Insuring Marriage,* plus a 96-page Leader's Guide to a 13-week Sunday school course.

We can help create Marriage Saver Churches that implement a loving ministry in which every marriage is cherished and strengthened to go the distance. St. Paul said pastors are to "equip the saints for ministry" or "train God's people for service" (Eph. 4:12). What more important ministry is there than saving marriages? And Marriage Savers, those with strong marriages, can be found in every congregation. Didn't Jesus send his disciples out "two by two"? (Luke 10). Could that not be husband-wife, husband-wife?

What God has joined together, let the church hold together.

J. Neil Tift

Civic leaders could dedicate themselves to weave together the fabric of community service with that of family involvement in five ways.

First, establish awards for businesses that provide the best environments for working fathers.

Second, sponsor a father's forum to help the local community determine the current needs of men as parents and then put programs in place to address them. Father's Resource Center and the National Fatherhood Initiative can provide resources for designing forums.

Third, establish mentor programs, such as Father-to-Father, a program created by Vice President Gore, that by pairing inexperienced fathers with experienced fathers, provides one-on-one opportunities to model healthy parenting techniques.

Fourth, take a leadership position in establishing community programs that focus on fathers' roles in ending family violence. Create networks with other men's organizations to promote non-violent problem solving. Spread the message: Raise our families, not our fists.

Fifth, encourage members to speak to schools and at brown bag lunch seminars for workplace employees on appropriate topics, such as the potential impact of teen pregnancies on families and students' futures or how to teach values to children.

Malcolm V. Williams and Matthew D. Buckwalter

Here are nine policy ideas for employers to use in reducing work-family conflicts which in turn increase employee productivity.

First, allow employees time off to be good dads. Encourage eligible fathers to take advantage of the Family and Medical Leave Act and to take time off upon the birth or adoption of a child. Give fathers a reasonable number of opportunities to attend special family events, such as a school play or sporting event, without fear of reprisals.

Second, implement a "Take Your Child to Work Day."

Third, encourage the use of flex-time, according to state laws, so workers may choose to exchange overtime hours for days off.

Fourth, allow some workers to tele-commute while providing management and technical support to prohibit these workers from feeling alienated and uninformed.

Fifth, initiate fatherhood education seminars just as businesses provide education on enhancing computer skills or organizing one's life. Fatherhood is a learned skill. Groups, such as the National Fatherhood Initiative, offer workplace-based fatherhood skills training.

Sixth, promote the use of leave banks, allowing workers with unused vacation or personal days to donate their extra time to employees who may need additional time to fulfill family obligations and commitments.

Seven, allow shift swapping so employees may exchange their work shifts with other employees. Fathers will then be free to take a child to the doctor, attend a child's sporting event, or meet other family obligations.

Eight, provide comprehensive health benefits that cover needs of growing families, and set up flexible spending accounts that allow employees to shelter some of their income from taxation for out-of-pocket medical expenses or child care.

Nine, allow job sharing where two part-time employees share the tasks of one full-time position.

Ruth A. Wooden

Those who wish to promote fatherhood through the media would do well to remember three things.

First, be not timid or leery of criticism. Tackle the controversy, even create it, for then the media will be interested in the story. Where controversy is involved, the press thrives. Media coverage by one network, magazine, or newspaper spawns more media coverage.

Second, give writers, broadcasters, and program sponsors facts about the fatherhood problem, and challenge them to create programs that treat fatherhood with dignity and importance. Use letters and meetings to communicate both cooperation and praise.

Third, speak out often about current trends, research, and surveys, using local dads to highlight or illustrate the message.

A Call to Fatherhood

One

We come together because we believe that every child deserves a loving, committed, and responsible father. Not just the lucky ones, but every child. We come together from across the nation and across the political spectrum, all dedicated to ending the curse of fatherlessness that is maiming our children and coarsening our society. We come together, inspired by the best of the American tradition, ready to declare our goal and seek the support of our fellow citizens. We come together to call for a fatherhood movement.

We come together as men and women, black and white, rich and poor, all committed to restoring the institution of loving fatherhood as the birthright of every child, the sure expectation of every mother, and the joyful obligation of every man who helps to bring a baby into this world.

We come together as liberal and conservative, and from every region of our nation, all believing that what divides us is far less important than what unites us. We come together as Catholics, Protestants, Jews, and Muslims, all asking for God's blessing and guidance, and all pledging our time, our energy, and our best ideas to achieving the great task before us.

We come together knowing that our journey will be difficult, but knowing we can do no other. For, whatever its other advantages, a society in which large and growing numbers of adult males cease to nurture their offspring is a failing society. Unless we reverse the trend of fatherlessness, no other set of accomplishments will arrest our social decay.

We come together to give life and energy to a fatherhood movement.

Two

We view fatherlessness as one of the greatest social evils of our generation. It is a principal cause of deteriorating child well-being in our society. It is also an engine driving our worst social problems, from crime and teen pregnancy to child poverty and domestic violence.

Today's mass separation of American fathers from their children is historically unprecedented. Never before in our nation's history—never before in any nation's history—have so many men been so radically estranged from their children and from the mothers of their children. Never before have so many children grown up without knowing what it means to have a father. Never before has the "father's name" on so many birth certificates been left blank.

Americans are increasingly familiar with the grim statistics of fatherlessness. Today, nearly 40 percent of all American children do not live with their fathers. Before they reach age 18, more than half of all U.S. children will spend at least a significant part of their childhood living apart from their fathers.

This astonishing absence—this large and growing hole in our society where fathers ought to be—stems demographically from two related behaviors: unwed childbearing and divorce. Today, never-married mothers and the males who impregnate them account for one of every three babies born. And though divorce rates have declined somewhat since the late 1980s, the United States remains by far the most divorcing society in the world. The result of these trends is the weakening of marriage and the loss of fatherhood for millions of families.

For at least the past decade, Americans have engaged in a loud and often needlessly polarizing debate over "the family" and "family values." Much of this debate has centered on the issue of family structure: whether or not the steady defection of fathers, and the resulting proliferation of mother-headed homes, amounts to a social crisis, a legitimate cause for alarm.

While we come from various points along America's political spectrum, we agree on one central point: The family debate of the past decade is over. It is over because everyone, or at least almost everyone, now realizes that fathers matter—not just a little or in some circumstances—but a lot, for every child. Increasingly, all our studies concur, all our experiences show the spread of fatherlessness in our generation is a profound social crisis and a legitimate cause for alarm.

The question, then, is no longer whether we have a problem. The question today is what, if anything, we are prepared to do about the problem. What we intend to do is express our commitment to giving life and energy to a fatherhood movement.

Three

We seek a fatherhood movement that is broadly based, overcoming barriers of income, race, and politics, represented by many voices and organizations, active at every level of our society.

We seek a fatherhood movement that is united by one idea: for every child, a loving, committed, and responsible father.

We seek a fatherhood movement that demands and teaches higher standards of male responsibility for children and higher standards of male accountability to mothers.

We seek a fatherhood movement premised upon equal regard between men and women, mothers and fathers, husbands and wives.

We seek a fatherhood movement that, while reaching out to divorced and unwed fathers, nevertheless, discourages divorce and unwed childbearing and insists upon the importance of marriage as a life goal worthy of the respect and commitment of young Americans.

We seek a fatherhood movement that recognizes cultural renewal and economic opportunity not as opposing ideas, but as two complementary and essential strategies for one idea: the fatherhood idea.

Four

The fatherhood movement we seek is more than a prediction, more than merely something that we hope will happen. It is already beginning to happen, embodied in the pioneering work of devoted leaders and new initiatives across the country.

Some of our colleagues focus on fatherhood education and skills training, reaching out especially to new fathers, teaching them better ways to care for their children and challenging them to become better men. We are thankful for their work and seek their leadership in a fatherhood movement.

Some of our colleagues work for economic empowerment and greater economic opportunity for young fathers, especially young African-American fathers in our urban centers, recognizing that, for many young men, economic prospects and fatherhood prospects are closely related and mutually reinforcing. We admire their accomplishments and seek their leadership for a fatherhood movement.

Some of our colleagues, rightly appalled by the prevalence of child poverty in this land of plenty, work to improve the conditions and life prospects of poor children and their families, recognizing that all children need fathers who will provide for and nurture them, and that the spread of fatherlessness in our generation is inextricably linked to the spread of child poverty. We share their goal and seek their leadership in a fatherhood movement.

Some of our colleagues are leaders in efforts to strengthen marriage. Some are active in efforts to reform no-fault divorce laws, advocating measures such as extending the waiting periods for divorce, requiring counseling for troubled marriages, and, in cases of contested divorces, ending or restricting the unilateral right to divorce on demand. Other colleagues are leaders in initiatives to improve marriage counseling and family therapy, urging their fellow professionals to approach their work with a bias in favor of marriage. Still others, working through their houses of worship and guided by the biblical premise that "God hates divorce," are leaders in efforts to improve pastoral counseling for engaged couples, create better faith-based marital enrichment programs, and establish new community-wide ecumenical policies aimed at strengthening marriage and reducing divorce. We are grateful for their work and seek their leadership for a fatherhood movement.

Many of our colleagues are women and men of religious faith, reminding us, in their words and deeds, that being a good father is part of being a righteous man, and viewing the renewal of fatherhood as one necessary part of a larger and much-needed spiritual rebirth in our society. Some of these leaders are active in the Promise Keepers. Others organized buses to the Million Man March. Others work as leaders in local men's ministries and other congregational and denominational outreach efforts. We are thankful for these important leaders, and seek their leadership in a fatherhood movement.

Some of our colleagues are community organizers. Some are business leaders. Some are scholars. Some are philanthropists and foundation officers. Some are writers and public speakers. Some are active in the mytho-poetic men's movements. Some are child and family advocates. Some are leaders in efforts to organize and represent the interests of divorced fathers who seek to remain active and committed parents. Some of our colleagues work in the media. Others work primarily with young people. Still others work in government and in public policy. All of these leaders have much to contribute. We seek their participation in a fatherhood movement.

Across the country, new leaders and new initiatives are emerging. The potential for real social change exists; the seeds of a movement have already been planted. The challenge now is to build further on these inspiring foundations—to deepen our commitment, to grow in wisdom, to win measurable victories, and to work together in trust and mutual commitment, striving to create a whole that is greater than the sum of its parts. The challenge is to ignite a broad-based movement for fatherhood.

Five

In an increasingly fatherless society, we come together to dedicate ourselves to a proposition: for every child, a loving, committed, and responsible father.

Some will disagree with this goal. Others, including many experts, will concede that fathers are important but will urge us to accept the current trend of fatherlessness with dispassion and equanimity. Rather than getting preachy about fatherhood, they will advise us, focus instead on more realistic solutions. More child support payments from absent fathers. More support for single mothers. More attempts to find adequate substitutes for the missing fathers.

While affirming the importance of reaching out with compassion to single mothers and fatherless children, this work, although necessary, is not sufficient. The truth is that the contributions fathers make to the well-being of children are unique and irreplaceable. Consequently, we assert that any fatherhood movement worthy of the name must ultimately be guided by this overriding goal: loving fathers for all our children. We assert this goal, not because we are unrealistic or lack compassion, but precisely because we wish to be as realistic and compassionate as possible.

We propose to reverse the deterioration of childhood by bringing back the fathers, for unless we reverse the trend of fatherlessness, we see no realistic possibility of reversing the current downward spiral for children.

Passivity in the face of this crisis is indefensible. We come together because we believe that our society can change for the better. We come together to call for fatherhood.

Endorsers
Affiliations listed for identification purposes only

KENT AMOS,
PRESIDENT
Urban Family Institute
Washington, DC

DAVID BLANKENHORN,
PRESIDENT
Institute for
   American Values
New York, NY

JEAN BETHKE ELSHTAIN
University of Chicago
Chicago, IL

CHARLES BALLARD,
PRESIDENT
National Institute for
   Responsible Fatherhood
Washington, DC

REGINALD BRASS,
FOUNDER/PRESIDENT
My Child Says Daddy
Los Angeles, CA

CHESTER E. FINN JR.,
PRESIDENT
Thomas B. Fordham
   Foundation
Washington, DC

PETER BAYLIES,
PUBLISHER
At-Home Dad Newsletter
North Andover, MA

ARMIN BROTT
Columnist and Author
Berkeley, CA

RABBI BARRY FREUNDEL
Kesher Israel Congregation
The Georgetown Synagogue
Washington, DC

REED BELL,
CO-DIRECTOR
Pensacola Fatherhood
   Initiative
Gulf Breeze, FL

KEN CANFIELD,
PRESIDENT
National Center for Fathering
Shawnee Mission, KS

MAGGIE GALLAGHER
Author and Columnist
Briarcliff Manor, NY

HENRY B. BILLER
University of Rhode Island
Kingsington, RI

ALLAN CARLSON,
PRESIDENT
Rockford Institute
Rockford, IL

WILLIAM A. GALSTON,
EXECUTIVE DIRECTOR
National Commission on Civic
   Renewal
College Park, MD

GREG BISHOP,
HEAD COACH
Boot Camp for New Dads
Irvine, CA

DON EBERLY,
DIRECTOR
Civil Society Project
Harrisburg, PA

ROBERT HAMRIN,
PRESIDENT
Great Dads Seminars
Fairfax Station, VA

RONALD K. HENRY
Men's Health Network
Washington, DC

WILLIAM MARSHALL,
PRESIDENT
Progressive Policy Institute
Washington, DC

MITCHELL PEARLSTEIN,
PRESIDENT
Center of the American
  Experiment
Minneapolis, MN

SYLVIA ANN HEWLETT,
PRESIDENT
National Parenting Association
New York, NY

WILLIAM R. MATTOX, JR.
Family Research Council
Washington, DC

FATHER VAL J. PETER,
EXECUTIVE DIRECTOR
Father Flanagan's Boys' Home
Boys Town, NE

WADE F. HORN,
PRESIDENT
National Fatherhood Initiative
Gaithersburg, MD

JAMES F.X. McLOUGHLIN,
PUBLISHER/EDITOR
Full Time Dads
Clifton, NJ

DAVID POPENOE,
PROFESSOR
Rutgers University
New Brunswick, NJ

JEFFREY JOHNSON
National Center for Strategic
  Nonprofit Planning and
  Community Leadership
Washington, DC

MICHAEL MEDVED,
Film Critic and Author
Mercer Island, WA

HILLARD POUNCY,
CONSULTANT
Wallingford, PA

JEFF KEMP,
EXECUTIVE DIRECTOR
Washington Family Council
Bellevue, WA

STUART MILLER
American Fathers' Coalition
Washington, DC

ROBERT RANNIGAN,
DIRECTOR
Father Development Project
Charlottesville, VA

RONALD L. KLINGER,
FOUNDER/PRESIDENT
Center for Successful
  Fathering
Austin, TX

RON MINCY
Ford Foundation
New York, NY

RON ROSE,
PRESIDENT
Faith in Families Ministry
Fort Worth, TX

DAVID LEVY,
PRESIDENT
Children's Rights Council
Washington, DC

JOSEPH NADEL,
FOUNDER/DIRECTOR
First State Fatherhood Center
Dover, DE

GLENN STANTON
Focus on the Family
Colorado Springs, CO

PAUL L. LEWIS,
PRESIDENT
Family University
San Diego, CA

MICHAEL NOVAK
George Frederick Jewett
Chair in Religion and Public
Policy
American Enterprise Institute
Washington, DC

BISHOP JAMES STANTON
Episcopal Diocese of Dallas
Dallas, TX

GLENN C. LOURY,
DIRECTOR
Institute on Race and Social
  Division
Boston, MA

MICHAEL O'DONNEL,
FOUNDER/EXECUTIVE
DIRECTOR
Center for Fathering
Abilene, TX

EDDIE F. STATON,
NATIONAL PRESIDENT
MAD DADS, Inc.
Omaha, NE

RICHARD LOUV
Author and Journalist
San Diego, CA

MARVIN OLASKY
University of Texas
Austin, TX

TOM TANCREDO
Independence Institute
Golden, CO

J. NEIL TIFT,
DIRECTOR
Fathers' Resource Center
Minneapolis, MN

WAYLON WARD,
PRESIDENT
Dallas Center for Fathering
Dallas, TX

ROBERT WOODSON,
PRESIDENT
National Center for
Neighborhood Enterprise
Washington, DC

P. JAY TRAY
Penn-Trafford School District
Harrison City, PA

BARBARA DAFOE
WHITEHEAD
Author and Social Historian
Amherst, MA

JUDITH WALLERSTEIN
Center for the Family in
Transition
Belvedere, CA

RUTH WOODEN,
PRESIDENT
The Ad Council
New York, NY

Index

About the Contributors

David Blankenhorn

David Blankenhorn is founder and president of the Institute for American Values, a private, nonpartisan organization devoted to research, publication, and education on issues of family well-being and civil society. He helped found the National Fatherhood Initiative and serves on its board as well as the board of National Parenting Association. The author of *Fatherless America: Confronting Our Most Urgent Social Problem* (Basic Books, 1995), Mr. Blankenhorn is the married father of three children.

Armin Brott

Armin Brott has written extensively on the subject of fatherhood for the *New York Times Magazine, Newsweek, Washington Post, Redbook, Parenting, Child,* and other national publications. A contributing writer to *BabyTalk* magazine, Mr. Brott's latest book is entitled *A Dad's Guide to the Toddler Years* (Abbeville Press, 1998). He is the father of two daughters and lives with his family in Berkeley, California.

Matthew D. Buckwalter

From 1996-1997, Mr. Buckwalter was the director of the Virginia Fatherhood Campaign (VFC), the nation's first state-wide effort to emphasize the responsibility and importance of fathers in the lives of their children. Prior to his work as director of the VFC, Mr. Buckwalter worked in developing curriculum and fatherhood policies that encourage individual and community strength in personal and civic responsibility.

Ken R. Canfield

Ken R. Canfield is president of the National Center for Fathering, an education and research center in Kansas City. The Center provides resources for dads including a variety of training seminars, a quarterly full-color magazine and an interactive website. Dr. Canfield is the author of several books, including *The Heart of a Father* (Northfield, 1996). He and his wife have been married 20 years and have five children.

Allan Carlson

Allan Carlson is president of The Howard Center for Family, Religion and Society, a nonprofit study center located in Rockford, Illinois. He is the author of three books, including *From Cottage to Work Station: The Family's Search for Social Harmony in the Industrial Age* (Ignatius Press, 1990). Dr. Carlson is married and the father of four children.

Dan Coats

Dan Coats is a U.S. Senator from the State of Indiana. During his tenure in Congress, Coats has dedicated himself to examining the relationship of government to the family. Senator Coats chairs the Senate Labor and Human Resources Subcommittee on Children and Families. Recently, he authored the Project for American Renewal, a legislative package designed to encourage the revival of civil society. He and his wife have been married 32 years and have three children and two grandchildren.

Don Eberly

Don E. Eberly is president and founder of the Civil Society Project in Harrisburg, Pennsylvania, a project committed to civic and democratic renewal. He is also the founder of the National Fatherhood Initiative. Mr. Eberly is the author of *Restoring the Good Society: A New Vision for Politics and Culture* (Baker Books, 1994) and the married father of three children.

Martha Farrell Erickson

Martha Farrell Erickson is director of the Children, Youth, and Family Consortium at the University of Minnesota, a national resource to link research, practice, and policy for the well-being of children and families. Dr. Erickson works with Vice President Al Gore on family policy issues, with a special focus on the role of men in children's lives, the impact of media on children and families, work/family issues, and parental involvement in education. For the fifth consecutive year, Dr. Erickson is the co-sponsor of Vice President Gore's Family Re-Union policy conference. She and her husband have been married for 28 years and have two children.

Chester E. Finn Jr.

Chester E. Finn Jr. is the John M. Olin Fellow at the Hudson Institute where he co-chairs the Educational Excellence Network and directs the project on "Charter Schools in Action." He also serves as president of the Thomas B. Fordham Foundation. Dr. Finn is professor of education and public policy at Vanderbilt University. He is the author of 10 books, including *The New Promise of American Life,* co-authored with Lamar Alexander (Hudson Institute, 1995). Dr. Finn lives with his wife in Chevy Chase, Maryland.

Maggie Gallagher

Maggie Gallagher is an affiliate scholar at the Institute for American Values and a nationally syndicated columnist with Universal Press Syndicate. She is currently engaged on a year-long research project investigating teen pregnancy. She is the author of *The Abolition of Marriage: How We Destroy Lasting Love* (Regnery, 1996). She lives with her husband and two children in Westchester, New York.

William A. Galston

From January 1993 through May 1995, William A. Galston served as deputy assistant to President Clinton for domestic policy. Dr. Galston currently teaches in the School of Public Affairs, University of Maryland at College Park and is director of the University's Institute for Philosophy and Public Policy. He is senior advisor to the Democratic Leadership Council and the Progressive Policy Institute. His six books include *Liberal Purposes: Goods, Virtues, and Diversity in the Liberal State* (Cambridge University Press, 1991). He is the married father of one son.

Stephen Goldsmith

Elected mayor of Indianapolis, Indiana, America's 12th largest city in November 1991, Stephen Goldsmith has earned a reputation as one of the nation's most innovative mayors. He is active in crime reduction, bureaucratic reform, tax reform, regulatory reform, and jobs creation. While in office, Mayor Goldsmith implemented a $500 million infrastructure improvement program called "Building Better Neighborhoods."

David L. Gutmann

David Gutmann is an emeritus professor of psychiatry at Northwestern University Medical School where he teaches, supervises, and does psychotherapy. His most recent book, *The Human Elder: In Nature, Society, and Culture* (Westview Press, 1997) is a collection of his major articles on the normal and abnormal psychology of aging. Married for 47 years, Dr. Gutmann and his wife have two grown children.

Ronald K. Henry

Ronald K. Henry is an attorney in Washington, D.C., whose pro bono activities focus on issues of family law reform and child advocacy. Mr. Henry serves on the American Law Institute's Family Law Project and is chair of the Joint Custody Task Force of the American Bar Association's Family Law Section. Mr. Henry is also an advisor to the Uniform Law Commissioner's Drafting Committee on Interstate Child Custody Jurisdiction and Enforcement. He is the married father of three children.

Wade F. Horn

Wade F. Horn is the president and co-founder of the National Fatherhood Initiative, an adjunct faculty member at Georgetown University's Public Policy Institute, an affiliate scholar with the Hudson Institute, and a member of the U.S. Advisory Board on Welfare Indicators. From 1989-1993, Dr. Horn served as the Commissioner for Children, Youth and Families and Chief of the Children's Bureau within the U.S. Department of Health and Human Services. Dr. Horn also served as a presidential appointee to the National Commission on Children and as a secretarial appointee to the National Commission on Childhood Disability. Dr. Horn is the author of numerous articles on children's issues, and is author of *Father Facts* (The National Fatherhood Initiative, 1998) and co-author of the *Better Homes and Gardens New Father Book* (Meredith Books, 1998). Dr. Horn lives in Gaithersburg, Maryland, with his wife and two daughters.

Michael C. Laracy

Michael C. Laracy is a senior program associate at the Annie E. Casey Foundation, a national philanthropy devoted to improving the life outcomes of America's disadvantaged children, where he is responsible for the foundation's initiatives and research on income security, welfare reform, and the "New Federalism." He is the married father of two young daughters.

David L. Levy

David L. Levy is co-founder of the Children's Rights Council (CRC), a nonprofit organization dedicated to assuring a child the right to two parents and extended family regardless of the parents' marital status. Dr. Levy's publications include the edited CRC volume, *The Best Parent is Both Parents* (1993). He lives in Maryland with his wife, a son from a previous marriage, and a daughter from his current marriage.

William R. Mattox Jr.

William R. Mattox Jr. is a writer who serves on the Board of Contributors for *USA Today*. Columns written by Mr. Mattox for the *Washington Post* and the *Wall Street Journal* have been recent award winners in the Amy Foundation's annual writing contest. Mr. Mattox also contributes considerable research and advertising work for the Family Research Council, where he is currently spearheading a public service ad campaign that features married couples who have found that persevering through tough times deepened their love and strengthened their marriage. He and his wife live in Virginia with their four children.

Michael J. McManus

Michael J. McManus is a syndicated newspaper columnist writing on issues of ethics and religion and the author of several books, including *Marriage Savers: Helping Your Friends and Family Avoid Divorce* (Zondervan, 1995). As president of the Marriage Savers Institute, Mr. McManus seeks to inspire and equip married couples to become mentors and to encourage communities to develop marriage strengthening strategies in their areas. He and his wife have been married 32 years and have three children.

Ronald B. Mincy

Ronald B. Mincy is the senior program officer for employment and welfare in the Ford Foundation's Human Development and Reproductive Health Program. He monitors activities and policy discussions in employment training and welfare and makes recommendations for the foundation's grant making in these two areas. His most recent book is *Nurturing Young Black Males: Challenges to Agencies, Programs, and Social Policy* (Urban Institute Press, 1994). He is the father of two sons.

Mitchell B. Pearlstein

Mitchell B. Pearlstein is president of Center of the American Experiment, a conservative and free-market think tank in Minneapolis. Dr. Pearlstein is also chairman of Minnesotans for School Choice and the Partnership for Choice in Education. Along with Katherine A. Kersten, he is coauthor of a forthcoming collection of their newspaper and magazine columns, *Close to Home*. He and his wife have four children, ranging in age from 26 to 7.

David Popenoe

David Popenoe is co-director of the National Marriage Project, a research and public education initiative, at Rutgers University, New Brunswick, New Jersey, where he is also professor of sociology and former social sciences dean. Dr. Popenoe's most recent book is *Life Without Father: Compelling New Evidence that Fatherhood and Marriage Are Indispensable for the Good of Children and Society* (Free Press, 1996). He has been married for 39 years and is the father of two married daughters.

Hillard Pouncy

Hillard Pouncy is a political scientist and independent consultant to several projects on youth opportunity, employment training, and education reform. He has published recently on school-to-career and child support enforcement policy, including the article, with Ronald B. Mincy, entitled "Paternalism, Child Support Enforcement and Fragile Families" for the Brookings Institution. He lives in Wallingford, Pennsylvania.

Irene Skricki

Irene Skricki is a program associate at the Annie E. Casey Foundation, where she works on welfare reform and income security issues. Prior to her position at the Casey Foundation, Ms. Skricki was a program assistant in the Urban Poverty Program at the Ford Foundation. She lives in Baltimore.

Glenn T. Stanton

Glenn T. Stanton is the vice president for policy and culture at the Palmetto Family Council, a nonprofit organization in South Carolina dedicated to the preservation of the family. Mr. Stanton is the author of *Why Marriage Matters* (Pinon Press, 1997). He and his wife have been married 15 years and are the parents of four children.

J. Neil Tift

J. Neil Tift is the co-founder and director of the Fathers' Resource Center in Minneapolis, Minnesota. Currently, Mr. Tift also serves on the adjunct faculty of Metropolitan State University where he teaches ethics, family studies, and human service administration. In addition, he is a deacon in the Catholic

Church and a family mediator with the Mediation Center in St. Paul. Mr. Tift contributed a chapter on single fathers to the text *Working with Fathers*. He is a father of three, a foster father, and a grandfather of three.

Judith S. Wallerstein

Judith S. Wallerstein is an internationally recognized researcher in marriage and divorce. She is the founder of the Judith Wallerstein Center for the Family in Transition in Corte Madera, California, and is Senior Lecturer Emerita, University of California at Berkeley. Dr. Wallerstein's most recent best-selling book, co-authored with Sandra Blakeslee, is entitled *The Good Marriage: How and Why Love Lasts* (Warner Books, 1995). Her other writings include two best-selling books on divorce and over 90 professional articles. She is married, the mother of three children and the grandmother of five.

Barbara Dafoe Whitehead

Barbara Dafoe Whitehead writes and speaks on issues of family and child well-being. She is author of the award-winning book *The Divorce Culture: Rethinking Our Commitments to Marriage and the Family* (Knopf, 1997) and currently serves as co-director of The National Marriage Project, a research and public education initiative based at Rutgers University, New Brunswick, New Jersey. Dr. Whitehead is the married mother of three children.

Malcolm V. Williams

Malcolm V. Williams is director of the National Fatherhood Initiative's National Resource Center and Clearinghouse. Prior to his affiliation with the NFI, Mr. Williams served as a research analyst with the Majority Policy Committee and Democratic Legislative Development in the Pennsylvania House of Representatives. He lives in Harrisburg, Pennsylvania.

Ruth A. Wooden

As president of The Advertising Council, Inc., Ruth A. Wooden serves as chief executive officer of an organization that mobilizes more than $900 million yearly of donated advertising space and time, the creative services of over 30 major advertising agencies, and related financial support from hundreds of corporations. Ms. Wooden has served as president of The Ad Council since 1987. She lives in New York City with her son.